Lecture Notes in Computer Science 16263

The series Lecture Notes in Computer Science (LNCS), including its subseries Lecture Notes in Artificial Intelligence (LNAI) and Lecture Notes in Bioinformatics (LNBI), has established itself as a medium for the publication of new developments in computer science and information technology research, teaching, and education.

LNCS enjoys close cooperation with the computer science R & D community, the series counts many renowned academics among its volume editors and paper authors, and collaborates with prestigious societies. Its mission is to serve this international community by providing an invaluable service, mainly focused on the publication of conference and workshop proceedings and postproceedings. LNCS commenced publication in 1973.

Belgacem Ben Hedia · Sébastien Bardin ·
Riadh Robbana
Editors

Verification and Evaluation of Computer and Communication Systems

18th International Conference, VECoS 2025
Paris, France, November 5–7, 2025
Proceedings

Editors
Belgacem Ben Hedia
CEA LIST Institute
Paris, France

Sébastien Bardin
CEA LIST Institute
Paris, France

Riadh Robbana
LRE, EPITA
Paris, France

ISSN 0302-9743 ISSN 1611-3349 (electronic)
Lecture Notes in Computer Science
ISBN 978-3-032-20439-4 ISBN 978-3-032-20440-0 (eBook)
https://doi.org/10.1007/978-3-032-20440-0

This Springer imprint is published by the registered company Springer Nature Switzerland AG
The registered company address is: Gewerbestrasse 11, 6330 Cham, Switzerland

If disposing of this product, please recycle the paper.

Preface

This volume contains the papers presented at the 18th International Conference on Verification and Evaluation of Computer and Communication Systems (VECoS 2025), held during November 5–6, 2025 in Paris, France. The conference was hosted by the CEA-LIST institute of the French Alternative Energies and Atomic Energy Commission (CEA).

This year's event continued the tradition of previous editions held in: 2007 in Algiers, 2008 in Leeds, 2009 in Rabat, 2010 in Paris, 2011 in Tunis, 2012 in Paris, 2013 in Florence, 2014 in Bejaïa, 2015 in Bucharest, 2016 in Tunis, 2017 in Montreal, 2018 in Grenoble, 2019 in Porto, 2020 in Xi'an (virtual), 2021 in Beijing (virtual), 2023 in Marrakech, and 2024 in Djerba.

As in previous editions, VECoS provided a forum for researchers and practitioners in the areas of verification, control, performance, and dependability evaluation to discuss the state of the art and challenges in modern computer and communication systems in which functional and extra-functional properties are strongly interrelated. The main motivation was to encourage the cross-fertilization between various formal verification and evaluation approaches, methods, and techniques, and especially those developed for concurrent and distributed hardware/software systems.

The Program Committee of VECoS 2025 was composed of 56 researchers from 16 countries. We received 29 full submissions from 10 countries. During a single blind review process with three reviwes for each paper and after a thorough and lively discussion phase, the committee decided to accept 13 regular papers. The topics presented covered a range of subjects, including approaches to improving the scalability and efficiency of formal verification and their applications. The conference also included two invited talks, one on the consistency checking problem and the other one on a fuzzing-based framework for the Cubicle model checker.

We are grateful to the program and organizing committee members, to the reviewers for their cooperation, and to Springer for their professional support during the production phase of the proceedings. We are also thankful to all authors of submitted papers, to the invited speakers, and to all participants in the conference. Their interest in this conference and their contributions are greatly appreciated.

VECoS 2025

November 2025

Belgacem Ben Hedia
Sébastien Bardin
Riadh Robbana

Organization

Executive Committee

Program Co-chairs

Sébastien Bardin	CEA-LIST Institute, France
Riadh Robbana	EPITA Research Lab, France

Publicity Co-chair

Belgacem Ben Hedia	CEA-LIST Institute, France

Local Organizers

Belgacem Ben Hedia	CEA-LIST, France
Sébastien Bardin	CEA-LIST Institute, France

Steering Committee

Djamil Aissani	LAMOS, Université de Bejaia, Algeria
Mohamed Faouzi Atig	Uppsala University, Sweden
Kamel Barkaoui (Chair)	CEDRIC CNAM Paris, France
Belgacem Ben Hedia	CEA-LIST Saclay, France
Hanifa Boucheneb	Veriform, Polytechnique Montréal, Canada
Gabriel Ciobanu	Romanian Academy, Romania
Karim Djouani	Tshwane University of Technology, South Africa
Francesco Flammini	Ansaldo STS, Milano, Italy
Antonín Kučera	Masaryk University, Czech Republic
Zhiwu Li	Xidian University, China
Yassine Maleh	Sultan Moulay Slimane University, Morocco
Ali Mili	New Jersey Institute of Technology, USA
Bruno Monsuez	ENSTA UIIS, France
Ayoub Nouri	Huawei France, France
Riadh Robbana	LRE-EPITA, France
Sofiène Tahar	Concordia University, Canada

Referees

P. A. Abdulla
D. Aissani
Y. Ait Ameur
M. Asavoae
M. Faouzi Atig
S. Bardin
K. Barkaoui
I. Ben Hafaiedh
B. Ben Hedia
M. T. Bennani
N. Ben Rajeb
P. Bonhomme
A. Bouajjani
A. Boudguiga
Z. Chen
G. Ciobanu
S. Dal Zilio
A. De Melo
I. Demongodin
M. Ghazel
S. Haddad
O. Hasan
M. Jmaiel
J. Julvez
K. Klai
M. Krichen
L. Kristensen
A. Kucera
O. Lengal
A. Lisitsa
G. Liu
Y. Maleh
F. Mallet
A. Methni
S. Merz
R. Meyer
A. Mili
B. Monsuez
A. Nouri
P. Ölveczky
S. Ouchani
M. Ouederni
A. Rabéa
R. Robbana
R. J. Rodríguez
O. H. Roux
M. A. Saied
L. Sliman
S. Tahar
X. Yin

Additional Reviewers

T. Haas
E. D. Gutierrez Mlot
S. Ashraf
Z. Sbaï
J. Tepe
O. Barhoumi
M. Nour
K. Trabelsi

Sponsoring Institutions

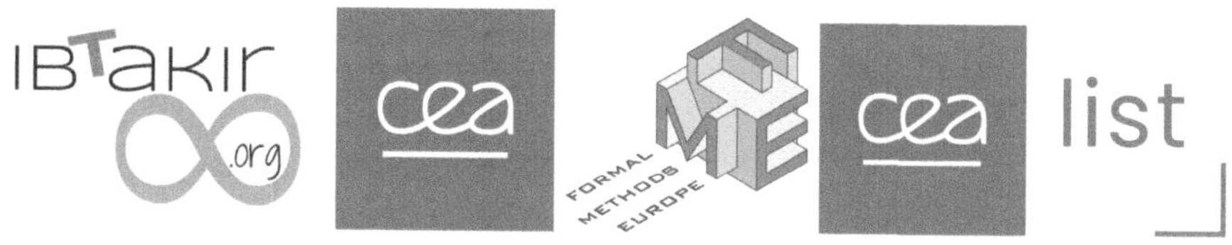

Keynote Speakers

The Consistency Checking Problem

Mohamed Faouzi Atig

Uppsala University, Sweden
mohamed_faouzi.atig@it.uu.se

Abstract. We study the consistency checking problem, which consists in determining whether, for a given program and a tracee.g., an execution graph, there exists an execution of the program that satisfies all the relations of the trace. This problem has been widely explored for various programming models In this work, we focus on event-driven programs, which extend concurrent shared-memory programs by allowing threads—called handlers—to send and receive messages. Each handler has a mailbox for incoming messages, which are processed sequentially. However, message executions of different handlers may interleave. We propose an equivalent axiomatic model for event-driven programs and analyze the complexity of their consistency checking problem.

The Cubicle Fuzzy Loop: A Fuzzing-Based Framework for the Cubicle Model Checker

Sylvain Conchon

Paris-Saclay University, France
sylvain.conchon@universite-paris-saclay.fr

Abstract. This talk presents the Cubicle Fuzzy LoopCFL, a fuzzing-based extension for Cubicle, a model checker for parameterized systems. To prove safety, Cubicle generates invariants, making use of forward exploration strategies like BFS or DFS on finite model instances. However, these standard algorithms are quickly faced with the state explosion problem due to Cubicle's purely nondeterministic semantics. This causes them to struggle at discovering critical states, hindering invariant generation. CFL replaces this approach with a powerful DFS-like algorithm inspired by fuzzing. Cubicle's purely nondeterministic execution loop is modified to provide feedback on newly discovered states and visited transitions. This feedback is used by CFL to construct schedulers that guide the model exploration. Not only does this provide Cubicle with a bigger variety of states for generating invariants, it also quickly identifies unsafe models. As a bonus, it adds testing capabilities to Cubicle, such as the ability to detect deadlocks. Our first experiments have yielded promising results. CFL effectively allows Cubicle to generate crucial invariants, useful to handle hierarchical systems, while also being able to trap bad states and deadlocks in hard-to-reach areas of such models.

Contents

Network Traversal Time (NTT) Analysis of ST Flows with Non-zero Arrival Jitter in TSN Networks

Pavan Kumar Kondooru(✉) and Deepak Gangadharan

IIIT Hyderabad, Hyderabad, India
pavan.kondooru@research.iiit.ac.in, deepak.g@iiit.ac.in

Abstract. Time-Sensitive Networking (TSN) is crucial for ensuring deterministic communication in real-time applications. In TSN, Network Traversal Time (NTT) is a critical metric that quantifies the timeliness of received data. Maintaining low NTT is essential for ensuring accurate system responses and to prevent outdated information from affecting real-time operations. However, the presence of non-zero arrival jitter negatively impacts NTT and poses challenges in providing predictable performance. When jitter increases, packets may arrive inconsistently, causing some to be delayed while others may arrive in bursts. To address this, we analyze the NTT bounds for time-critical flows, influenced by arrival jitter. We propose an analytical framework to estimate best- and worst-case ST slots for data transmission, considering interference from higher priority flows and establishing data reachability along the network path across the switches. To validate our analysis, we conducted experiments using both a synthetic task set and an automotive use case. We also analyzed the impact of flow parameters on NTT determination, which, in some scenarios, led to pessimistic bound estimations.

Keywords: ST slot · arrival jitter · gate schedule · TSN switch

1 Introduction

Modern vehicular embedded platforms consist of multiple distributed electronic control units (ECUs), which interact by communicating over real-time communication medium. The in-vehicle communication protocol that has been traditionally used in vehicle platforms is controller area network (CAN) [3]. However, CAN protocol is limited by its low data rate thereby making it difficult to deploy several new functionalities requiring high data rate information to provide timely responses to the inputs. An alternative communication standard which is gaining attention recently is the IEEE Time-sensitive Networking (TSN) standard [9] due to its high-bandwidth and low-latency communication support. This will enable enhanced real-time communication between distributed ECUs, thereby satisfying the requirements of many time critical automotive applications such as Advanced Driver Assistance Systems (ADAS) [1].

B. Ben Hedia et al. (Eds.): VECoS 2025, LNCS 16263, pp. 1–16, 2026.
https://doi.org/10.1007/978-3-032-20440-0_1

Information is exchanged within vehicular systems using messages. In TSNs, this message transmission across several TSN switches is considered as a flow [2]. The flow starts when the first task, which reads input from the environment (external physical world the vehicle interacts with), executes and produces an output that is then transmitted across several switches. These flows are generated at specific times, either periodically, sporadically, or on demand. Each time a flow is generated, it is referred to as a flow instance, which traverses the same predetermined route from source to destination. Each egress port in a TSN switch is associated with transmission queues, which are prioritized and utilized for the transmission of different types of flows, including Scheduled Traffic (ST), Audio-Video Bridging Traffic (AVB), and Best-Effort Traffic (BE). ST flows, which are time-critical, are shaped using the Time-Aware Shaper (TAS) [10], while AVB and BE flows are managed using a hierarchical strategy involving the Credit-Based Shaper (CBS) [10] and TAS.

Most studies assume that the gates of ST flows open in non-overlapping time intervals to prevent interference from other ST flows. However, ST traffic may not always fully utilize the allocated time intervals, leading to bandwidth wastage [15]. Additionally, isolating ST flows from one another can overly restrict schedule generation for specific TSN applications [13]. Also, TSN relies on the premise that end-systems can release and transmit time-sensitive data precisely according to predetermined schedules. In practice, however, this premise is often challenged in current end-system architectures. Factors such as shared bus contention, unpredictable context switching, and queuing delays within the Network Interface Controller (NIC) introduce jitter, which disrupts the task release, execution, and timely transmission of critical flows [7]. These variations in ST flow generation and transmission times at the source node lead to inconsistent arrival times at the switch, resulting in arrival jitter. Considering ST flow isolation, such jitter can affect the ability of ST flows to meet their transmission timing requirements within the allocated intervals, further reducing bandwidth efficiency. To address this, we adopt the design from [15] where all ST queues are allowed to transmit during the assigned time intervals. If multiple ST flows are ready for transmission, the flow with the highest priority is selected.

At each switch, a flow experiences delays due to other higher priority flows utilizing the switch. Hence, different flow instances experience different timing behavior as the path from source to destination varies temporally. Also, the arrival jitter in message transmission also has its effect on the timing behavior of the flows. In this work, we propose an analytical framework to derive the upper and lower bounds on the timing behavior called *Network Traversal Time* (NTT), which aids in the analysis of systems with multiple ST flows operating in overlapping time intervals.

To analyze the impact of arrival jitter on a flow's traversal path, which is the route taken by the flow through transmission intervals across switches from the source node to the destination switch, consider two periodic ST flows, F_0 and F_1 (priority: $F_0 > F_1$), and two TSN switches, SW_0 and SW_1. In Fig. 1, s_a, s_b, s_c and s_d denote the time intervals during which ST flows are transmitted in

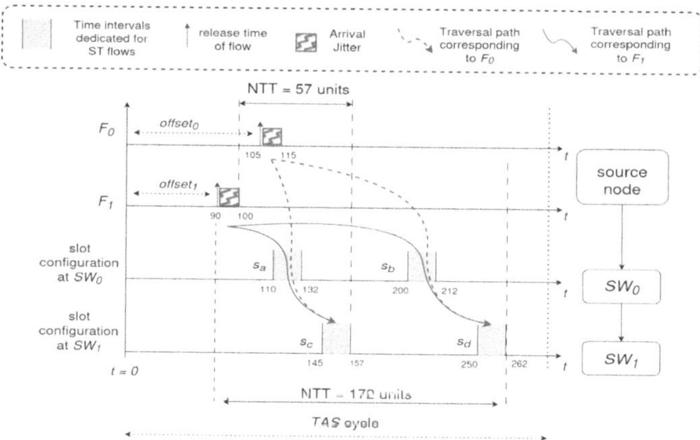

Fig. 1. An example shows how arrival jitter affects traversal paths, leading to varying NTT for f_0^1,f_1^1.

the network. These flows have initial offset, period and maximum arrival jitter as follows: F_0 (105, 500, 10) and F_1 (90, 500, 10). For a flow F_k, pth periodic instance is denoted as f_k^p, where $p \geq 1$.

Consider a scenario where the first instance of flow F_0, denoted as f_0^1, is generated at $t = 105$, and the first instance of F_1, denoted as f_1^1, is generated at $t = 90$. As f_0^1 has higher priority, it is transmitted via s_a and s_c through switches SW_0 and SW_1, while f_1^1 uses s_b and s_d. The NTT of a flow is the time it spends along its traversal path, from its release at the source to its consumption at the destination switch (the last switch traversed). As shown in the Fig. 1, the NTT for f_1^1 is 172 time units. In another scenario, with f_0^1 generated at $t = 115$ and f_1^1 at $t = 100$, f_1^1 is transmitted via s_a and s_c, and f_0^1 via s_b and s_d, resulting in a NTT value of 57 time units for f_1^1.

This example illustrates how arrival jitter can result in multiple paths, affecting NTT in a TSN network. Through our work, we conduct a comprehensive analysis to evaluate all potential paths, accounting for the effects of arrival jitter.

Contribution: Following are the contributions of the paper:

- Through our work, we determine the upper and lower bounds of NTT for ST flows, where the flows experience variable arrival jitter.
- The above proposed framework was applied to TSN switches, where the transmission of ST flows is regulated by TAS, followed by a strict priority transmission mechanism.
- A comprehensive experimental evaluation was conducted with synthetic task sets and an automotive use case to assess the framework's reliability, the impact of flow parameters on bound determination, and analyze the simulation time complexity.

In Sect. 2, we discuss the related works, focusing on previous studies that analyze the timing of ST flows. We introduce the system model in Sect. 3 and present the main contribution of our work: determining the NTT bounds in Sect. 4. Section 5 discusses our experimental evaluation and finally, we conclude our paper in Sect. 6.

2 Related Works

Performance analysis techniques have been a focus of research, addressing challenges related to worst-case delay and schedulability analysis. As discussed in [16], delay analysis techniques are generally classified into three categories: (1) simulation-based, (2) model-checking based exhaustive search, and (3) analytical methods. Our work falls into the third category.

Few research studies have focused on improving end-to-end delay analysis for ST flows in TSN. Zhao et al. [17] developed a Network Calculus-based approach to analyze worst-case latencies for critical flows by relaxing strict isolation among critical traffic classes and removing constraints on Gate Control List (GCL) configurations, thereby permiting overlapping transmission windows. Later, Seliem et al. [14] proposed another Network Calculus framework for analyzing TSN-based industrial networks with preemptive traffic. Their approach computes upper bounds on worst-case delays, which are validated through simulations and compared against existing frameworks. A worst-case response time analysis for ST, AVB class A and B flows—considering interference from both higher and same priority flows, as well as the effects of traffic shaping—was developed in [8]. Houtan et al. [5] observed that existing delay analyses tend to be pessimistic for synchronized nodes. To address this, they proposed an end-to-end data propagation delay analysis. Their work assumes deterministic data transmission across switches and introduces a reachability-based timed path estimation from the last link to the destination node. Srinivasan et al. [15] proposed best- and worst-case latency analysis for ST flows in a TSN switch and suggested an extension for end-to-end analysis. The approach assumes that TAS gates for multiple traffic classes can be open simultaneously, and if multiple flows are present, the transmission is determined based on flow priority.

While prior works offer limited exploration of end-to-end network traversal analysis in the presence of jitter, this work addresses that gap by proposing a formal NTT analysis. Most existing models ignore jitter from end-systems, whereas our approach considers its impact to provide traversal time guarantees.

3 System Model

This section presents the network model, outlining its characteristics, followed by an analysis of the traffic model, focusing on flow attributes and their transmission mechanism.

3.1 Network Model

We model the network as a directed graph $G(V, E)$ where V represents the set of vertices corresponding to end-systems and TSN switches, and E represents the set of edges denoting the links between an end system and a TSN switch or between TSN switches. End-systems refer to source or destination nodes in the network, representing compute nodes that generate or consume traffic flows. For any two vertices $v_a \in V$ and $v_b \in V$, the link connecting them is represented as an ordered tuple $(v_a, v_b) \in V \times V$. Each flow in the system, traveling from sender node v_a to destination node v_b through $\mathbb{M}$ switches, follows the same sequence of links: $\{(v_a, v_0), (v_0, v_1), ..., (v_{\mathbb{M}-2}, v_{\mathbb{M}-1}), (v_{\mathbb{M}-1}, v_b)\}$.

TAS defines a schedule at every port of TSN switch, specifying gate opening/closing events, and repeats periodically with period T_{sch} [10]. A TAS cycle refers to the repeating time period T_{sch} in which the shaper operates to control the flow transmission. The cycle is segmented into multiple time slots, enabling the transmission of time-critical and non-time-critical flows within non-overlapping intervals. Time-critical ST flows are allocated specific ST slots, while non-time-critical flows are accommodated within the remaining time intervals [10]. In [10], two TAS configurations were analyzed for AVB delay analysis in TSN: one with a single ST slot per cycle (called as single protected window in their approach) and another with multiple ST slots per cycle (called as multiple protected windows). In this work, we adopt the latter, where multiple ST slots are generated and each slot is utilized to transmit one ST frame.

ST Slot Model. The schedule at any switch v_x operates throughout its life time and consists of N_{ST}^x slots in a TAS cycle. Each slot is uniquely identified as s_i^x, where i represents the slot index. The properties of s_i^x are described as follows:

$$s_i^x := \langle \eta^x(i), \rho^x(i), \psi^x(i) \rangle \tag{1}$$

$\eta^x(i)$ represents the TAS cycle to which s_i^x belongs, while $\rho^x(i)$ and $\psi^x(i)$ denote the relative position and start time of the slot from the beginning of the TAS cycle, respectively, obtained from Eqs. (2) and (3).

$$\eta^x(i) = \lfloor \frac{i}{N_{ST}^x} \rfloor \tag{2}$$

$$\rho^x(i) = i \ mod \ N_{ST}^x \tag{3}$$

Since the schedule is predetermined, the start time of s_i^x, $\psi^x(i)$ for $0 \le i \le N_{ST}^x - 1$ is given. For ST slots in consequent TAS cycles, where $i \ge N_{ST}^x$, the start time relative to the beginning of the cycle remains the same as that of the slot with the identical $\rho^x(i)$ in the 0th TAS cycle. So, for $i \ge N_{ST}^x$,

$$\psi^x(i) = \psi^x(i - \eta^x(i).N_{ST}^x) \tag{4}$$

As mentioned, in ST slot duration, all queues associated with ST flows are opened for transmission. During remaining time intervals, flow transmission is regulated by the CBS mechanism. Since the proposed work focuses on the transmission of ST flows—during which AVB and BE flows are restricted—the discussion of CBS and non-ST flow transmission is beyond the scope of this work.

3.2 Traffic Model

The traffic model is a mathematical representation of various types of flows present in the system. In our work, the traffic model is denoted by $F_k = F(\Phi_k, C_k, T_k, D_k, \delta_k^{max})$, where F_k is the kth periodic flow. The lower the value of k, higher is its priority. Then, the set of periodic flows of size $\mathbb{N}$ is represented as $S = \{F_k\}\ \forall k \in [0, \mathbb{N} - 1]$. F_k is characterized using the following properties: initial offset Φ_k, transmission time C_k, time period T_k, relative deadline D_k, and the maximum arrival jitter δ_k^{max}. In contrast to traditional TSN models that assume perfectly periodic and jitter-free transmission, our model explicitly incorporates jitter at the source nodes. This allows the model to capture real-world uncertainties which can affect the precise timing of ST frames.

In our model, each instance of a periodic ST flow consists of a single frame of Maximum Transmission Unit (MTU). The pth instance of flow F_k is denoted as f_k^p. In the transmission mechanism, ST frames that enter the queue immediately after the ST slot has started are allowed to transmit in the next available slot. The slot-based access aligns with the TSN paradigm, where each switch follows a predefined schedule for gate control and slot allocation. Our model adheres to this scheduling structure, ensuring compatibility with TAS, while accounting for jitter. For a flow to get transmitted via s_i^x from switch v_x and subsequently transmitted via s_j^{x+1} from v_{x+1}, the minimum separation between the end time of s_i^x and start time of s_j^{x+1} is denoted as X. X represents the propagation and switch fabric delay for a flow and is considered constant. While checking the possibility of flow transmission via s_i^x and s_j^{x+1}, minimum separation criteria is already considered and is not explicitly mentioned in further discussions.

4 Proposed Approach

In this section, we introduce our analytical framework for determining the NTT bounds of a kth periodic ST flow F_k in a TSN environment, where all flows follow the same sequence of links. The proposed approach begins by considering the release of a flow instance f_k^p. Initially, all potential transmission slots at the source switch are identified. For each of these candidate slots, the corresponding reachable slots at the intermediate switches are then determined. These slot estimations are subsequently used to identify all feasible traversal paths. By analyzing these paths, the minimum and maximum NTT values are computed. This process is repeated across all flow instances, and the resulting NTT bounds are reported. Initially, we derive the slot estimation at the source switch, followed by its computation at all intermediate switches.

4.1 Slot Determination at Source Switch

The transmission of f_k^p, the pth instance of F_k, through a given ST slot is influenced by the k higher-priority flows that have already been generated. Theorem 1 provides a method to find the instances of higher-priority ST flows that may interfere with the transmission of f_k^p in the presence of arrival jitter.

Theorem 1. *Let s_i^0 be the slot of interest for the transmission of f_k^p from source switch v_0. Given the arrival jitter $\delta_0, ..., \delta_{k-1}$ for k higher-priority flows, the number of instances of these flows generated prior to s_i^0 is determined by Eq. (5).*

$$hpInst(s_i^0, k, \delta_0, \ldots, \delta_{k-1}) = \sum_{l=0}^{k-1} \left(1 + \left\lfloor \frac{\eta^0(i).T_{sch} + \psi^0(i) - X - \Phi_l - \delta_l}{T_l} \right\rfloor\right) \tag{5}$$

The proof follows by analyzing the time window in which higher-priority flows may be released and potentially interfere with the transmission of f_k^p through s_i^0. For a flow F_l with period T_l, the number of interfering instances is given by the ratio of the window length to T_l. Summing over k higher-priority flows yields the total number of interfering instances, as expressed in Eq. (1). The proof is omitted due to space and is provided in Sect. 1 of the technical report [6].

From Eq. (5), the number of k higher priority instances generated ahead of s_i^0 depends on δ, where $\delta \in [0, \delta^{max}]$. It can be observed that $hpInst()$ value is higher when δ_l has a lower value since $\eta^0(i).T_{sch} + \psi^0(i) - X - \Phi_l$ is constant for a slot and a flow. Hence,

$$hpInst(s_i^0, k, \delta_0^{max}, .., \delta_{k-1}^{max}) \leq hpInst(s_i^0, k, 0, .., 0) \tag{6}$$

This jitter variability allows us to determine the minimum and maximum number of higher-priority releases, as given by Eq. (7) and (8).

$$min\_hpInst(s_i^0, k) = hpInst(s_i^0, k, \delta_0^{max}, \ldots, (\delta_{k-1}^{max})) \tag{7}$$

and

$$max\_hpInst(s_i^0, k) = hpInst(s_i^0, k, 0, \ldots, 0) \tag{8}$$

Now, we determine the earliest and latest slots for transmission at the source switch.

Slot Allotment. Arrival jitter introduces uncertainty in the number of releases of the k higher-priority flows interfering with f_k^p, making it necessary to estimate both the earliest and latest possible transmission slots for f_k^p.

Earliest Slot Assignment. Minimum interference for the transmission of f_k^p through s_i^0 occurs when the fewest higher-priority instances are generated and the maximum number of these are transmitted before s_i^0 begins. The expression for minimum interference at s_i^0 is given as follows:

$$min\_interference(s_i^0, k) = min\_hpInst(s_i^0, k) - max\_slotfilling(s_i^0, k) \quad (9)$$

$max\_slotfilling(s_i^0, k)$ refers to maximum number of k higher priority flows that are transmitted before the start of s_i^0. Corresponding expression is presented in the next section. If $min\_interference(s_i^0, k) \neq 0$, we check s_{i+1}^0.

Table 1. Slot Parameters and Their Definitions

Slot Parameter	Type	Description
$s_i^x.min\_fill$	Boolean	True if s_i^x can be filled by higher priority flows with minimum interference.
$s_i^x.max\_fill$	Boolean	True if s_i^x can be filled by higher priority flows with maximum interference.
$s_i^x.no\_min$	Integer	Number of slots filled so far with minimum interference, including s_i^x.
$s_i^x.no\_max$	Integer	Number of slots filled so far with maximum interference, including s_i^x.

Latest Slot Assignment. Maximum interference occurs when the largest number of higher priority instances are generated and the fewest are transmitted before the slot's start time. Slots ahead of worst-case release time of f_k^p are checked sequentially to arrive at the latest slot. Considering s_{i+r}^0, expression for maximum interference is presented below:

$$max\_interference(s_{i+r}^0, k) = max\_hpInst(s_{i+r}^0, k) - min\_slotfilling(s_{i+r}^0, k) \quad (10)$$

In some cases, previous instances of the flow may also influence slot estimation. The detailed discussion is provided in Sect. 2 of the technical report [6].

4.2 Slot Determination at Intermediate Switches

In this subsection, we analyze all potential slots at switch v_x, given the transmitted slot information from v_{x-1}.

In order to determine these slots, we firstly define slot parameters as described in Table 1 for each ST slot in the TSN network. These parameters are different for different k values and are independent of the flow instance p.

Slot Parameters at Source Switch. If least number of higher priority instances are generated and all those are transmitted until s^0_{i-1}, then no frame is transmitted through s^0_i. Otherwise, s^0_i is occupied by a higher priority flow. Expressions for $s^0_i.no\_min$ and $s^0_i.min\_fill$ are described below:

$$s^0_i.no\_min = \begin{cases} s^0_{i-1}.no\_min, & \text{if } min\_hpInst(s^0_i, k) - s^0_{i-1}.no\_min = 0, \\ s^0_{i-1}.no\_min + 1, & \text{otherwise} \end{cases} \tag{11}$$

$$s^0_i.min\_fill = \begin{cases} False, & \text{if } min\_hpInst(s^0_i, k) - s^0_{i-1}.no\_min = 0, \\ True, & \text{otherwise} \end{cases} \tag{12}$$

If maximum number of higher priority instances are generated ahead of s^0_i and all those are transmitted until s^0_{i-1}, then no frame get transmitted through s^0_i. So, $s^0_i.no\_max = s^0_{i-1}.no\_max$ and $s^0_i.max\_fill = False$. Otherwise, $s^0_i.no\_max = s^0_{i-1}.no\_max + 1$ and $s^0_i.max\_fill = True$.

As described in the previous section, $max\_slotfilling(s^0_i, k) = s^0_{i-1}.no\_max$ and $min\_slotfilling(s^0_i, k) = s^0_{i-1}.no\_min$.

Slot Parameters at Intermediate Switches. Now, we define the parameters for s^x_i at switch v_x, considering s^{x-1}_r to be the immediate previous slot at switch v_{x-1}. The minimum number of higher-priority flow transmissions up to s^x_i depends on the number of such transmissions from the preceding switch v_{x-1}, which must also be minimal. So, if only the minimum number of higher-priority flows are transmitted up to s^{x-1}_r from v_{x-1}, and subsequently forwarded up to s^x_{i-1} from v_x, then no frame is transmitted via s^x_i. Otherwise, s^x_i is occupied with a higher-priority flow.

Similarly, for $s^x_i.no\_max$ and $s^x_i.max\_fill$ we consider maximum higher priority transmissions up to s^{x-1}_r and further maximum transmissions till s^x_{i-1} from v_x. The expressions are omitted for brevity, as they follow the similar logical pattern to that of the slot parameters at the source switch. Detailed expressions for slot parameters at source and intermediate switches are presented in Sect. 3 of the technical report [6].

Using these parameters, we now determine the best and worst reachable paths for transferring a flow through s^x_i from switch v_x to v_{x+1}. The best reachable path is the traversal path with the shortest time duration from s^x_i to a potential transmission slot in v_{x+1}. Conversely, the traversal path with the longest time duration represents the worst reachable path.

Best-Case Reachability. Let s^{x+1}_j be the slot of interest for identifying the least timed traversal path. To check if a flow can use s^{x+1}_j under best-case timing assumptions, we evaluate the net effect of interfering higher-priority flows by subtracting the maximum number of flows that could have been transmitted before s^{x+1}_j from the minimum number of flows arriving from the previous switch.

We define a Boolean function $bforward(s_i^x \to s_j^{x+1})$ that returns true if the flow can reach s_j^{x+1} from s_i^x with minimal interference. Since multiple slot pairs may satisfy the condition, the least-timed path is established by selecting the first pair that meets the requirements. Based on this, we define the best-case reachability condition as follows:

$$best\_reachable(s_i^x \to s_j^{x+1}) = bforward(s_i^x \to s_j^{x+1}) \wedge \neg bforward(s_i^x \to s_w^{x+1})$$
$$\forall w \in [0, j-1] \tag{13}$$

The different timing scenarios under which $bforward()$ evaluates to true are discussed in detail in Sect. 4 of the technical report [6].

Worst-Case Reachability. We analyze the same scenarios to estimate the worst-case reachable path, considering both the maximum input flow transmissions from v_x and the minimum subsequent transmissions from v_{x+1}. The case condition now considers $s_i^x.no\_max$. The slots satisfying the conditions of both scenarios are determined by $wforward()$. The worst-case reachability condition is given as follows:

$$\begin{aligned} worst\_reachable(s_i^x \to s_j^{x+1}) = wforward(s_i^x \to s_j^{x+1}) \wedge \\ \neg wforward(s_i^x \to s_w^{x+1}) \forall w \in [0, j-1] \end{aligned} \tag{14}$$

4.3 NTT Bounds Determination

In this section, we compute the NTT bounds for F_k, where each slot is associated with a rel_list to track the flow instance release times. The NTT is calculated as the time interval between the release time of f_k^p and the moment when f_k^p is completely transmitted from $v_{\mathrm{M}-1}$, as determined by Algorithm 1.

- The first step is to estimate the earliest and latest slot assignments at the source switch for all flow instances of F_k, that are released within the observation window(OW) duration (Lines 2–4).
- For each slot s_u^0 within the earliest and latest slot range for a flow instance f_k^p, the minimum and maximum release times, which depend on δ_k, are stored in $rel\_list(s_u^0)$ (Lines 5–6).
- Next, for each s_q^0 with non-empty rel_list, we compute the best- and worst-case reachable slots, denoted by $s_{best_q}^1$ and $s_{worst_q}^1$ at v_1 (Lines 8–10). This step helps in establishing all possible traversal paths from v_0 to v_1 for transmission of F_k.
- For every reachable slot s_u^1, where $u \in [best_q, worst_q]$, we store maximum and minium values of $rel\_list(s_q^0)$ (Lines 11–12). Among all traversal paths derived in the previous step, we retain only those with the maximum and minimum NTT values, eliminating the intermediary ones to propagate further in the estimation.
- This process is continued for all the slots across the switches till the destination switch (Lines 7–12).

For any slot $s_r^{\mathbb{M}-1}$ at $v_{\mathbb{M}-1}$, the minimum and maximum NTT values are computed as follows:

$$\tau_{ntt}^{min}(s_r^{\mathbb{M}-1}) = [\eta^{\mathbb{M}-1}(r).T_{sch} + \psi^{\mathbb{M}-1}(r) + C_k] - max(rel\_list(s_r^{\mathbb{M}-1})) \quad (15)$$

$$\tau_{ntt}^{max}(s_r^{\mathbb{M}-1}) = [\eta^{\mathbb{M}-1}(r).T_{sch} + \psi^{\mathbb{M}-1}(r) + C_k] - min(rel\_list(s_r^{\mathbb{M}-1})) \quad (16)$$

The minimum and maximum values are computed for all slots at $v_{\mathbb{M}-1}$ with non-empty *rel_list*. Utilizing these values, overall maximum and minimum NTT values for F_k are reported(Lines 13 - 15).

The proposed approach is detailed for ST flows that follow the same sequence of links. An analysis of the algorithm's time complexity, which is $\mathcal{O}(n^2)$, along with an extension to support flows originating from different source switches, is presented in Sects. 5 and 6 of the technical report [6], respectively.

Algorithm 1: Computation of NTT bounds

Input: k, $F(\Phi_k, T_k, \delta_k)$
Output: min_NTT, max_NTT
1 $min\_NTT \leftarrow \infty$; $max\_NTT \leftarrow -1$;
2 **foreach** f_k^p ***where*** $\Phi_k + p.T_k + \delta_k^{max} < OW$ **do**
3 $\quad s_{ear_p}^0 \leftarrow earliest\_slot\_assign(f_k^p)$;
4 $\quad s_{lat_p}^0 \leftarrow latest\_slot\_assign(f_k^p)$;
5 $\quad$ **foreach** $u \in \{ear_p, lat_p\}$ **do**
6 $\quad\quad rel\_list(s_u^0).\mathrm{add}(\Phi_k + pT_k, \Phi_k + pT_k + \delta_k^{max})$;
7 $\quad$ **for** $v \leftarrow 0$ ***to*** $\mathbb{M} - 2$ **do**
8 $\quad\quad$ **foreach** s_q^v ***where*** $rel\_list(s_q^v).size \neq 0$ **do**
9 $\quad\quad\quad s_{best_q}^{v+1} \leftarrow best\_reachable(s_q^v)$;
10 $\quad\quad\quad s_{worst_q}^{v+1} \leftarrow worst\_reachable(s_q^v)$;
11 $\quad\quad\quad$ **foreach** $u \in \{best_q, worst_q\}$ **do**
12 $\quad\quad\quad\quad rel\_list(s_u^{v+1}).\mathrm{add}(\max(rel\_list(s_q^v)), \min(rel\_list(s_q^v)))$;
13 $\quad$ **foreach** $s_r^{\mathbb{M}-1}$ ***where*** $rel\_list(s_r^{\mathbb{M}-1}).size \neq 0$ **do**
14 $\quad\quad min\_NTT \leftarrow \min(min\_NTT,\ \tau_{ntt}^{min}(s_r^{\mathbb{M}-1}))$;
15 $\quad\quad max\_NTT \leftarrow \max(max\_NTT,\ \tau_{ntt}^{max}(s_r^{\mathbb{M}-1}))$;

5 Evaluation

We evaluate our framework for NTT bounds using experiments on synthetic task set and an automotive use case, conducted on a system equipped with an Intel i5-11300H processor and 8GB RAM.

5.1 Synthetic Task Set

A dumbbell topology network with four TSN switches is used for the experiments, with the TAS cycle length T_{sch} set to 500 µs [10]. The number of ST streams, $\mathbb{N}$, is selected from the set $\{5, 6, 7, 8, 9\}$. Flow periods are drawn from the pool $\{200, 500, 1000, 2000, 5000\}$µs [4], and the offset for each flow, is randomly chosen from the interval $(0,\ T_k)$ [12]. Considering link speed of 1 Gbit/s and MTU size per each frame, the transmission time for a frame is $12.336\,\mu$s. For the experiments, the slot duration is approximated to $12\,\mu$s. A random gate schedule is generated for each experiment by selecting the number of slots in a TAS cycle from the interval $[y.Slt,\ z.Slt]$, where $y \leq z \leq 1$. The value of Slt is computed using Eq. (17), by considering maximum possible flow releases per cycle. To determine the actual NTT values, we introduce a random arrival jitter from the predefined range and then analyze the resulting traversal paths.

$$Slt = \sum_{k=0}^{\mathbb{N}-1} \left\lceil \frac{T_{sch}}{T_k} \right\rceil \tag{17}$$

Experiment 1. We evaluated the NTT variation for all flows, considering $\mathbb{N} = 7$ with flow periods of [2000, 2000, 1000, 1000, 5000, 2000, 5000]μs and δ_k^{max} is set to be 1% of its respective period. Simulation is conducted over a time duration equivalent to 9 times the LCM of the ST flow periods and the TAS cycle with $y = 0.2$ and $z = 0.5$.

As shown in Fig. 2a, the NTT bounds exhibit both increasing and decreasing trends; however, the overall tendency is an increase in traversal time as the priority decreases. The proposed bounds closely align with the actual values for higher-priority flows; but, as priority decreases, the actual NTT diverges, resulting in greater differences from the proposed values. This is because the higher-priority flows encounter minimal interference, yielding tighter bounds. The non-coinciding bound for the highest-priority flow in this scenario is due to the presence of jitter. In contrast, lower-priority flows experience significant interference from higher-priority flows, leading to an increase in NTT. The decrease in NTT for certain flows is influenced by slot configuration and the parameters of higher-priority flows. In Fig. 2a, the flow with priority 2 has a shorter period than the higher-priority flows. As a result, every alternate instance of this flow encounters minimal interference, leading to a reduced NTT value.

Experiment 2. In this experiment, we considered $\mathbb{N} = 8$ and evaluated fluctuations in NTT for one of the flows, where δ_k^{max} varies from 0.25% to 3.75% of its period. The experiment was conducted using two different sets of flow parameters and gate schedules. The first set includes flow periods of [200, 500, 2000, 200, 2000, 1000, 200, 1000]μs, while the second set consists of [1000, 2000, 2000, 5000, 2000, 2000, 500, 500]μs. We considered the flow with priority 3, whose period is 200μs in the first set and 5000 μs in the second set. The plots for these two sets are presented in Figs. 2b and 2c, respectively. It was observed that Set

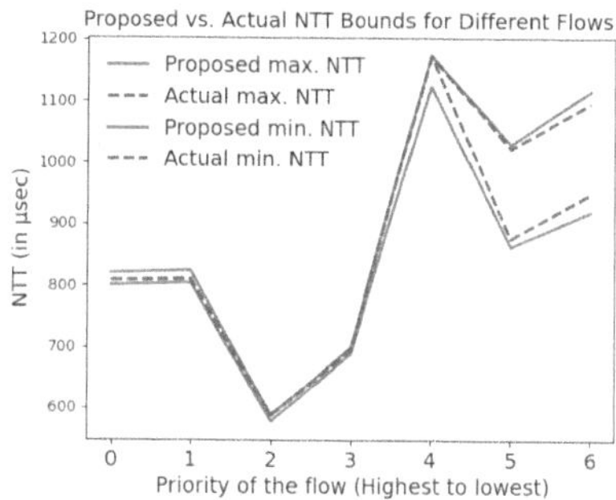

(a) NTT variation for periodic flows, where (δ^{max}) is 1% of the period.

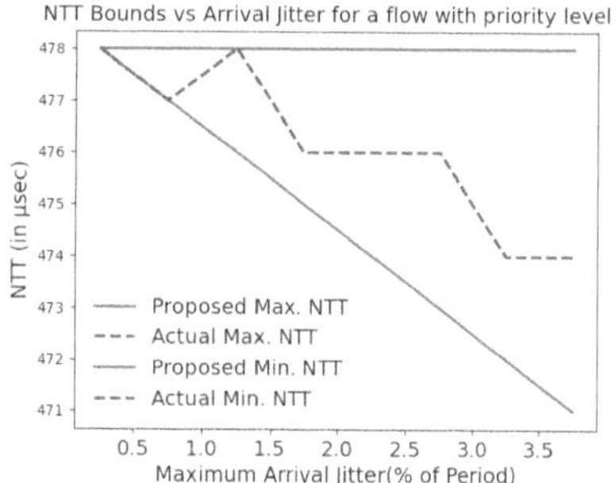

(b) NTT variation with maximum arrival jitter for a periodic flow with priority 3

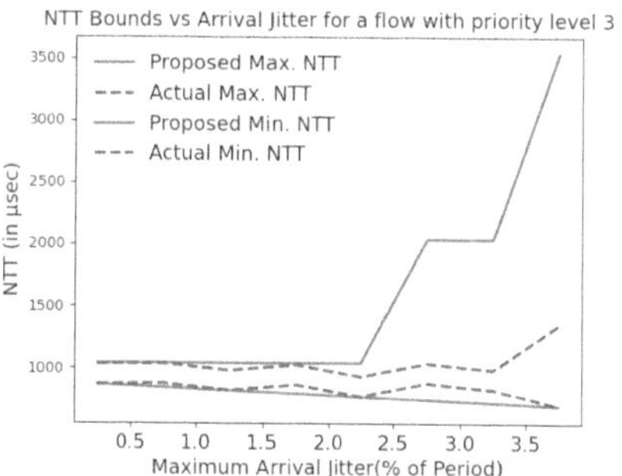

(c) Impact of interference on NTT bound pessimism for a flow with priority 3

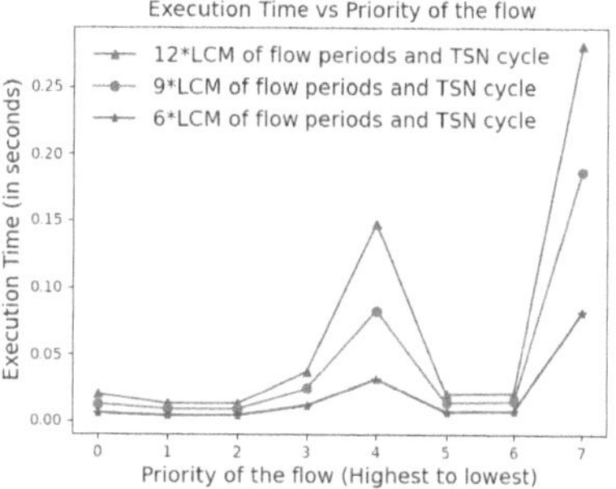

(d) Computation time of NTT bounds for priority flows for different OWs

Fig. 2. Experiments on Synthetic task set

2 resulted in more pessimistic bounds compared to Set 1. This difference can be attributed to the time periods of higher-priority flows and the number of slots available at each switch. In Set 1, the periods of higher-priority flows are greater than or equal to that of considered flow, leading to less interference due to fewer instance releases. In contrast, Set 2 reflects a scenario in which higher priority flows have shorter periods, causing more frequent interference. The proposed worst-case bound exhibits an absolute pessimism of 2187μs over the observed maximum. Another contributing factor is the number of slots per TAS cycle: Set 1 includes three slots per cycle, whereas Set 2 has only two. Additionally, at low jitter, the proposed bounds and actual values are nearly identical. This is because the variability introduced in Eq. 5 is minimized, resulting in relatively closer earliest and latest slot transmissions at each switch.

Experiment 3. This experiment analyzed the simulation time for each flow, with $\mathbb{N} = 8$, by varying the observation window (OW) - used to compute all possible traversal paths in the system - to 6, 9 and 12 times the LCM of the flow periods and the TAS cycle length. As shown in the Fig. 2d, the maximum simulation times for each OW are 0.074, 0.169 and 0.318 s, respectively. This demonstrates the feasibility of observing trends across different OW lengths. For this experiment, the following periods were considered: [1000, 5000, 5000, 1000, 200, 5000, 5000, 200]μs. The increase in execution time for the flow with priority 4 is attributed to its shorter period compared to higher-priority flows. This results in both the earliest and latest slots being assigned to a larger number of flow instances, which in turn leads to the computation of more traversal paths.

5.2 Automotive Use Case

The automotive network described in [11] includes time-critical, audio, video, and event-driven flows. To evaluate our approach, we conducted experiments on an isolated subsystem comprising two TSN switches that connect sensors to a central controller, ensuring that flows from other switches were excluded, as the proposed approach is detailed for flows following the same sequence of links. The payload size was set to the MTU, with padding added for smaller frames.

Experiment. In this experiment, we analyzed the NTT variation for a subset of time-critical flows within the network architecture, specifically HeartBeat, TelematicsData, LiDAR, and RADAR, listed in order of priority. The periods for these flows are [6000,10000,1300,2500]μs, and δ_k^{max} for each stream is set to 0.5% of its respective period. The offset determination and simulation parameters were configured the same as those used for the synthetic task set.

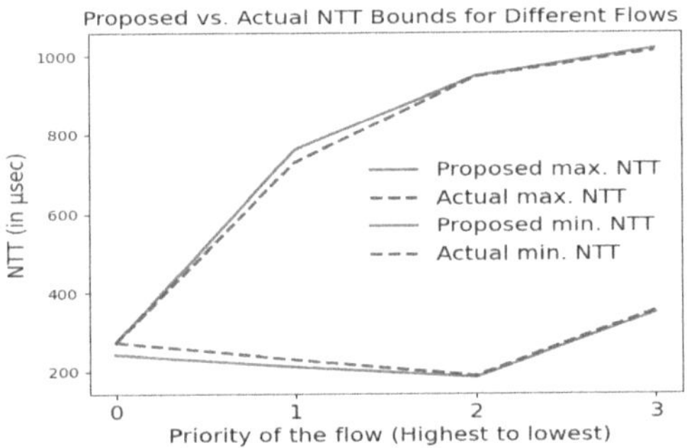

Fig. 3. NTT variation for periodic flows in the automotive use case where δ^{max} for each flow is set to 0.5% of its period.

From Fig. 3, we observe an increasing trend as the flow priority decreases from highest to lowest. However, a slight decrease in NTT for the flow with priority 2 can be attributed to its shorter period. In this setup, the maximum difference between the actual and the proposed values across the flows is 32μs.

6 Conclusion

NTT is a key metric for evaluating latency in TSN, crucial for meeting real-time deadlines and ensuring deterministic communication. This work presents a systematic NTT analysis framework under arrival jitter, estimating the best- and worst-case ST slot allocations for a flow instance as it traverses multiple switches. The proposed approach efficiently computes NTT bounds by systematically pruning the paths through each slot across switches whose NTT values are ineffective for bound determination. To evaluate the efficacy of our framework, we conducted experiments on both a synthetic task set and an automotive use case, analyzing the trends in the bounds across different priority flows. Future research directions include the development of an optimized gate scheduling algorithm that minimizes NTT while accounting for arrival jitter.

References

1. Alieiev, R., Kwoczek, A., Hehn, T.: Automotive requirements for future mobile networks. In: 2015 IEEE MTT-S International Conference on Microwaves for Intelligent Mobility (ICMIM), pp. 1–4 (2015)
2. Barzegaran, M., Reusch, N., Zhao, L., Craciunas, S.S., Pop, P.: Real-time traffic guarantees in heterogeneous time-sensitive networks. In: Proceedings of the 30th International Conference on Real-Time Networks and Systems, p. 46–57 (2022)
3. Chen, H., Tian, J.: Research on the controller area network. In: 2009 International Conference on Networking and Digital Society, vol. 2, pp. 251–254 (2009)
4. Houtan, B., Ashjaei, M., Daneshtalab, M., Sjödin, M., Mubeen, S.: Synthesising schedules to improve QoS of best-effort traffic in TSN networks. In: Proceedings of the 29th International Conference on Real-Time Networks and Systems, p. 68–77 (2021)
5. Houtan, B., Ashjaei, M., Daneshtalab, M., Sjödin, M., Mubeen, S.: Supporting end-to-end data propagation delay analysis for TSN-based distributed vehicular embedded systems. J. Syst. Architect. **141**, 102911 (2023)
6. Kondooru, P.K., Gangadharan, D.: Technical Report: Network Traversal Time (NTT) Analysis of ST Flows in TSN networks. Technical report (2025). https://github.com/Pavankumarkondooru/NTT-Analysis/blob/main/Technical_report.pdf, Accessed 25 Jul 2025
7. Li, C., Li, Z., Li, T., Li, C., Wang, B.: A deterministic embedded end-system tightly coupled with TSN schedule. IEEE Trans. Comput. Aided Des. Integr. Circuits Syst. **42**(11), 3707–3719 (2023)
8. Lo Bello, L., Ashjaei, M., Patti, G., Behnam, M.: Schedulability analysis of time-sensitive networks with scheduled traffic and preemption support. J. Parallel Distrib. Comput. **144**, 153–171 (2020)
9. Lo Bello, L., Steiner, W.: A perspective on IEEE time-sensitive networking for industrial communication and automation systems. Proc. IEEE **107**(6), 1094–1120 (2019)
10. Maxim, D., Song, Y.Q.: Delay analysis of AVB traffic in time-sensitive networks (TSN). In: Proceedings of the 25th International Conference on Real-Time Networks and Systems, p. 18–27. RTNS '17 (2017)

11. Patti, G., Bello, L.L., Leonardi, L.: Deadline-aware online scheduling of TSN flows for automotive applications. IEEE Trans. Industr. Inf. **19**(4), 5774–5784 (2023)
12. Pellizzoni, R., Lipari, G.: Feasibility analysis of real-time periodic tasks with offsets. Real-Time Syst. **30**(1–2), 105–128 (2005)
13. Reusch, N., Zhao, L., Craciunas, S.S., Pop, P.: Window-based schedule synthesis for industrial IEEE 802.1Qbv TSN networks. In: 2020 16th IEEE International Conference on Factory Communication Systems (WFCS), pp. 1–4 (2020)
14. Seliem, M., Zahran, A., Pesch, D.: Delay analysis of TSN based industrial networks with preemptive traffic using network calculus. In: 2023 IFIP Networking Conference (IFIP Networking), pp. 1–9 (2023)
15. Srinivasan, S., Nelissen, G., Bril, R.J., Meratnia, N.: Analysis of TSN time-aware shapers using schedule abstraction graphs. In: 36th Euromicro Conference on Real-Time Systems (ECRTS 2024), pp. 16:1–16:24 (2024)
16. Zhao, L., He, F., Li, E., Lu, J.: Comparison of Time Sensitive Networking (TSN) and TTEthernet. In: IEEE/AIAA DASC, pp. 1–7 (2018)
17. Zhao, L., Pop, P., Craciunas, S.S.: Worst-case latency analysis for IEEE 802.1Qbv time sensitive networks using network calculus. IEEE Access **6**, 41803–41815 (2018)

Dead Transitions Analysis and Resolution in Dual-Time Petri Nets

Shu Zhang[1], Ruotian Liu[2], Yufeng Chen[1], Maria Pia Fanti[2(✉)], Wei Wei[3], and Boyu Dong[3]

[1] School of Electro-Mechanical Engineering, Xidian University, Xi'an 710071, China
[2] Department of Electrical and Information Engineering, Polytechnic University of Bari, 70126 Bari, Italy
{ruotian.liu,mariapia.fanti}@poliba.it
[3] Beijing NAURA Microelectronics Equipment Co., Ltd., Beijing 100176, China
{weiwei01,boyu.dong}@naura.com

Abstract. This paper investigates the impact of static temporal parameters on the behavior of timed discrete event systems modeled using dual-time Petri nets. In such models, the firing of transitions is essential to ensure correct system evolution. However, improperly configured temporal constraints may result in dead transitions, where certain transitions are prevented from firing despite being enabled with respect to markings, thereby disrupting expected system behavior. To address this issue, we analyze the conditions under which dead transitions occur due to invalid temporal functions within the net structure. Based on this analysis, a set of adjustment options is introduced to resolve a dead transition, designed to restore an invalid firing window by modifying temporal parameters. Furthermore, we propose a cost-based adjustment strategy that iteratively derives a valid temporal function, ensuring the absence of dead transitions in the revised system. At each iteration, the strategy selects the adjustment option with the lowest associated cost to resolve a specific dead transition. To validate the effectiveness of the proposed approach, an extended state class graph is employed as a structural representation of D-TPN evolution, enabling verification of the resolution of dead transitions under each revised temporal function.

Keywords: Discrete event system · deadlock analysis · time Petri net

1 Introduction

Petri nets are a widely used mathematical formalism for modeling and analyzing discrete event systems [1–3], providing both an intuitive and explicit representation of system behavior. Among various extensions, dual-time Petri nets (D-TPNs) [4] incorporate temporal parameters associated with both places and transitions, offering a more compact and expressive framework for representing diverse temporal behaviors. However, improperly configured temporal constraints may lead to a dead transition problem, where an enabled transition

B. Ben Hedia et al. (Eds.): VECoS 2025, LNCS 16263, pp. 17–31, 2026.
https://doi.org/10.1007/978-3-032-20440-0_2

cannot fire due to an unsatisfied firing window, thereby hindering the system's evolution. Consequently, addressing this problem is essential for ensuring system liveness, that is, the property that guarantees every transition can eventually fire within the net.

Deadlocks have been extensively studied in the literature as a major liveness issue in discrete event systems. Within the classic Petri net formalism, several approaches have been developed for deadlock control. These include reachability graph analysis, which aims to derive optimal (maximally permissive) deadlock controllers [5–8]; structural analysis, which focuses on siphons, place invariants, and other structural objects to design deadlock prevention and recovery mechanisms [9–12]; and parametric model checking, where control strategies are formulated by assigning temporal constraints to transitions to prevent deadlocks [13,14].

Given the increasing importance of temporal aspects in real-world systems, significant efforts have been dedicated to liveness enforcement in time-dependent Petri nets. One of the earliest contributions is the supervisory control framework proposed in [15], which aims to prevent deadlocks in timed discrete event systems. This work was extended in [16], where control synthesis is performed over state regions with a focus on safety properties defined by the markings of Petri nets. To address real-time scheduling problems without an exhaustive state space exploration, a method for enforcing transition firing deadlines is proposed in [17]. Building on this, a forward on-the-fly method is introduced based on the exploration of the state class graph, achieving both safety and maximal permissiveness [18]. Recently, several studies have focused on enforcing deadlock-freeness in a class of Petri nets where temporal intervals are assigned to transitions, known as transition-time Petri nets. These studies operate under logical control specifications, such as generalized mutual exclusion constraints [19], aiming to ensure deadlock-freeness in a maximally permissive manner [20–23]. Moreover, parametric model checking techniques developed in [13,14] can be applied to verifying whether appropriate restrictions on the firing intervals of controllable transitions, can enforce deadlock-freeness; the study in [24] introduces a control pattern defined over system states to guide the evolution of the controlled model, effectively prohibiting the firing of illegal transitions. This method reduces the computational overhead typically associated with parametric approaches, thereby enhancing the practical applicability of supervisory control in time-constrained systems.

Despite these advances, the issue of dead transitions, arising from temporal constraints rather than marking conditions, has received relatively little attention. In complex systems with complex temporal dependencies, system blocking caused by temporal coupling can lead to degraded performance and reduced resource utilization, thereby posing a challenge to ensuring system liveness. To address these problems, this study focuses on the analysis and resolution of dead transitions in D-TPNs, a formalism well-suited for capturing temporal coupling due to its temporal semantics, laying the foundation for ensuring system liveness under complex temporal constraints.

The main contributions of this paper are summarized as follows: (1) We formulate the verification problem of a temporal function to determine the presence of dead transitions in a D-TPN, and analyze the conditions under which such transitions arise due to an invalid temporal function within the net structure. (2) A set of adjustment options that modify specific temporal parameters to restore the firing window of a given dead transition is introduced, and a cost function is defined to quantify the impact of modification on the temporal parameters. (3) We propose a cost-based strategy to derive a valid temporal function that ensures the absence of dead transitions in the revised system. Specifically, an iterative algorithm is developed to resolve each dead transition individually by selecting the adjustment option with the minimum associated cost at each iteration, until returning a valid temporal function.

The remainder of this paper is organized as follows. Section 2 provides basic concepts on D-TPNs. We characterize the conditions under which dead transitions arise and propose adjustment options for their resolution in Sect. 3. Section 4 presents a cost-based strategy, implemented as an iterative algorithm, to derive a valid temporal function of the net structure. Finally, Sect. 5 concludes the paper and discusses potential directions for future research.

2 Preliminaries

2.1 Dual-Time Petri Nets

Let $\mathbb{N}$ be the set of non-negative integers and $\mathbb{R}_0^+$ be the set of non-negative real numbers. We denote by $\Omega = \{[a,b] \mid \langle a,b\rangle \in \mathbb{R}_0^+ \times (\mathbb{R}_0^+ \cup \{\infty\}) \wedge a \leq b\}$ a set of closed intervals whose lower and upper bounds are in $\mathbb{R}_0^+$ and $\mathbb{R}_0^+ \cup \{\infty\}$, respectively.

Definition 1. *A dual-time Petri net (D-TPN) is a five-tuple $N_t = (P, T, Pre, Post, \mathcal{I}s)$, where*

- *P is a set of n_p places;*
- *T is a set of n_t transitions;*
- *$Pre : P \times T \to \mathbb{N}$ is the* pre-*incidence function that specifies the arcs directed from places to transitions;*
- *$Post : P \times T \to \mathbb{N}$ is the* post-*incidence function that specifies the arcs directed from transitions to places;*
- *$\mathcal{I}s : P \cup T \to \Omega$ is a temporal function that assigns to a place $p_i \in P$ or a transition $t_j \in T$ a static interval, denoted by $\mathcal{I}s(p_i) = [a_i, b_i]$ and $\mathcal{I}s(t_j) = [l_j, u_j]$, respectively.* □

Let $C = Post - Pre$ be the incidence matrix of the net. For a transition $t_j \in T$, its preset is defined as ${}^\bullet t_j = \{p_i \in P \mid Pre(p_i, t_j) > 0\}$ and its postset is defined as $t_j{}^\bullet = \{p_i \in P \mid Post(p_i, t_j) > 0\}$. A marking is a mapping $M : P \to \mathbb{N}$ that assigns to a place a non-negative integer number of tokens. $M(p)$ represents the number of tokens in place p at marking M. A pair $\langle N_t, M_0\rangle$ is called a D-TPN system, where N_t is a D-TPN and M_0 is an initial marking.

The static temporal attributes associated with a place affect the tokens it holds. The interval $\mathcal{I}s(p_i) = [a_i, b_i]$ denotes the token availability in p_i. Specifically, when a token is deposited in p_i, it remains unavailable until a_i time units have elapsed; it is available during the interval $[a_i, b_i]$; and it becomes expired after b_i time units. Token availability plays distinct roles in the net evolution: the unavailable and available tokens, both called *effective* tokens, participate in enabling and firing transitions, while expired tokens are considered ineffective and cannot contribute to enabling transitions. For concise, at marking M, let q_v^i be a specific token in $p_i \in P$ with an index $v \in \{1, 2, \cdots, M(p_i)\}$, $\mathcal{K}_i^e(M)$ be the set of effective tokens in place p_i at M.

Definition 2. *Given a transition t_j in a D-TPN N_t, it is enabled at marking M if for all $p_i \in {}^\bullet t_j$, $|\mathcal{K}_i^e(M)| \geq Pre(p_i, t_j)$, where $|\mathcal{K}_i^e(M)|$ is the number of effective tokens in place p_i at M.* □

A transition $t_j \in T$ in N_t is said to be enabled at marking M if there are enough effective tokens in each of its input places. At M, we denote the set of enabled transitions by $\mathcal{E}_l(M)$ and the set of tokens by $\mathcal{K}(M)$.

Definition 3. *A state of a D-TPN N_t is a pair $S = (M, \mathcal{I}d)$, where M is a marking and $\mathcal{I}d : \mathcal{K}(M) \cup \mathcal{E}_l(M) \rightarrow \Omega$ is a function that assigns a dynamic interval to a token $q \in \mathcal{K}(M)$ or a transition $t \in \mathcal{E}_l(M)$, which corresponds to the time window during which the token is available and the transition fires, respectively.* □

At state S, the *available window* of a token q is denoted as $\mathcal{I}d(q) = [\mathscr{L}(q), \mathscr{U}(q)]$, where $\mathscr{L}(q)$ is the *earliest available time instant* at which token q becomes available for consumption, and $\mathscr{U}(q)$ is the *latest available time instant*, representing the moment when token q expires. Upon the deposition of token q in place p_i, its available window is initially set to $\mathcal{I}s(p_i) = [a_i, b_i]$.

Definition 4. *Let $S = (M, \mathcal{I}d)$ be a state in a D-TPN N_t, q be a token with availability window $\mathcal{I}d(q) = [\mathscr{L}(q), \mathscr{U}(q)]$. At state S, a token q is said to be expired if $\mathscr{U}(q) < 0$.* □

Whether an enabled transition can fire depends on the duration for which the required tokens remain available in its input places. Let $\mathscr{C}_j(M)$ be the set of consumed tokens with respect to (w.r.t) a transition t_j, following the *first-in-first-out rule* [25]. Formally, $\mathscr{C}_j(M) = \{qc_m^i = arg\min_{q_v^i \in \mathcal{K}_i^e(M) \setminus \{\bigcup_{k=1}^{m-1}\{qc_k^i\}\}} \{\mathscr{L}(q_v^i)\} \mid p_i \in {}^\bullet t_j, m = 1, 2, \ldots, Pre(p_i, t_j)\}$. Specifically, for an enabled transition t_j, its firing window $\mathcal{I}d(t_j) = [\mathscr{L}(t_j), \mathscr{U}(t_j)]$, determined by the availability of tokens in $\mathscr{C}_j(M)$ and its predefined static interval $\mathcal{I}s(t_j) = [l_j, u_j]$, is specified in a calculation rule:

$$\mathcal{I}d(t_j) = [\mathscr{A}_q(t_j) + l_j, \min\{\mathscr{A}_q(t_j) + u_j, \mathscr{E}_q(t_j)\}] \tag{1}$$

where $\mathscr{A}_q(t_j) = \max_{qc_m^i \in \mathscr{C}_j(M)}\{\mathscr{L}(qc_m^i)\}$ represents the time instant when all tokens in $\mathscr{C}_j(M)$ become available and $\mathscr{E}_q(t_j) = \min_{qc_m^i \in \mathscr{C}_j(M)}\{\mathscr{U}(qc_m^i)\}$ represents the time instant that a token in $\mathscr{C}_j(M)$ becomes expired.

Definition 5. *Let $S = (M, \mathcal{I}d)$ be a state in a D-TPN, t_j be an enabled transition at M, and $\mathscr{C}_j(M)$ be the set of consumed tokens w.r.t t_j. At state S, an enabled transition t_j, associated with $\mathcal{I}s(t_j) = [l_j, u_j]$, is said to be firable if $l_j \leq \mathscr{E}_q(t_j) - \mathscr{A}_q(t_j) \leq u_j$, and dead otherwise.* □

The dynamic evolution of a D-TPN system through both continuous (time elapses) and discrete (transitions fire) semantics, where the following policies [26, 27] are considered: (i) *strong time semantics*: a firable transition must fire unless it is disabled by the firing of another transition; (ii) *single-server policy*: a transition can fire only one enabling instance at a time; (iii) *enabling memory policy*: a transition does not retain any memory of previous enabling.

The semantics of a D-TPN is formalized as a timed transition system, represented by a tuple $\mathcal{S}_{N_t} = (\mathrm{Q}, S_0, \rightarrow)$, where Q is the set of reachable states; $S_0 \in \mathrm{Q}$ is an initial state; $\rightarrow$ is a transitive relation. A D-TPN system $\langle N_t, M_0 \rangle$ evolves from a state $S = (M, \mathcal{I}d)$ as follows:

A continuous transition relation is defined as $(M, \mathcal{I}d) \xrightarrow{\theta_j} (M, \mathcal{I}d_c)$ for all $\theta_j \in \mathbb{R}_0^+$ if $\theta_j \leq \min_{t_s \in \mathcal{E}_l(M)}\{\mathscr{U}(t_s)\}$, where for each $x \in \mathcal{K}(M) \cup \mathcal{E}_l(M)$, $\mathcal{I}d(x) = [\mathscr{L}(x), \mathscr{U}(x)]$ and $\mathcal{I}d_c(x) = [\max\{0, \mathscr{L}(x) - \theta_j\}, \mathscr{U}(x) - \theta_j]$. A discrete transition relation is defined as $(M, \mathcal{I}d) \xrightarrow{t_j} (M', \mathcal{I}d')$ for all $t_j \in T$ if

$$\begin{cases} \text{(a) } |\mathcal{K}_i^e(M)| \geq Pre(p_i, t_j) & \forall p_i \in {}^\bullet t_j \\ \text{(b) } \mathscr{U}(t_j) \geq \mathscr{L}(t_j) & \\ \text{(c) } M' = M + C(\cdot, t_j) & \\ \text{(d) } \mathcal{I}d'(q_v^i) = [a_i, b_i] & \forall q_v^i \in \mathcal{K}(M') \setminus \mathcal{K}(M) \\ \text{(d}'\text{) } \mathcal{I}d'(q_v^i) = \mathcal{I}d(q_v^i) & \forall q_v^i \in \mathcal{K}(M') \cap \mathcal{K}(M) \\ \text{(e) } \mathcal{I}d'(t_f) = [\mathscr{L}'(t_f), \mathscr{U}'(t_f)] & \forall t_f \in \mathcal{X}_l^{t_j}(M) \\ \text{(e}'\text{) } \mathcal{I}d'(t_f) = \mathcal{I}d(t_f) & \forall t_f \in \mathcal{E}_l(M') \setminus \mathcal{X}_l^{t_j}(M) \end{cases} \tag{2}$$

Note that $\mathcal{X}_l^{t_j}(M)$ denotes by the set of newly enabled transitions resulting from the firing of t_j at marking M, defined by $\mathcal{X}_l^{t_j}(M) = \{t' | t' \in \mathcal{E}_l(M + C(\cdot, t_j)) \wedge (t' \notin \mathcal{E}_l(M - Pre(\cdot, t_j)) \vee (t' = t_j)\}$. Constraint (2.a) guarantees that t_j is enabled at M; the condition that t_j is firable at state S is ensured by Constraint (2.b); Constraint (2.c) shows the marking evolution by the firing of transition t_j; the dynamic windows of tokens and enabled transitions at state S' are updated due to Constraints (2.d, 2.d′) and (2.e, 2.e′), where $\mathscr{L}'(t_f)$ and $\mathscr{U}'(t_f)$ are computed following the calculation rule (1).

A state S is reachable if there exists at least one run π such that $S_0 \xrightarrow{\theta_0} S_0' \xrightarrow{t_0} S_1 \xrightarrow{\theta_1} S_1' \xrightarrow{t_1} S_2 \cdots S_n \xrightarrow{\theta_n} S_n' \cdots$, where S_0 is the initial state. A marking M is reachable if there exists a reachable state $S = (M, \mathcal{I}d) \in \mathrm{Q}$. State S is said to be a time-induced dead if all enabled transitions are dead at S.

2.2 Extend State Class Graphs

For a D-TPN, an extended state class graph (ESCG), which serves as a structural abstraction of the system's dynamic behavior, offers insights into the system's behavior and properties [4].

Definition 6. *Given a D-TPN system $\langle N_t, M_0\rangle$, an extended state class graph is a finite directed graph $\mathcal{G} = (\mathcal{C}, \mathcal{E}, \Gamma, C_0)$ such that*

- *$\mathcal{C} \subseteq S_s^d$ is the set of nodes, where each node C corresponds to a distinct state;*
- *$\mathcal{E} \subseteq \mathcal{C} \times (T \times \Omega) \times \mathcal{C}$ is the set of edges, where each edge is labeled with a pair $(t, \Delta) \in (T \times \Omega)$;*
- *$\Gamma : \mathcal{C} \rightarrow 2^{\mathcal{E}}$ is a function that maps each node $C \in \mathcal{C}$ to the set of its outgoing edges;*
- *$C_0 \in \mathcal{C}$ is the root node.* □

The ESCG of a D-TPN is a directed graph in which nodes represent classes, and edges indicate the evolution of these nodes as a result of transition firings. A node $C_k \in \mathcal{C}$ corresponds to a class associated with the state $S_k = (M_k, \mathcal{I}d_k)$, encompassing all reachable states from S_k that maintain the same marking M_k throughout the system's continuous evolution. As time elapses, a transition in S_k may fire, leading to the creation of a new node C_{k+1}, which corresponds to the new state S_{k+1}. Each outgoing edge from node C_k in $\Gamma(C_k)$ is labeled with a pair (t_j, Δ_j^k), where t_j is the firing transition, and $\Delta_j^k \in [\mathscr{L}(t_j), \min_{t_s \in \mathcal{E}_l(M_k)}\{\mathscr{U}(t_s)\}]$ represents the time duration the system remains in C_k before the firing of t_j. The notation $C_k[\Gamma(C_k)\rangle C_{k+1}$ indicates the discrete evolution that creates a new node. Due to space limitations, the step-by-step procedure for constructing an ESCG $\mathcal{G}$ is introduced in [4]. It is worth noting that an ESCG is finite if a bounded D-TPN does not contain repetitive sequences that may fire in zero time.

Example 1. To illustrate the notations and key concepts related to D-TPNs and the ESCG, consider the D-TPN system depicted in Fig. 1 [4], initialized with the temporal function $\mathcal{I}s_0$. The corresponding ESCG, shown in Fig. 2, is constructed within the initial state space Q_0. The ESCG comprises nine nodes, capturing all reachable states of the system in a structural representation, modeling both the discrete and continuous semantics of the D-TPN.

For example, class C_2 (represented by state S_2) is characterized by marking M_2 and a set of constraint inequalities associated with the enabled transitions t_1 and t_3, as well as tokens q_2^1, q_1^3, and q_1^4 at M_2. At state S_2, according to Equation (1), the firing window of transition t_1 is given by $\mathcal{I}d(t_1) = [18, 60]$, where $\mathscr{L}(t_1) = \mathscr{A}_q(t_1) + l_1 = \max\{0, 10\} + 8 = 18$, and $\mathscr{U}(t_1) = \min\{\mathscr{A}_q(t_1) + u_1, \mathscr{E}_q(t_1)\} = \min\{10 + 80, 60, \infty\} = 60$. Under strong time semantics, transition t_1 may fire as soon as 18 time units have elapsed, and must fire no later than 30 time units have elapsed, which corresponds to the upper bound of transition t_3 in state S_2. Assume that transition t_1 fires after $\Delta_1^2 \in [18, 30]$ time units have elapsed in state S_2, and the system evolves to a new state S_3. This evolution is represented in the ESCG by an edge from node C_2 to node C_3, labeled with the pair (t_1, Δ_1^2), where Δ_1^2 denotes the time duration the system remains in C_2 before the firing of t_1. In state S_3, transition t_3 remains enabled; thus its firing interval is reduced by Δ_1^2, reflecting the elapsed time since it became enabled.

The ESCG exploration terminates at two nodes: C_5 and C_8. State S_8 corresponds to a target state of the system, while state S_5 is identified as time-induced dead, since its only enabled transition t_2 cannot fire due to a violated firing window. □

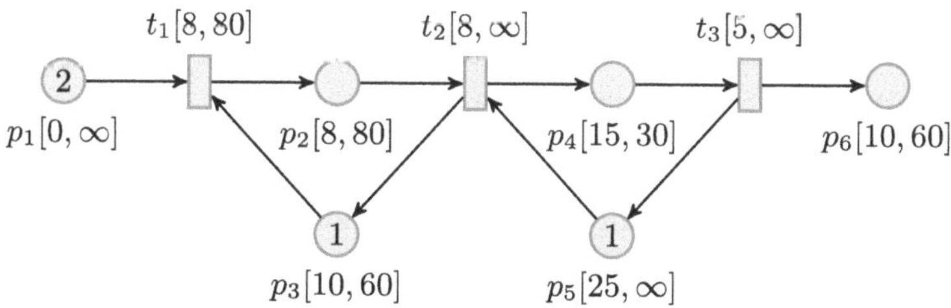

Fig. 1. A D-TPN system

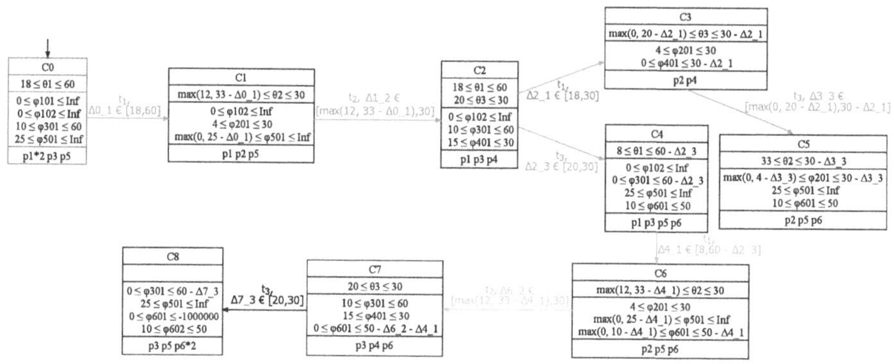

Fig. 2. An ESCG Example

3 Problem Statement

Within the D-TPN framework, improperly configured temporal constraints may result in dead transitions, where certain transitions are enabled with respect to marking conditions but cannot fire due to invalid firing windows, thereby disrupting the expected system behavior. This section examines how inappropriate static temporal parameters result in such dead transitions, and introduces a set of adjustment options, along with the corresponding cost function, to facilitate their resolution.

3.1 Dead Transition Analysis

In the semantics of D-TPNs, a transition $t_j \in T$ is firable at a state if its dynamic firing window is satisfied. This firing condition is governed by both the availability of the required tokens and the static temporal parameters associated with the transition. Based on Eq. (1), we examine two key conditions under which an enabled transition t_j is firable at a given state S, specifically, whether the inequality $\mathscr{L}(t_j) \leq \mathscr{U}(t_j)$ holds at S.

Case 1: $\mathscr{A}_q(t_j) + u_j \leq \mathscr{E}_q(t_j)$. The firing window of transition t_j is given by $[\mathscr{L}(t_j), \mathscr{U}(t_j)] = [\mathscr{A}_q(t_j) + l_j, \mathscr{A}_q(t_j) + u_j]$. It follows that $\mathscr{L}(t_j) \leq \mathscr{U}(t_j)$ due to $l_j \leq u_j$ by Definition 1, ensuring that the transition t_j is firable at S.

Case 2: $\mathscr{A}_q(t_j) + u_j > \mathscr{E}_q(t_j)$. The upper bound of the firing window is constrained by $\mathscr{E}_q(t_j)$, holding $[\mathscr{L}(t_j), \mathscr{U}(t_j)] = [\mathscr{A}_q(t_j) + l_j, \mathscr{E}_q(t_j)]$. Depending on the relationship between $\mathscr{A}_q(t_j) + l_j$ and $\mathscr{E}_q(t_j)$, two sub-cases are then discussed:

- Sub-case 2.1: $\mathscr{A}_q(t_j) + l_j \leq \mathscr{E}_q(t_j)$. The firing window of transition t_j satisfies the condition $\mathscr{L}(t_j) \leq \mathscr{U}(t_j)$, ensuring that the transition is firable at S.
- Sub-case 2.2: $\mathscr{A}_q(t_j) + l_j > \mathscr{E}_q(t_j)$. The transition cannot fire due to the violation of firing window. This situation arises when the availability windows of the required tokens do not sufficiently overlap with the transition's static temporal constraints.

Based on the above analysis, we can now characterize the condition under which a dead transition occurs. A transition t_j is considered dead at state S if the inequality $\mathscr{E}_q(tj) < \mathscr{A}_q(tj) + l_j$ holds. This condition implies the transition cannot fire, as its firing window is no longer satisfied. In fact, this situation results from a misalignment between token availability and the static temporal constraints of the transition.

Remark 1. It is worth noting that the condition $\mathscr{E}_q(t_j) < \mathscr{A}_q(t_j)$ indicates that certain tokens may expire before they can be consumed, preventing the firing of associated transitions. Moreover, the presence of such expired tokens adversely affects the enabling condition of transitions. Consequently, the appropriate configuration of temporal parameters is essential to ensure the correct evolution of the system.

3.2 Adjustment Options and Costs for Dead Transitions

When restoring a firing window by reconfiguring static temporal parameters to resolve a dead transition, broad modifications should be avoided. Instead, adjustments should be targeted specifically at the parameters that directly contribute to the unsatisfied firing window of the dead transition, ensuring a cost-effective resolution.

Consider a dead transition t_j that fails to satisfy its firing condition $\mathscr{L}(t_j) \leq \mathscr{U}(t_j)$. We define an adjustment parameter set $\mathcal{P}(t_j)$, comprising the static temporal parameters that directly influence the computation of the dynamic bounds $\mathscr{L}(t_j)$ and $\mathscr{U}(t_j)$. Formally, $\mathcal{P}(t_j) = \{l_j\} \cup \mathcal{P}_a \cup \mathcal{P}_b$, where l_j is the static lower bound of transition t_j; $\mathcal{P}_a = \{a_i \mid qc^i_m \in \mathscr{C}_j(M), \mathscr{L}(qc^i_m) = \mathscr{A}_q(t_j)\}$ and $\mathcal{P}_b(t_j) = \{b_i \mid qc^i_m \in \mathscr{C}_j(M), \mathscr{U}(qc^i_m) = \mathscr{E}_q(t_j)\}$ represent the sets of static lower and upper bounds of places whose consumed tokens determine $\mathscr{A}_q(t_j)$ and $\mathscr{E}_q(t_j)$, respectively.

To restore the firing condition of a dead transition t_j, the following three adjustment options can be applied to the parameters in $\mathcal{P}$ to ensure $\mathscr{L}(t_j) \leq \mathscr{U}(t_j)$:

(*O*1) Reduce the transition-related parameter l_j;
(*O*2) Reduce the set of place-related parameters $\mathcal{P}_a$ associated with consumed tokens w.r.t t_j, thereby decreasing $\mathscr{A}_q(t_j)$;
(*O*3) Increase the set of place-related parameters $\mathcal{P}_b$ associated with consumed tokens w.r.t t_j, thereby increasing $\mathscr{E}_q(t_j)$.

Before formulating the problem, we introduce the notion of an optimality criterion, namely the minimum adjustment cost. The adjustment cost is formalized through a cost function $\mathbf{C} = \omega \cdot \Upsilon$, where $\omega : \mathcal{P}(t_j) \rightarrow \mathbb{N}$ assigns a non-negative weight to each temporal parameter in the parameter adjustment set $\mathcal{P}(t_j)$, reflecting the expense associated with the modification; and $\Upsilon : \mathcal{P}(t_j) \rightarrow \mathbb{N}$ denotes the magnitude of the modification applied to each parameter, as designed through the adjustment options (*O*1)–(*O*3). Note that the quantification of adjustment weights should consider not only the impact of their modifications on system behavior but also the fulfillment of system requirements, such as resource utilization and efficiency objectives.

Example 2. Consider a dead transition detected in the ESCG shown in Fig. 2. At state S_5, the enabled transition t_2 fails to fire due to an unsatisfied firing window. Specifically, the lower bound is calculated as $\mathscr{L}(t_2) = \max\{0, 4 - \Delta^3_3, 25\} + 8 = 33$, which exceeds its upper bound, given by $\mathscr{U}(t_2) = \min\{\max\{0, 4 - \Delta^3_3, 25\} + \infty, 30 - \Delta^3_3, \infty\} = 30 - \Delta^3_3$.

According to adjustment options (O1)–(O3), the temporal parameters $l_2 = 8$, $a_5 = 25$, and $b_4 = 30$ are candidates for modification to resolve the constraint violation associated with transition t_2, i.e., $\mathcal{P}(t_2) = \{l_2, a_5, b_4\}$. Given that $\Delta^3_3 \in [0, 12]$, the upper bound $\mathscr{U}(t_2)$ is restricted to the interval $[18, 30]$. To satisfy the condition $\mathscr{L}(t_2) \leq \mathscr{U}(t_2)$, the required adjustment magnitudes must meet (i) $3 \leq \Upsilon_{l_2} \leq 8$, (ii) $3 \leq \Upsilon_{a_5} < \infty$, assuming the upper bound remains fixed at 30, and (iii) $3 \leq \Upsilon_{b_4} < \infty$, if $\mathscr{L}(t_2) = 33$ is fixed.

Based on the physical constraints of the system, the adjustment weights are assumed to be $\omega_{l_2} = 2$, $\omega_{a_5} = 3$, and $\omega_{b_4} = 3$. Therefore, the minimum-cost solution for resolving the dead transition t_2 is achieved by modifying the parameter l_2 from 8 to 5, with an adjustment cost of $\mathbf{C} = 2 \cdot 3 = 6$. □

Definition 7. *Given a D-TPN N_t, a temporal function $\mathcal{I}s$ is said to be valid if N_t is free of dead transitions.* □

Problem 1: Given a D-TPN N_t, determine whether a temporal function $\mathcal{I}s$ is valid. If not, derive a valid temporal function $\mathcal{I}s'$ such that the revised system N_t' is free of dead transitions.

A valid adjustment strategy addresses Problem 1 by computing a revised temporal function $\mathcal{I}s'$ such that, for every enabled transition t_j, the firing condition $\mathscr{L}(t_j) \leq \mathscr{U}(t_j)$ is satisfied at all reachable states throughout the system's evolution. This work develops a strategy that, for each dead transition, iteratively selects the adjustment option with the minimum cost. The presence of dead transitions is then re-verified in the revised system, and this process repeats until a valid temporal function is obtained.

4 Temporal Parameter Adjustment Strategy

This subsection presents a parameter adjustment strategy for resolving dead transitions in D-TPNs. The proposed method iteratively derives a valid temporal function that ensures the absence of dead transitions in the revised system. During each iteration, all adjustment options associated with a given dead transition, either a transition-related parameter or a set of place-related parameters, are evaluated. The option yielding the minimal adjustment cost is selected for resolving the specific dead transition. The detailed step-by-step procedure of this method is outlined in Algorithm 1.

Algorithm 1 begins with a set of dead transitions $\mathcal{D}$ and an initial temporal function $\mathcal{I}s$ within the initial state space Q. The temporal function $\mathcal{I}s$ is considered valid if $\mathcal{D}$ is empty (Step 2). During each iteration (Steps 2–22), the algorithm contains two sets: $\mathcal{R}$ and $\mathcal{C}$, which respectively store temporal functions for which the revised system is free of dead transitions, and those resolve the current dead transition. In Steps 8–15, the algorithm applies three adjustment options $(O1)$–$(O3)$ to satisfy the firing condition of a given dead transition t_d, involving in the modification of temporal parameters $\mathcal{P}(t_d) = \{l_d, a_{i,k_1}, b_{i,k_2} \mid p_i \in {}^\bullet t_d, k_1 \in 1, \ldots, |\mathcal{P}_a|, k_2 \in 1, \ldots, |\mathcal{P}_b|\}$. This results in a set of updated temporal functions $\mathcal{A} = \{\mathcal{I}s_{l_d}^{(Q)} \cup \mathcal{I}s_{a_{i,k_1}}^{(Q)} \cup \mathcal{I}s_{bi,k_2}^{(Q)}\}$. For each adjustment option, a new state space Q^x (with $x \in \mathcal{A}$) is generated, and the corresponding adjustment cost $\mathbf{C}^x$ is computed. If the resulting system contains no dead transitions, i.e., $\mathcal{D}^x = \emptyset$, the associated temporal function is added to $\mathcal{R}$ (Steps 16–19); Otherwise, it is stored in $\mathcal{C}$. If all adjustment options cannot resolve the set of dead transitions in $\mathcal{D}$, i.e., $\mathcal{R} = \emptyset$, the algorithm proceeds iteratively to resolve dead transitions in a revised system with the revised temporal function whose associated adjustment cost is minimal among adjustment options in $\mathcal{C}$ (Steps 20–22). The algorithm terminates when a valid temporal function with the minimum total adjustment cost is obtained. If all iterations are exhausted without yielding such a function, the algorithm returns "No solution".

Algorithm 1: A single-option parameter adjustment strategy

Input: A D-TPN N_t, state space Q, a set of dead transitions $\mathcal{D}$, a temporal function $\mathcal{I}s$.

Output: A valid temporal function $\mathcal{I}s_v$.

Initialize $iter \leftarrow 0$, $\mathbf{C} \leftarrow 0$;
while $\mathcal{D} \neq \emptyset$ *and* $iter \leq N$, **do**
  foreach *dead transition* $t_d \in \mathcal{D}$, **do**
    initialize resolved solution set $\mathcal{R} \leftarrow \emptyset$;
    initialize alternative adjustment set $\mathcal{C} \leftarrow \emptyset$;
    $iter \leftarrow iter + 1$;
    design the set of temporal functions $\mathcal{A}$ following adjustment options (O1)–(O3);
    foreach $\mathcal{I}s^x \in \mathcal{A}$, **do**
      evaluate the new state space Q^x under $\mathcal{I}s^x$;
      update the new dead transition set $\mathcal{D}^x$;
      if $\mathcal{D}^x = \emptyset$, **then**
        add $\mathcal{I}s^x$ to $\mathcal{R}$;
      else
        add $\mathcal{I}s^x$ to $\mathcal{C}$;
      compute adjustment cost $\mathbf{C}^x$;
    if $\mathcal{R}$ *is not empty,* **then**
      select $\mathcal{I}s^x \in \mathcal{R}$ with the minimum $\mathbf{C}^x$;
      $\mathcal{I}s_v \leftarrow \mathcal{I}s^x$ and $\mathbf{C} \leftarrow \mathbf{C} + \mathbf{C}^x$;
      return $\mathcal{I}s_v$ *and* $\mathbf{C}$;
    else
      select $\mathcal{I}s^x \in \mathcal{C}$ with the minimum $\mathbf{C}^x$;
      update $Q \leftarrow Q^x$, $\mathcal{D} \leftarrow \mathcal{D}^x$, $\mathcal{I}s \leftarrow \mathcal{I}s^x$ and $\mathbf{C} \leftarrow \mathbf{C} + \mathbf{C}^x$.

Let v be the number of dead transitions in the initial system and N be the maximum number of adjustment iterations required to obtain a valid temporal function. In each iteration, a state space abstraction is performed, with an associated computational cost denoted by C_c. For each of the v dead transitions, Algorithm 1 considers up to $K = 3$ candidate adjustment options. As a result, the maximum number of system verifications per iteration is bounded by $K \cdot v$. Since each verification involves a state space abstraction, the computational complexity per iteration is $\mathcal{O}(K \cdot v \cdot C_c)$. Therefore, the total computational complexity of Algorithm 1 is $\mathcal{O}(N \cdot K_1 \cdot v \cdot C_c)$.

Proposition 1. *Algorithm 1 returns a valid temporal function $\mathcal{I}s_v$ if it holds an empty set $\mathcal{D}^x$ in the revised system.*

Proof. The proof is straightforward from Algorithm 1. In each iteration, the algorithm evaluates all adjustment options $\mathcal{A}$. For each option $x \in \mathcal{A}$, it generates the revised state space Q^x and updates the corresponding set of dead transitions $\mathcal{D}^x$. If a revised system is free of dead transitions, i.e., $\mathcal{D}^x = \emptyset$, the corresponding temporal function $\mathcal{I}s_x$ is added to the resolved solution set $\mathcal{R}$. The algorithm returns the temporal function in $\mathcal{R}$ with the minimum total adjustment cost. If none yields a temporal function for which the revised system is free of dead transitions within the maximum number of iterations, the algorithm terminates and returns "No solution". Thus, a temporal function $\mathcal{I}s_v$ ($\mathcal{I}s^x$) is returned if and only if it produces a revised system in which $\mathcal{D}^x = \emptyset$. ■

The proposed strategy offers a straightforward and computationally efficient approach for deriving a valid temporal function in a revised system that is free from dead transitions. Unlike previous methods that constrain system behavior through control synthesis [20–23], this study emphasizes the restoration of desired system evolution by appropriately configuring static temporal parameters of the net.

Example 3. Consider again the D-TPN model depicted in Fig. 1, where the cost-based parameter adjustment strategy is employed to resolve the dead transition t_2 at state S_5, as detected in Fig. 2. Based on the analysis in Example 2, the adjustment magnitudes for the parameters l_2, a_5 and b_2 are determined as: $\Upsilon_{l_2} \in [3, 8]$, $\Upsilon_{a_5} \in [3, 25]$, and $\Upsilon_{b_4} \in [3, \infty)$, with associated adjustment weights of $\omega_{l_2} = 2$, $\omega_{a_5} = 3$, and $\omega_{b_4} = 3$, respectively.

Algorithm 1 is initialized with the initial temporal function $\mathcal{I}s_0$, along with empty sets for candidate solutions $\mathcal{R}$ and subsequent adjustment options $\mathcal{C}$. Based on adjustment options $(O1)$–$(O3)$, three temporal functions are designed: $\mathcal{I}s^{l_2}$, $\mathcal{I}s^{a_5}$, and $\mathcal{I}s^{b_4}$. The updated temporal intervals, each corresponding to an adjustment magnitude of $\Upsilon = 3$, are given by: $\mathcal{I}s^{l_2}(t_2) = [5, \infty)$, $\mathcal{I}s^{a_5}(p_5) = [22, \infty)$, and $\mathcal{I}s^{b_4}(p_4) = [15, 33]$.

The corresponding ESCGs for these revised D-TPN models (see Fig. 3) indicate that no dead transitions remain. As a result, three temporal functions are added to the resolved solution set, given by $\mathcal{R} = \{\mathcal{I}s^{l_2}, \mathcal{I}s^{a_5}, \mathcal{I}s^{b_4}\}$. The associated adjustment costs are computed as $\mathbf{C}^{l_2} = 6$, $\mathbf{C}^{a_5} = 9$, and $\mathbf{C}^{b_4} = 9$, respectively. Among these, the temporal function $\mathcal{I}s^{l_2}$ is selected as a valid temporal function to return, as it yields the minimum total adjustment cost. □

Remark 2. For systems characterized by complex interdependencies among temporal parameters, the proposed single-option parameter adjustment strategy may exhibit limitations in computational efficiency and optimality of total adjustment cost. This deficiency stems from the fact that a greedy strategy, which applies a single adjustment option per dead transition in each iteration, can fail to identify the globally optimal, more cost-effective solution. To overcome this limitation, a multi-options parameter adjustment strategy can be adopted, where multiple parameters are simultaneously considered to capture their joint influence on the temporal behavior of the system.

Such a strategy facilitates the formulation of dead transition resolution as a mathematical optimization problem. The objective is to minimize the total adjustment cost, subject to the condition that no reachable state contains violated temporal constraints, that is, ensuring that no dead transitions and expired tokens exist. Consequently, this approach enables the efficient exploration of the

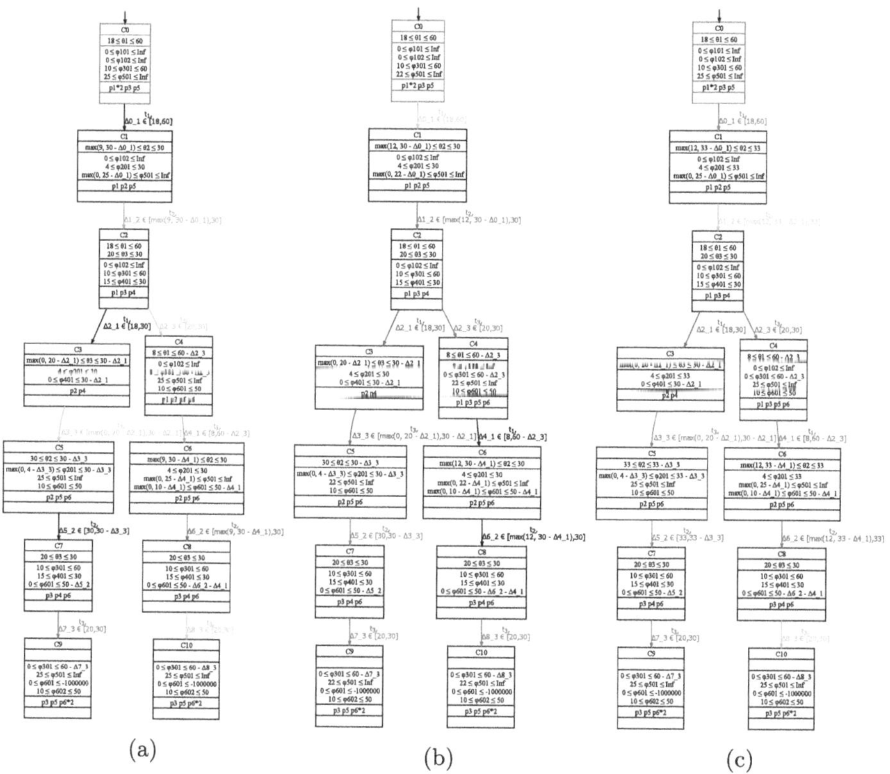

Fig. 3. (a) an ESCG with $\mathcal{I}s^{l_2}$, (b) an ESCG with $\mathcal{I}s^{a_5}$, and (c) an ESCG with $\mathcal{I}s^{b_4}$.

solution space through established optimization techniques, including integer linear programming. The development and evaluation of such a multi-option parameter optimization framework will be the focus of future work.

5 Conclusions

This work proposes a cost-based approach for resolving dead transitions in D-TPNs through the modification of static temporal parameters. A detailed analysis of the conditions under which dead transitions arise is first conducted, highlighting the role of static temporal parameters in constraining the firing of transitions. Building on this analysis, a set of parameter adjustment options is developed to enable the resolution of a dead transition by restoring its unsatisfied firing window. A cost-based adjustment strategy is then introduced, aiming to derive a valid temporal function that ensures a revised system is free of dead transitions. By iteratively selecting the adjustment option associated with the minimum cost for each dead transition, the total adjustment cost is locally minimized. The effectiveness of the proposed method is demonstrated through an example, in which the ESCG is employed to verify if the revised systems are free of dead transitions. While the approach is computationally efficient and straightforward, it provides only locally optimal solutions. Future work will focus on extending the strategy to support multi-parameter and hybrid adjustment mechanisms, with the object of achieving globally optimal solutions that offer a better trade-off between computational efficiency and total adjustment cost.

Acknowledgments. This work is supported by "the Fundamental Research Funds for the Central Universities" under Grants ZYTS25045 and YJSJ25003.

Disclosure of Interests. The authors have no competing interests to declare that are relevant to the content of this article.

References

1. Giua, A., Seatzu, C.: Petri nets for the control of discrete event systems. Softw. Syst. Model. **14**, 693–701 (2015)
2. Liu, R., Ammour, R., Brenner, L., Demongodin, I.: Event-driven control of hybrid systems using batches Petri nets: Application to high throughput manufacturing systems. IEEE Trans. Autom. Sci. Eng. **22**, 11 906–11 919 (2025)
3. Liu, R., Mangini, A.M., Fanti, M.P.: Synthesis of optimal stealthy attacks against diagnosability in labeled Petri nets. IEEE/CAA J. Autom. Sinica **12**(8), 1661–1672 (2025)
4. Zhang, S., Liu, R., Chen, Y., Cong, X., Fanti, M.P.: Modeling and analysis of time dependent Petri nets. In: Proceeding of the 20th IEEE Conference on Automation Science and Engineering, pp. 2140–2145 (2024)
5. Liu, G., Chao, D.Y.: Further reduction of minimal first-met bad markings for the computationally efficient synthesis of a maximally permissive controller. Int. J. Control **88**(8), 1423–1428 (2015)
6. Uzam, M.: An optimal deadlock prevention policy for flexible manufacturing systems using Petri net models with resources and the theory of regions. Int. J. Adv. Manuf. Technol. **19**, 192–208 (2002)
7. Liu, G., Li, P., Li, Z., Wu, N.: Robust deadlock control for automated manufacturing systems with unreliable resources based on Petri net reachability graphs. IEEE Trans. Syst. Man Cybern.: Syst. **49**(7), 1371–1385 (2018)
8. Hu, Y., Ma, Z., Liu, R., Fanti, M.P., Li, Z.: Supervisor synthesis using labeled Petri nets for forbidden state specifications. IEEE Trans. Syst. Man Cybern.: Syst. (2024)
9. Liu, G.Y., Chao, D.Y., Uzam, M.: A merging method for the siphon-based FMS maximally permissive controllers with simpler structures. IMA J. Math. Control. Inf. **31**(4), 551–573 (2014)
10. Huang, Y.-S., Jeng, M., Xie, X., Chung, D.-H.: Siphon-based deadlock prevention policy for flexible manufacturing systems. IEEE Trans. Syst. Man Cybern.-Part A: Syst. Hum. **36**(6), 1248–1256 (2006)
11. Chen, Y., Pan, L., Li, Z.: Design of optimal supervisors for the enforcement of nonlinear constraints on Petri nets. IEEE Trans. Autom. Sci. Eng. **20**(1), 611–623 (2022)

12. Liu, R., Ammour, R., Brenner, L., Demongodin, I.: On/off control for reaching a steady state attractive region in batches Petri nets. IFAC-PapersOnLine **56**(2), 9618–9623 (2023)
13. Boucheneb, H., Barkaoui, K., Xing, Q., Wang, K., Liu, G., Li, Z.: Time based deadlock prevention for Petri nets. Automatica **137**, 110119 (2022)
14. Zhai, Q., Hu, X., El-Sherbeeny, A.M., Li, Z.: A deadlock prevention strategy for Petri nets through tuning time constraints. IEEE Access (2024)
15. Brandin, B.A., Wonham, W.M.: Supervisory control of timed discrete-event systems. IEEE Trans. Autom. Control **39**(2), 329–342 (1994)
16. Gardey, G., Roux, O., Roux, O.H.: Safety control synthesis for time Petri nets. In: 8th International Workshop on Discrete Event Systems, pp. 222–228. IEEE (2006)
17. Wang, H., Grigore, L., Buy, U., Lehene, M., Darabi, H.: Enforcing periodic transition deadlines in time Petri nets with net unfoldings. IEEE Trans. Syst. Man Cybern.-Part A: Syst. Hum. **41**(3), 522–539 (2010)
18. Heidari, P., Boucheneb, H.: Maximally permissive controller synthesis for time Petri nets. Int. J. Control **86**(3), 493–511 (2013)
19. Giua, A., DiCesare, F., Silva, M.: Generalized mutual exclusion contraints on nets with uncontrollable transitions. In: Proceeding of the IEEE International Conference on Systems, Man, and Cybernetics, pp. 974–979. IEEE (1992)
20. Chen, Y., Li, Z., Khalgui, M., Mosbahi, O.: Design of a maximally permissive liveness-enforcing Petri net supervisor for flexible manufacturing systems. IEEE Trans. Autom. Sci. Eng. **8**(2), 374–393 (2010)
21. Li, L., Basile, F., Li, Z.: An approach to improve permissiveness of supervisors for GMECs in time Petri net systems. IEEE Trans. Autom. Control **65**(1), 237–251 (2019)
22. Li, L., Basile, F., Li, Z.: Closed-loop deadlock-free supervision for GMECs in time Petri net systems. IEEE Trans. Autom. Control **66**(11), 5326–5341 (2020)
23. Basile, F., Cordone, R., Piroddi, L.: Supervisory control of timed discrete-event systems with logical and temporal specifications. IEEE Trans. Autom. Control **67**(6), 2800–2815 (2021)
24. Qin, T., Dong, Y., Yin, L., Li, Z.: Liveness enforcement for production systems modeled by time Petri nets. Inf. Sci. **648**, 119564 (2023)
25. Boucheneb, H., Bullich, A., Roux, O.H.: FIFO time Petri nets for conflicts handling. IFAC Proc. Vol. **45**(29), 143–148 (2012)
26. Bérard, B., Cassez, F., Haddad, S., Lime, D., Roux, O.H.: Comparison of different semantics for time Petri nets. In: Proceeding of the 3rd International Conference on Automated Technology for Verification and Analysis, pp. 293–307 (2005)
27. Wang, J.: Timed Petri Nets: Theory and Application, vol. 9. Springer (2012)

A Multivariate Stochastic Ordering for Analysis of Task Graphs with Correlated Random Durations

Jean-Michel Fourneau[1,2(✉)], Soumeya Kaada[2], and Nihal Pekergin[3]

[1] INRIA ARGO, Paris, France
[2] DAVID, Univ. Paris-Saclay, UVSQ, Versailles, France
Jean-Michel.Fourneau@uvsq.fr
[3] LACL, Univ. Paris Est-Créteil, Créteil, France
nihal.pekergin@u-pec.fr

Abstract. This paper presents an approach to provide stochastic bounds for models based on task graphs completion when the elementary durations are stochastic and not independent. When the parameters are deterministic, the complexity of computing the completion time is polynomial. Here, we consider the much more complex case where the durations are discrete random variables. Such an assumption drastically changes the complexity of the problem. Furthermore, we assume that these random variables are somehow correlated. We propose to give stochastic bounds based on the stochastic order for discrete multivariate random vectors to compute bounds on the completion time.

Keywords: Completion Time · Stochastic Task Graph · Stochastic bounds · Discrete Correlated Distributions

1 Introduction

The Completion Time of a task graph is an important model for performance evaluation and operation research as it represents the execution time of a parallel program (also known as stochastic PERT). Unfortunately this problem turns out to be very difficult when the delays are random variables (see [AK89, BAmL93]). Here, we also assume that these delays are somehow correlated. To the best of our knowledge, it is the first approach to consider dependent random variables in this context. We present a general framework which can be associated with stochastic orderings to obtain stochastic bounds of the Completion Time of the task graph. The main idea is to use discrete distributions to describe the random variables and to compute with numerical algorithms the Completion Time. Two difficulties arise: the computations require that the random variables are independent and the number of atoms in the distributions can grow exponentially with the steps of the computation. We assume that the input distributions came from measurements. In that context, the dependence between random variables

B. Ben Hedia et al. (Eds.): VECoS 2025, LNCS 16263, pp. 32–47, 2026.
https://doi.org/10.1007/978-3-032-20440-0_3

came from a sensor which measure two quantities at the same time. Similarly the size of the distributions is a consequence of the precision of the sensor. We claim that stochastic comparison can help to solve both problems by providing stochastic bounds.

The technical part of the paper is as follows. In Sect. 2 we present the known results for the analysis the Completion Time of a task graph with random durations. As many of these approach are based on the stochastic comparison of durations, we also give a brief introduction of the theory of stochastic ordering. In Sect. 3, we present the algorithmic aspect of the stochastic comparison of discrete distributions. These algorithms only consider univariate random variables and their application to the Completion Time is limited to the case where the random variables are all independent and univariate. This approach has already been presented in [ACC+12]. Section 4 is devoted to the first extension to multivariate random variables: the orthant orderings. We present an algorithm to check the comparison and we prove an algorithmic method to build an upper bound and a lower bound according to the orthant ordering such that the size of the support is smaller. This algorithm is the multivariate extension of the key basic action of the algorithm proposed in [ACC+12]. In Sect. 5, we study the multivariate strong stochastic ordering and we prove that the algorithm proposed in the former section also gives lower and upper bounds for this ordering. We also present several new algorithms to analyze the Completion Time of stochastic task graph with dependent random delays. In this paper we will denote by atoms the elements of the support of any discrete finite distribution.

2 Stochastic Task Graphs

We consider the following simple performance evaluation problem for a task graph. We consider a general Directed Acyclic Graph $G = (V, E)$ with number of edges Nv. We distinguish two nodes of V: the source s and the sink t. Let e be the cardinality of E. The nodes are labelled with positive random delays $(w_i)_{i \in V}$. Computing the Completion Time is polynomial when the delays are deterministic. Unfortunately, it is not true anymore when the nodes are associated with random variables (see [BCP95] for a survey on the complexity for various delays and flow problems for networks or graphs with random discrete costs or durations). As it is difficult to solve the problem, several approaches have been proposed to obtain approximations or bounds. We briefly reviewed some of these approaches based on stochastic bounds and suggest to refer to the following surveys [AK89, BAmL93].

Note that it is still possible to solve the problem for small instances where the sizes of the supports are very small and the random variables are independent. It is sufficient to use the Total Probability Theorem after conditioning on the states of all the random variables. Let X_i be the discrete multivariate random vector associated with the distribution of the delays. We assume that the support of X_i is finite. Let S_i be the size of the support of X_i. We denote by Ω the Cartesian product of the support of the input distributions. Under these assumptions, the probability of $(d_1,,,,d_k)$ is given by:

$$Pr(d_1, ..., d_k) = \prod_{i=1}^{k} Pr(X_i = d_i).$$

Thus, some approaches try to minimize the number of nodes where we must have a conditioning to be able to analyze large graphs (see for instance the conditioning set approach by O'Connor [O'C06] and the Uniformly Directed Cutset by Sigal et al. [SPS79]). We now present the definition of the conditioning set as we generalize it in Sect. 5.

Definition 1 (conditioning set). *Any node i is a C-node (conditioning node) if it has 2 or more immediate successors, or any successor of node i is a C-node. The set of C-nodes is a conditioning set. Note that we can remove nodes s and t in the conditioning set as they belong to all the paths we study.*

When the graph has a special structure (the so called serie-parallel graph) it is possible to give a closed form expression for the delay from s to t.

Definition 2 (serie-parallel graph). *A graph is serie-parallel if it is recursively built as follows. It is either: a single node, or some serie-parallel graphs connected in serie, or some serie-parallel graphs connected in parallel.*

Even if we obtain a closed form expression, it remains to explicitly compute the distribution in the discrete case. Such a problem also leads to a combinatorial explosion during the numerical computation. This problem is addressed in Sect. 3.

A more sophisticated approach is based on a property of the paths from s to t: positively associated random variables [Sho77, YPV91]. Intuitively positively associated random variables are positively correlated, a property which holds for the paths from s to t as they may share some nodes and some durations.

More generally, strong stochastic bounds are often used even if the arguments are not always explicit [Dod85, CPT00]. We begin with a definition and the fundamental property which justifies the approach.

Definition 3 (strong stochastic ordering). *Let X and Y be two random variables, $X \preceq_{st} Y$ iff for all increasing function Φ, $\mathbf{E}[\phi(X)] \leq \mathbf{E}[\phi(Y)]$ if the expectations exist. Another definition is $X \preceq_{st} Y$ iff $Pr(X > x) \leq Pr(Y > x)$ for all x.*

Proposition 1 *(Theorem 1.A.3 item b [SS07]). Let $X_1, ..., X_m$ be a set of independent random variables, let $Y_1, Y_2, ..., Y_m$, be another set of independent random variables. If $X_i \preceq_{st} Y_i$ for all i, then, for any increasing function $\psi : R^m \rightarrow R$, one has $\psi(X_1, X_2, ..., X_m) \preceq_{st} \psi(Y_1, Y_2, ..., Y_m)$.*

Thus bounding the input distributions with the $\preceq_{st}$ ordering will provide a univariate stochastic bound on the output when function ψ associated with the problem is increasing.

The univariate strong stochastic ordering is closed under mixtures and this property will be used when we compute and combine conditional distributions.

Proposition 2 (Theorem 1.A.3 item d), [SS07]). *Let X, Y and Θ be random variables such that $[X|\Theta = \theta] \preceq_{st} [Y|\Theta = \theta]$ for all θ in the support of Θ. Then $X \preceq_{st} Y$.*

The main characterization of the Completion Time problem is an extension of monotony related to various stochastic orderings. Let us define first the generic Ψ−monotony. We will use the $\preceq_{st}$ −monotony in this section.

Definition 4 (Ψ−Monotony). *A function f is Ψ−monotone if for all X and Y random variables such that $X \preceq_{\psi} Y$, then $f(X) \preceq_{\psi} f(Y)$.*

The increasing convex ordering is also used. It is defined as follows:

Definition 5 (Increasing convex ordering). *Let X and Y be two random variables, $X \preceq_{icx} Y$ if for all increasing convex function Φ, $\mathbf{E}[\phi(X)] \leq \mathbf{E}[\phi(Y)]$ if the expectations exist.*

Proposition 3. *The Completion Time problem is monotone for the strong univariate stochastic ordering and the increasing convex ordering (see [BAmL93] or [YPV91]).*

The key idea to derive bounds consists in deleting or adding nodes or edges to obtain some families of graphs where the analysis is simpler (for instance the serie-parallel graphs) and which provide bounds for general graphs. The arguments used in the deletion of nodes or edges is simply based on the monotonicity of the Completion Time problem and $0 \preceq_{st} X$ for all X as the random variables are all positive. Unfortunately, independence among the elementary task durations is a mandatory assumption for all these approaches. Thus we have to generalize the techniques to deal with more complex orderings for dependent variables.

Here, we assume that the input distributions (i.e. the elementary delays of the task) are discrete positive random variables with some kind of dependence among them. Let us first illustrate using a small numerical example that one must take into account the dependence between the random variables. We consider the following small graph with 3 nodes depicted in left part of Fig. 1. X, Y and Z represent the delays associated with respectively the first, second and third node. Clearly, the time needed to execute the program associated to this graph is $X + Y + Z$. The distributions are computed after conditioning on the value of the random variables to obtain a problem with deterministic delays which is easily solved. We now assume that the measurements provide a coupled results for X and Y. It is the main reason why we have dependent random variables: the sensors measure two quantities at the same time and one cannot prove that they are independent. We report in the following two tables the assumed values of the distribution of these random variables. We also report the value for the distribution of Z (Table 1). Note that (X, Y) and Z have the same number of atoms but this is not mandatory. Note that if the distributions are independent, the execution time can be exactly computed by the convolution of the distribution of X, Y and Z. However X and Y are dependent.

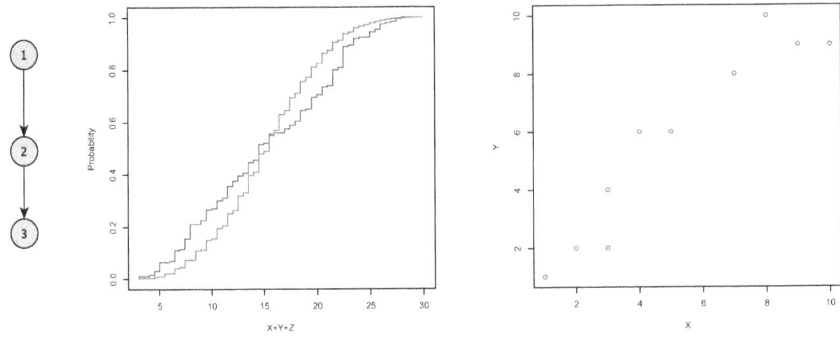

Fig. 1. Simple task graph (left), Completion Time for the simple task graph with correlated random delays: exact distribution in blue and independence approximation in red (center), X vs Y (right). There is a clear positive correlation (i.e. 0.944). (Color figure online)

In the left part of Fig. 1 we have depicted the cumulative distribution function of the exact result (in blue) and the one of the approximation based on independence (in red). Clearly the approximation is not a strong stochastic bound of the exact result as the two curves cross. The difference between the exact distribution and the approximation is due to the correlation between the random variables X and Y which is shown in the right part of Fig. 1. The coefficient of correlation is 0.944, X and Y are clearly dependent and positively correlated (Table 1).

Table 1. Measurements for Z and (X, Y).

Z	Pr(Z)	Z	Pr(Z)
1	1/20	5	5/20
2	1/20	7.5	1/10
2.5	1/20	8	1/20
3	1/10	8.5	1/20
4	5/20	10	1/20

(X,Y)	Pr((X,Y))	(X,Y)	Pr((X,Y))
(1,1)	0.1	(5,6)	0.1
(3,2)	0.1	(9,9)	0.1
(2,2)	0.1	(7,8)	0.1
(3,4)	0.1	(8,10)	0.1
(4,6)	0.1	(10,9)	0.1

Thus, when the measurements show some correlations between the variables, one must take them into account during the numerical analysis and the bounding operations. We now present the algorithmic approaches to deal with discrete random variables in Sect. 3 and we generalize them to multivariate orderings in Sect. 4 and 5 to deal with dependence.

3 Algorithmic Stochastic Bounds

In [ACC+12] we have proposed an approach to obtain distributions which are stochastic bounding distributions according to the strong stochastic ordering of univariate random variables. Using a real trace with an efficient measurement tools, the number of elements in the distribution is too large for many algorithms. Indeed, some numerical algorithms produce an output distribution with a much larger number of atoms than the input distributions. For instance, the convolution of two distributions with 1000 atoms may lead to a distribution with 10^6 atoms. Thus, we derive upper and lower stochastic bounds (we only present below the algorithm for an upper bound) with a smaller support. These bounding distributions have less atoms to facilitate the numerical computations on the model. The number of atoms we want to keep is a parameter of the algorithms we have designed and it gives us a tradeoff between the complexity and the accuracy [ACC+12]. More precisely, for an arbitrary distribution (probability vector) **D** with size N and any positive increasing reward function **r**, we have proved in [ACC+12] an algorithm to find the distributions **D1** and **D2** with size $K < N$ such that

- $\mathbf{D1} \preceq_{\mathbf{st}} \mathbf{D} \preceq_{\mathbf{st}} \mathbf{D2}$
- **D1** and **D2** are optimal bounds according to the expectation of function r.

The optimality of **D1** means that if we found a distribution **D3** such that $\mathbf{D3} \preceq_{\mathbf{st}} \mathbf{D}$ and $\sum_i \mathbf{r(i)D1(i)} \leq \sum_\mathbf{i} \mathbf{r(i)D3(i)} \leq \sum_\mathbf{i} \mathbf{r(i)D(i)}$, then $\mathbf{D3} = \mathbf{D1}$ or $\mathbf{D3} = \mathbf{D}$. The optimality of **D2** is defined in a similar manner. Note that, as function r is increasing, $\mathbf{D1} \preceq_{\mathbf{st}} \mathbf{D}$ implies that $\sum_i \mathbf{r(i)D1(i)} \leq \sum_\mathbf{i} \mathbf{r(i)D(i)}$. This algorithm uses as an elementary block the following operation which provides an upper bound for the univariate strong stochastic ordering with one atom less:

Definition 6 (Max Compression Operation). *Let X be an arbitrary discrete distribution with support $\mathcal{S}_X$ and probability Pr_X. Let a and b two atoms of $\mathcal{S}_X$ such that $a < b$. We build Y as follows:*

- *Y is a discrete distribution with support $\mathcal{S}_X - \{a\}$*
- *for all x in $\mathcal{S}_X - \{a\}$, $Pr_Y(x) = Pr_X(x)$,*
- *$Pr_Y(b) = Pr_X(a) + Pr_X(b)$.*

Choosing the optimal atoms a and b to minimizes the difference between the distribution with respect to a reward function **r** defined by the modeler is based on a graph representation of the distribution and the Guerin and Orda algorithm [GO02]. This algorithm uses a dynamic programming approach and its complexity is $O(K\ N^2)$. We also derive a faster heuristic which computes a stochastic bound which is not optimal. It is based on a the perturbation created by the fusion of atoms. **D2** is initialized as **D** and the MaxCompression operator adds a quantity $(\mathbf{r(b)} - \mathbf{r(a)})\mathbf{D2(a)}$ when it moves atom a to atom b and removes atom a. The heuristic finds at each step the atoms such that the perturbation is minimal and perform the Max Compression operation to delete one atom.

After $N - K$ iterations, the size of the distribution is K. Note that there is no proof that this myopic strategy is optimal for the global compression of the distribution.

Algorithm 1 Heuristic to build an $\preceq_{st}$ upper bound with less atoms.

Input: input distribution $\mathbf{D}$, input size N, output size K.
Output: Output distribution $\mathbf{D2}$.

Let $\mathbf{D2} = \mathbf{D}$.
for all atoms a and b of $\mathbf{D2}$ **do**
  Compute and store $\Gamma(a, b) = (\mathbf{r(b)} - \mathbf{r(a)})\mathbf{D2(a)}$.
end for
for i $= N$ down to $K + 1$ **do**
  Search for the couple of atoms (a, b) of $\mathbf{D2}$ (with $a < b$) which minimizes $\Gamma(a, b)$.
  Apply the MaxCompression operator on a and b in $\mathbf{D2}$. And update matrix Γ.
end for

However when we deal with multiple distributions, this approach supposes independence. As this assumption may be sometimes questionable when the sensors measuring the system provide several quantities at the same time instants, we propose to extend this approach to random vectors (instead of random variables) and multivariate ordering (instead of univariate).

4 Multivariate Stochastic Bounds: the Orthant Orderings and Their Algorithmic Aspects

We assume in the following that we measure vectors of values instead of independent values. Therefore we must generalize to random vectors the comparison results obtained for random variables. More precisely, we assume that there exists a proper partition of V: $(V_1, V_2, .., V_k)$ such that inside a subset V_i all delays are dependent while the delays in V_i are independent of the delays in V_j with $j \neq i$. In the paper, the comparison of vectors (denoted by $\leq$) is made component-wise. We consider multivariate order in R^n for an arbitrary n. However the figures were drawn for $n = 2$. Due to size limitation, we only present the upper bounds results.

Definition 7 (upper orthant ordering). *Let X and Y be two random vectors in R^n , $X \preceq_{uo} Y$ if for all $\boldsymbol{x}$ in R^n, we have: $Pr(X > \boldsymbol{x}) \leq Pr(Y > \boldsymbol{x})$.*

Definition 8 (lower orthant ordering). *Let X and Y be two random vectors in R^n, $X \preceq_{lo} Y$ if for all $\boldsymbol{x}$ in R^n, we have: $Pr(X \leq \boldsymbol{x}) \geq Pr(Y \leq \boldsymbol{x})$.*

Definition 9 (upper orthant and lower orthant). *For all $\boldsymbol{x}$ in R^n, upper orthant $x \uparrow$ is the set of vectors $\boldsymbol{y}$ such that $\boldsymbol{x} \leq \boldsymbol{y}$. Similarly, lower orthant $x \downarrow$ is the set of vectors $\boldsymbol{y}$ such that $\boldsymbol{x} \geq \boldsymbol{y}$.*

Orthant orderings are used to study the dependence among components of a random vector.

Definition 10 (independent version). *Let* $X = (X_1, .., X_n)$ *a random vector in* R^n. *Let* X^I *denote a random vector of* R^n *where* $X_j =_{st} X_j^I$ *for all* j, *and* $X_1^I, X_2^I, .., X_n^I$ *are independent.*

Definition 11 (positively upper orthant dependent). *Let* $X = (X_1, .., X_n)$ *a random vector in* R^n. *We say that* X *is positively upper orthant dependent (PUOD) if* $X^I \preceq_{uo} X$.

We first address the question of an algorithmic comparison of discrete random vectors for the orthant orders. The main question is to find a necessary and sufficient set of orthants to perform the algorithmic verification. Indeed once an orthant is chosen, computing the probability to be in that orthant is straightforward.

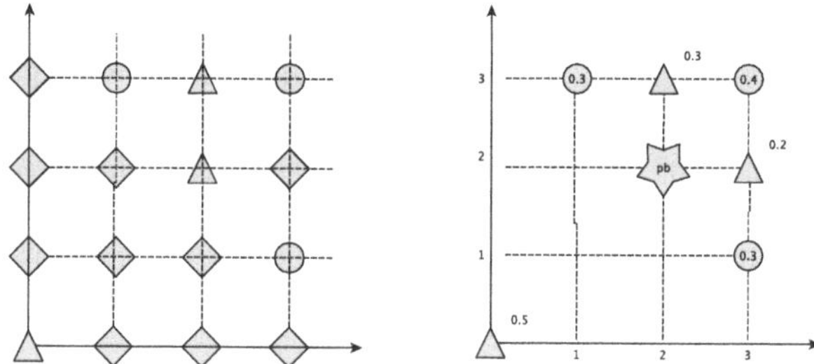

Fig. 2. Set $\mathcal{P}$ for $n = 2$. The nodes of $\mathcal{S}_X$ are depicted as circles, the nodes of $\mathcal{S}_Y$ as triangles, and the remaining nodes of $\mathcal{P}$ are represented as diamonds (left), Counter-example (right).

Proposition 4. *Assume that* X *and* Y *are discrete random vectors. Let* $\mathcal{S}_X$ *and* $\mathcal{S}_Y$ *be respectively the support of* X *and* Y. *Let* $\mathcal{S} = \mathcal{S}_X \cup \mathcal{S}_Y$ *and* $\mathcal{S}_i$ *be the projection of* $\mathcal{S}$ *on the i-th coordinates. Finally, we define* $\mathcal{P} = \mathcal{S}_1 \times \mathcal{S}_2 \times .... \times \mathcal{S}_n$ *where* $\times$ *is the Cartesian product. By construction,* $\mathcal{P}$ *is a lattice. It is sufficient to check the constraint for the orthant ordering (lower or upper) for elements of* $\mathcal{P}$ *to prove the comparison.*

Proof: Consider x an arbitrary vector of R^n and upper orthant $x \uparrow$. Assume that $x \notin \mathcal{P}$. Now let us define set $\mathcal{C}_x$ as follows: $\mathcal{C}_x = \{y \in \mathcal{P} \mid y \geq x\}$. This set may be empty. Otherwise let Sup_x be the smallest node of $\mathcal{C}_x$. Sup_x is unique because $\mathcal{P}$ is a lattice.

- If $\mathcal{C}_x = \emptyset$, then $Pr(X \geq x) = 0 = Pr(Y \geq x)$
- Otherwise, $Pr(X \in x \uparrow) = Pr(X \in Sup_x \uparrow)$ and $Pr(Y \in x \uparrow) = Pr(Y \in Sup_x \uparrow)$. Therefore it is sufficient to verify the constraint for upper orthant $Sup_x \uparrow$, which is by definition a node of $\mathcal{P}$.

Thus we have to check the condition on the upper orthants defined by $\mathcal{P}$.

Proposition 5. *Assume that X and Y are discrete random vectors. Let $\mathcal{S}_X$ and $\mathcal{S}_Y$ be respectively the support of X and Y. Let $\mathcal{S} = \mathcal{S}_X \cup \mathcal{S}_Y$. Checking the constraint for the orthant ordering for elements of $\mathcal{S}$ is not sufficient.*

Proof: by a counter-example depicted in Fig. 2. The atoms of $\mathcal{S}_Y$ are depicted with circles while the atoms of S_X are represented by triangles. The probabilities for Y are 0.3 in $(1,3)$, 0.4 in $(3,3)$ and 0.3 in $(3,1)$ while probabilities for X are 0.5 in $(0,0)$, 0.3 in $(2,3)$ and 0.2 in $(3,2)$. One can check easily that for all x in $\mathcal{S}$ the difference $(Pr(Y \geq x) - Pr(X \geq x)$ is non negative (see the results in the following table). But if we consider $x = (2,2)$ which is not in $\mathcal{S}$, we clearly have $Pr(X \geq x) = 0.5$ and $Pr(Y \geq x) = 0.4$. Thus inequality $Pr(X \geq x) \geq Pr(Y \geq x)$ does not hold and $X \preceq_{uo} Y$ is false.

Atoms	(0,0)	(1,3)	(2,3)	(3,1)	(3,2)	(3,3)
$Pr(X \geq x)$	1	0.3	0.3	0.2	0.2	0
$Pr(Y \geq x)$	1	0.7	0.4	0.7	0.4	0.4

Let m be the size of $\mathcal{S}$. When we consider multivariate distributions with large support, both m and n can be large and the use of conditioning is computationally prohibitive. Therefore it is important to find a smaller set to check the conditions for comparing distributions.

Proposition 6. *Let $\mathcal{S} = \mathcal{S}_X \cup \mathcal{S}_Y$. Let $\mathcal{L}$ be the semi-lattice for the "min" operator generated by the nodes of $\mathcal{S}$. Checking the constraint for orthant ordering for elements of $\mathcal{L}$ is sufficient.*

Proof: First as $\mathcal{L} \subset \mathcal{P}$, it is necessary to check the nodes of $\mathcal{L}$. it remains to prove that this is sufficient. Assume that there exists a vector (say y) in $\mathcal{P}$ and not in $\mathcal{L}$ such that $Pr(X \geq y) > Pr(Y \geq y)$, and assume that for all x in $\mathcal{L}$ we have: $Pr(X \geq x) \leq Pr(Y \geq x)$. Now let $\mathcal{C}_y$ be the largest set of nodes of $\mathcal{L}$ (for the inclusion) which are larger than y. This set may be empty. Otherwise let Sup_y be the smallest node of $\mathcal{C}_y$. Again Sup_y is unique because $\mathcal{C}_y$ is a lattice.

- If $\mathcal{C}_y = \emptyset$, then $Pr(X \geq y) = 0 = Pr(Y \geq y)$. We have a contradiction.
- Otherwise we have by construction $Pr(X \geq y) = Pr(X \geq Sup_y)$ because $\mathcal{C}_y$ is maximal for the inclusion of nodes of $\mathcal{L}$ (and therefore $\mathcal{S}$). Similarly $Pr(Y \geq y) = Pr(Y \geq Sup_y)$. As $Sup_y \in \mathcal{L}$ we have $Pr(X \geq Sup_y) \leq Pr(Y \geq Sup_y)$. Again a contradiction.

Thus it is sufficient to check the condition on the upper orthants defined by $\mathcal{L}$. The algorithm to generate the semi-lattice is well-known (see for instance [NR99]). We now propose some algorithms to derive stochastic bounds with less atoms. We begin with a basic algorithm which provides an upper bound for the $\preceq_{uo}$ ordering with one atom less (or two atoms if $max(a,b) \in \mathcal{S}_X$).

Definition 12 (Max2 Transform). *Let X be an arbitrary discrete distribution with support $\mathcal{S}_X$ and probability Pr_X. Let a and b two atoms of $\mathcal{S}_X$. $Y = Max2(a,b,X)$ is a discrete distribution with support $\mathcal{S}_Y$ and probability Pr_Y such that: (note that $max(a,b)$ is in $\mathcal{S}_Y$ by construction but it may also be in $\mathcal{S}_X$)*

- $\mathcal{S}_Y = \mathcal{S}_X - \{a,b\} \cup max(a,b)$ *where* $max(a,b)$ *is defined component-wise,*
- *for all* x *in* $\mathcal{S}_X - \{a,b,max(a,b)\}$, $Pr_Y(x) = Pr_X(x)$,
- $Pr_Y(max(a,b)) = Pr_X(a) + Pr_X(b) + Pr_X(max(a,b))$.

Proposition 7. *Let X be an arbitrary discrete distribution, and a and b be two arbitrary atoms of its distribution, then $X \preceq_{uo} Max2(a,b,X)$.*

Proof: Consider an arbitrary x in $\mathcal{P}$. We have four cases to consider:

- $a \in x \uparrow$ and $b \in x \uparrow$. Clearly, $max(a,b) \in x \uparrow$. Therefore $Pr(X \geq x) = Pr(Y \geq x)$.
- $a \in x \uparrow$ and $b \notin x \uparrow$. $max(a,b) \geq a \geq x$. Thus, $max(a,b) \in x \uparrow$ also holds. Therefore, assuming that the probability of b is positive, $Pr(X \geq x) < Pr(Y \geq x)$.
- $a \notin x \uparrow$ and $b \in x \uparrow$. Same as the previous case due to the symmetry.
- $a \notin x \uparrow$ and $b \notin x \uparrow$. Therefore $S_X \cap x \uparrow \quad \subset \quad S_Y \cap x \uparrow$ as $max(a,b) \geq x$ may hold. Thus, $Pr(X \geq x) \leq Pr(Y \geq x)$.

Thus, $Pr(X \geq x) \leq Pr(Y \geq x)$ always holds. The proof is complete.

We then define some heuristics to iterate on operation Max2. The key idea is to find some atoms a and b to perform the reduction. We define a cost matrix related to the replacement of atoms a and b by atom $max(a,b)$. Let Δ be the matrix defined as follows:$\Delta(a,b) = \sum_{i=1}^{n} c_i|a(i) - b(i)|$, where c_i is the unit cost associate to dimension i of the problem. All c_i are positive and are chosen to take into account some aspects of the model. When $c_i = 1$ for all i, $\Delta(a,b) = ||a-b||_1$.

5 Multivariate Strong Stochastic Bounds

Definition 13 (Upper Set). *$\mathcal{U}$ is an upper set of R^n if for all $x \in \mathcal{U}$ and for all $y \geq x$, then $y \in \mathcal{U}$.*

Definition 14 (Multivariate strong stochastic ordering). *Let X and Y be two random vectors, $X \preceq_{st} Y$ if for all upper set $\mathcal{U}$ in R^n, we have: $Pr(X \in \mathcal{U}) \leq Pr(Y \in U)$.*

Proposition 8. *The following properties, proved in [SS07], are the key ideas for our method:*

- *Let X and Y be arbitrary discrete distributions. If $X \preceq_{st} Y$, then $X \preceq_{uo} Y$ and $X \preceq_{lo} Y$.*

Algorithm 2 Algorithm for an upper bound for $\preceq_{uo}$ order (and $\preceq_{st}$ order).

Input: input distribution **D1**, input size N.
Output: Output distribution **D2**, output size K.

Let **D2** = **D1**.
for all atoms a and b **do**
  Compute and store $\Delta(a, b)$.
end for
for i = N down to $K + 1$ **do**
  Search for the couple (a, b) which minimizes $\Delta(a, b)$.
  Make the fusion of a and b in **D2** with Max2Transform. Let c be the atom created by the fusion.
  Update matrix Δ: remove the entries related to a and b, add the new entries related to c.
end for

– *(Thm 6.B.16 item b) Let $X_1, ..., X_m$ be a set of independent random vectors where the dimension of X_i is k_i, let $Y_1, Y_2, ..., Y_m$, be another set of independent random vectors where the dimension of Y_i is k_i. Denote $k = \sum_i k_i$. If $X_i \preceq_{st} Y_i$ for all i, then, for any increasing function $\psi : R^k \rightarrow R$, one has $\psi(X_1, X_2, ..., X_m) \preceq_{st} \psi(Y_1, Y_2, ..., Y_m)$.*

Theorem 1. *Let X be an arbitrary discrete distribution, and a and b be two arbitrary atoms of its distribution, then $X \preceq_{st} Max2(a, b, X)$. A lower bound is also proved but it is omitted.*

Proof: We consider an arbitrary upper set $\mathcal{U}$. As the random variable is discrete, we have:

$$\begin{aligned} Pr(X \in \mathcal{U}) &= \textstyle\sum_{x \in S_X} 1_{x \in \mathcal{U}} Pr_X(x) \\ &= \textstyle\sum_{x \in S_X / \ \{a,b,max(a,b)\}} 1_{x \in \mathcal{U}} Pr_X(x) + 1_{a \in \mathcal{U}} Pr_X(a) \\ &+ 1_{b \in \mathcal{U}} Pr_X(b) + 1_{max(a,b) \in \mathcal{U}} Pr_X(max(a, b)). \end{aligned}$$

Now, let $Y = Max2(a, b, X)$. By construction of Y, we have:

$$\begin{aligned} Pr(Y \in \mathcal{U}) &= \textstyle\sum_{x \in S_Y} 1_{x \in \mathcal{U}} Pr_X(x) \\ &= \textstyle\sum_{x \in S_Y / \ \{max(a,b)\}} 1_{x \in \mathcal{U}} Pr_Y(x) + 1_{max(a,b) \in \mathcal{U}} Pr_Y(max(a, b)). \end{aligned}$$

Remember that $S_X / \ \{a, b, max(a, b)\} = S_Y / \ \{max(a, b)\}$ and that for all x in $S_X / \ \{a, b, max(a, b)\}$, we have $Pr_X(x) = Pr_Y(x)$. Moreover, $Pr_Y(max(a, b)) = Pr_X(a) + Pr_X(b) + Pr_X(max(a, b))$.Therefore,

$$\begin{aligned} Pr(Y \in \mathcal{U}) - Pr(X \in \mathcal{U}) = &\ (1_{max(a,b) \in \mathcal{U}} - 1_{a \in \mathcal{U}}) Pr_X(a) \\ &+ (1_{max(a,b) \in \mathcal{U}} - 1_{b \in \mathcal{U}}) Pr_X(b). \end{aligned}$$

Remember that $\mathcal{U}$ is an upper set. Clearly $max(a, b) \geq a$. Therefore if $a \in \mathcal{U}$, then $max(a, b) \in \mathcal{U}$. and we have the same result for b. Thus,$Pr(Y \in \mathcal{U}) - Pr(X \in \mathcal{U}) \geq 0$.

Corollary 1. *Let X be an arbitrary discrete distribution. Let a and b be two arbitrary atoms of its distribution, then:*

$$X \preceq_{lo} Max2(a,b,X) \text{ and } X \preceq_{uo} \mathrm{Max2(a,b,X)}.$$

Proof: Because of Theorem 1 and the first item in property 8.

Thus, Algorithm 2 also provides multivariate strong stochastic ordering and we will use it to reduce the number of sub-problems we have to solve to get a bound of the Completion Time. We propose a numerical technique to provide stochastic bounds for the distribution of the Completion Time when the delays are correlated. We consider the following graph (depicted in Fig. 3) to illustrate our approach. Let X_i be the delay of node i. We assume that $X2$, $X3$ and $X5$ are correlated. The joint distribution is modeled by atoms $((4,2,3),(5,2,4),(5,3,4),(6,3,5),(5,3,3),(6,3,4),(6,4,4),(6,4,5))$ with respective probabilities $(1/24, 3/24, 2/24, 6/24, 1/24, 3/24, 2/24, 6/24)$. All the others delays are independent. The method provides upper and lower bounding distributions but we only present the upper bound for the sake of conciseness.

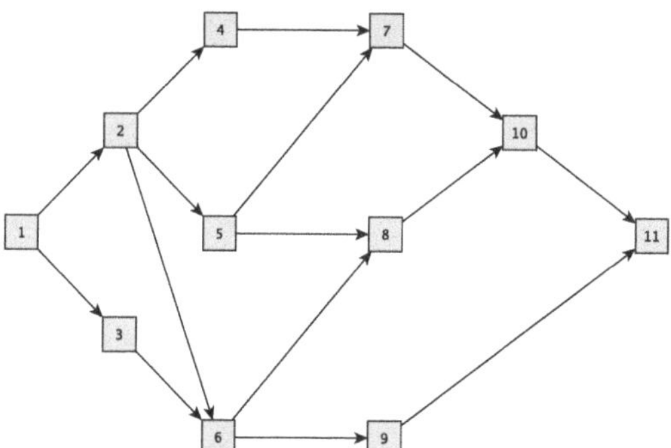

Fig. 3. The task graph.

We assume that X_1, X_4, X_6, X_7, X_8, X_9, X_{10} and X_{11} are uniformly distributed between 1 and 10. The naive approach to compute the distributions requires 8 10^8 computations of deterministic problems and the size of the distribution may be as large as this quantity. We can enumerate the paths from $s = 1$ to $t = 11$. The Completion Time can be computed as:

$$\begin{aligned} CT = max\ (&X_1 + X_2 + X_4 + X_7 + X_{10} + X_{11}, X_1 + X_2 + X_5 + X_7 + X_{10} + X_{11},\\ &X_1 + X_2 + X_5 + X_8 + X_{10} + X_{11}, X_1 + X_2 + X_6 + X_8 + X_{10} + X_{11},\\ &X_1 + X_2 + X_6 + X_9 + X_{11}, X_1 + X_3 + X_6 + X_8 + X_{10} + X_{11},\\ &X_1 + X_3 + X_6 + X_9 + X_{11}) \end{aligned}$$

where X_i is the random variable representing the delay of task i.

Our approach is based on two properties. First, if we are able to factorize the equation which describes the Completion Time such that all the delays appear only once in the equation, we obtain a constructive way to compute and bound this distribution. This is the idea used in the serie-parallel decomposition (the equation is a recursive construction), and in the conditioning set and the Uniformly Directed Cutset (the equation is associated with a tree). Second, Prop. 8 states that we can consider stochastic bounds of the input and obtain stochastic bounds for the Completion Time. Indeed the Completion Time is a function defined with "Max" and "Sum" operators and it is increasing. This is the key idea to reduce the number of sub-problems we want to solve. A sub-problem is the computation of an exact conditional distribution or upper and lower univariate strong stochastic bounds of the conditional distribution. Finally we combine these bounds using the Total Probability theorem and the property that univariate strong stochastic bounds are closed under mixtures (see Prop. 2). We combine stochastic bounds on the conditional probability and stochastic bounds on the conditioning variables.

Proposition 9 *Let X, Y, Θ_1 and Θ_2 four random variables. Assume that:*

- $\Theta_1 \preceq_{st} \Theta_2$
- *for all* θ, $[X|\Theta_2 = \theta] \preceq_{st} [Y|\Theta_2 = \theta]$
- $[X|\Theta_1 = \theta]$ *is a non decreasing function of* θ.

Then, $X \preceq_{st} Y$.

Proof:

$$\begin{aligned} Pr(X > x) &= \textstyle\sum_\theta Pr(X > x|\Theta_1 = \theta)Pr(\Theta_1 = \theta) \\ &\leq \textstyle\sum_\theta Pr(X > x|\Theta_2 = \theta)Pr(\Theta_2 = \theta) \\ &\leq \textstyle\sum_\theta Pr(Y > x|\Theta_2 = \theta)Pr(\Theta_2 = \theta) \\ &\leq Pr(y > x). \end{aligned}$$

The first and the fourth lines are the Total Probability Theorem. The first inequality is consequence of the strong stochastic ordering of Θ_1 and Θ_2 and the fact that the $Pr(X > x|\Theta_2 = \theta)$ is a non decreasing reward in θ. The second inequality is a consequence of the stochastic ordering of the conditional distributions.

Let S_{obj} be the size of the distribution we want to obtain and N_{obj} the number of sub-problems we want to solve. The first step is to evaluate the size of $\Omega = \prod_{i \in ECS} S_i$ the number of conditioning we have to perform. If the size of Ω is larger than N_{obj} we use Algorithm 2 to reduce the size certain variables in the conditioning set. During the evaluation of the conditional distribution, we use Algorithms 1 to reduce the size of the distributions if it is larger than S_{obj}.

Definition 15 (extended conditioning set). *The extended conditioning set (called ECS in the following) is the conditioning set as defined by O'Connor in [O'C06] completed by the nodes associated with dependent random variables.*

Note that the ECS may contains all the variable. In that case, the approach is equivalent to the naive technique. For the graph example (i.e. in Fig. 3), the conditioning set consists in nodes 2, 5 and 6. As we assume that the delays of nodes 2, 3 and 5 are correlated, we add them in the extended conditioning set. Therefore, $ECS = \{2, 3, 5, 6\}$. Furthermore assuming that we have conditioned on the random variables of the extended conditioning set, the conditional distribution of the Completion Time is (a, b, c and d are respectively the value of X_2, $X_2 + X_5$, $X_3 + X_6$ and $X_2 + X_6$):

$$\begin{aligned}[CT|X_2, X_3, X_5, X_6] = X_1 + X_{11} \\ + max[X_9 + max(c, d), X_5 + X_{10} + max(b, c, d), \\ X_6 + X_7 + max(a + X_4, b)]\end{aligned}$$

Proposition 10. *The equation obtained after conditioning on the random variables and the random vectors of the extended conditioning set, is associated with an evaluation tree where the internal nodes are associated with "max" or "+" operators, the leaves are independent random variables and the resulting distribution is associated with the root of the tree.*

Proof: By construction of the extended conditioning set, the remaining variables are associated with the leaves of a tree [O'C06] and they are independent. The evaluation tree for the example is depicted in Fig. 4. Using a bottom up approach, one can evaluate the distribution of the random variables at each node of the tree until we obtain the result. At each step, we compute the output distribution for the gate and we apply the bounding algorithms for univariate distribution presented in Sect. 3 is the size of the output distribution is larger than N_{obj}. This is needed because the gates "Max" and "+" increase the sizes of the distribution.

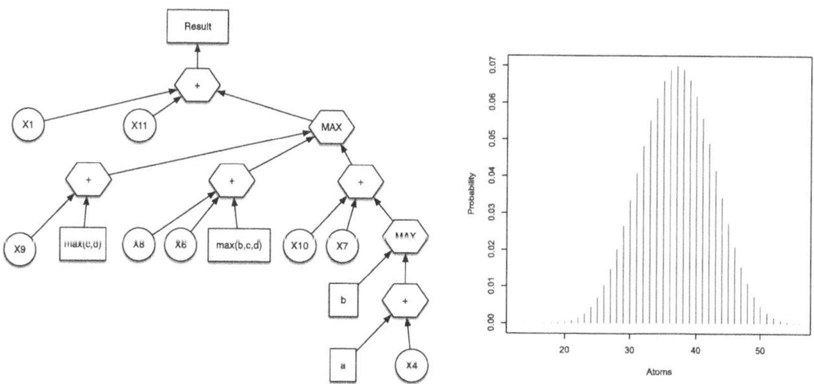

Fig. 4. Example: Evaluation tree (left), Stochastic upper bounds (right).

Proposition 11. *Consider a gate with two input distributions. Assume that the input distributions has respectively size* N_1 *and* N_2*, and let* $N = N1 + N2$*, then if the gate is a "+" operator, we compute the convolution of the distributions (remember that the random variables in the evaluation tree are independent). Thus the size of the output distribution may be as large as* $N_1 \times N_2$*. If the gate is a "Max" operator, the complexity of an efficient algorithm based on sorted lists insertion is* $O(N)$ *and the size of the output distribution is at most* $N - 1$*.*

The method is used on the example graph with the following constraint. We compute a stochastic upper bound with size $S_{obj} = 100$ using $N_{obj} = 9$ sub-problems (i.e. conditional distributions). The initial number of sub-problems was 80. We use an upper multivariate strong stochastic bound for distribution of (X_2, X_3, X_5) as follows: we use a support with atoms $(5, 3, 4), (6, 3, 5), (6, 4, 5)$ and a distribution on these atoms equal to $(9/24, 7/24, 8/24)$. Similarly, the distribution of X_6 is bounded by a distribution with atoms 3, 7 and 10 and probabilities $(3/10, 4/10, 3/10)$. The results are reported in Fig. 4.

6 Conclusion

Like in [ACC+12], we propose a tradeoff between complexity and tightness of the bound, therefore one has to chose between the quality of the bounds and the time needed to compute them. As our approach is based on the operators used in the optimization process, the approach can provide bound for many optimization problems which looks distinct but which are built with operators: "Max", "Min" and "+" and are non decreasing [FPT20]. We plan to add these methods in the XBorne tool [FMQV16] to make it available for analysis of larger models.

Acknowledgment. This work was supported by a public grant as part of the "Investissement d'avenir" project, reference ANR-11-LABX-0056-LMH, LabEx LMH, in a joint call with Gaspard Monge Program for optimization and operations research.

References

[ACC+12] Ait Salaht, F., Cohen, J., Castel Taleb, H., Fourneau, J.M., Pekergin, N.: Accuracy vs. complexity: the stochastic bound approach. In: 11th International Workshop on Discrete Event Systems (WODES), Mexico (2012)

[AK89] Adlakha, V.G., Kulkarni, V.G.: Classified bibliography of research on stochastic pert networks: 1966–1987. Infor **27**(3), 272–296 (1989)

[BAmL93] Baccelli, F., Jean-marie, A., Liu, Z.: A survey on solution methods for task graph models. INRIA Report, Sophia Antipolis, France (1993)

[BCP95] Ball, M., Colbourn, C.J., Provan, J.S.: Network reliability. Handb. Oper. Res. Manage. Sci. **7**, 673–762 (1995)

[CPT00] Colajanni, M., Lo Presti, F., Tucci, S.: A hierarchical approach for bounding the completion time distribution of stochastic task graphs. Perform. Eval. **41**(1), 1–22 (2000)

[Dod85] Dodin, B.: Bounding the project completion time distribution in pert networks. Oper. Res. **33**(4), 862–881 (1985)

[FMQV16] Fourneau, J.M., Mahjoub, Y.A.E., Quessette, F., Vekris, D.: XBorne 2016: a brief introduction. In: Czachórski, T., Gelenbe, E., Grochla, K., Lent, R. (eds.) ISCIS 2016. CCIS, vol. 659, pp. 134–141. Springer, Cham (2016). https://doi.org/10.1007/978-3-319-47217-1_15

[FPT20] Fourneau, J.-M., Pekergin, N., Tan, S.: Stochastic bounds for some stochastic optimisation problems. In: 13th ACM-EAI ValueTools, Japan, pp. 112–119. ACM (2020)

[GO02] Guérin, R., Orda, A.: Computing shortest paths for any number of hops. IEEE/ACM Trans. Netw. **10**(5), 613–620 (2002)

[NR99] Nourine, L., Raynaud, O.: A fast algorithm for building lattices. Inf. Process. Lett. **71**(5–6), 199–204 (1999)

[O'C06] O'Connor, D.: Exact and approximate distributions of stochastic PERT networks. Dublin University College (2006)

[Sho77] Shogan, A.W.: Bounding distributions for a stochastic pert network. Networks **7**, 359–381 (1977)

[SPS79] Sigal, C.E., Pritsker, A.A.B., Solberg, J.J.: The use of cutsets in Monte Carlo analysis of stochastic networks. Math. Comput. Simul. **21**(4), 379–384 (1979)

[SS07] Shaked, M., Shantikumar, J.G.: Stochastic Orders. Springer, New York (2007)

[YPV91] Yazici-Pekergin, N., Vincent, J.-M.: Stochastic bounds on execution times of parallel programs. IEEE Trans. Softw. Eng. **17**(10), 1005–1012 (1991)

Transformation of DES Formalisms with the Assistance of Generative AI

Celina Lemmouchi and Rim Saddem-Yagoubi(✉)

Aix Marseille Univ, CNRS, LIS, Marseille, France
rim.saddem@lis-lab.fr

Abstract. In a context where the increasing complexity of discrete event systems (DES) makes flexible modeling tools essential, interoperability between different formalisms has become a central challenge. This work addresses this issue by exploring the transformation between three widely used formalisms: automata, Petri Nets, and DEVS models (Discrete Event System Specification).

The proposed approach involves two main steps. First, a systematic review of existing transformation rules reported in the literature is conducted. Second, generative artificial intelligence is employed to automatically generate transformation rules. The rules derived from the literature and those generated by the AI are then compared.

Based on this comparison, a refined set of transformation rules was manually defined. These rules were applied to a practical case study: modeling the behavior of an autonomous cleaning robot. The robot's behavior was initially modeled as an automaton and then transformed into a Labelled Petri Net using the defined rules. This transformation was implemented in Python, enabling automated validation of the correspondence between the two formalisms while preserving the system's behavioral logic.

Keywords: Discrete Event Systems · Automata · Labelled Petri Net · Transformation Methods · Hybrid Approach · Generative IA

1 Introduction

Discrete event systems are characterized by state changes triggered by discrete events, often in contexts involving concurrency and reactivity. To describe their behavior, several modeling formalisms have been developed, each offering a specific approach in terms of representation and analysis. Among the most widely used are finite automata, Petri nets, and DEVS models (Discrete Event System Specification).

Each of these formalisms provides a unique perspective on the structure and dynamics of systems, with its own specific advantages—such as expressiveness, simulation capability, and modularity—but also with inherent limitations. However, this diversity introduces a major challenge: interoperability between formalisms. Being able to transform a model from one formalism to another, while preserving its behavioral remains an open problem, especially in the context of integrated engineering.

B. Ben Hedia et al. (Eds.): VECoS 2025, LNCS 16263, pp. 48–65, 2026.
https://doi.org/10.1007/978-3-032-20440-0_4

The issue of interoperability has already been addressed in numerous studies, mostly focusing on formal and manual transformation methods that are often tailored to specific use cases. While these classical approaches are effective in well-defined contexts, they struggle to adapt to the growing variety and complexity of modern systems. At the same time, the rise of generative artificial intelligence tools, such as ChatGPT or Mistral AI, offers new opportunities for the automatic generation of transformation rules between formalisms.

This is the context in which the present work is situated. It proposes a hybrid method for the automatic transformation between formalisms, based on the combination of transformation rules drawn from scientific literature with rules automatically generated by generative AI tools.

The main contributions of this work are as follows:

- A systematic review of existing transformation rules between formalisms.
- The automatic generation of transformation rules using AI tools.
- A small comparison of the generated rules (AI vs literature).
- The application of the method to an academic use case: the modeling of an autonomous cleaning robot.
- A Python implementation enabling the automated transformation of a finite automaton into a Labelled Petri Net.

This work thus stands at the intersection of formal modeling and artificial intelligence, offering an original contribution to the interoperability problem between formalisms, and paving the way for automated modeling support tools in the domain of discrete event systems.

The remainder of this paper is organized as follows:

- **Section** 2 presents the background and related work on the main modeling formalisms and existing transformation approaches.
- **Section** 3 provides formal definitions of the three main formalisms used in this study: finite automata, Petri nets, and DEVS.
- **Section** 4 compares the transformation rules from automata to Petri nets, contrasting literature based methods with those generated by generative AI tools, and presents a critical analysis of AI-generated transformation rules.
- **Section** 5 introduces a hybrid transformation method that integrates AI-generated rules with those from the literature to improve reliability and automation.
- **Section** 6 illustrates the application of the hybrid method to a real-world case study involving the behavioral modeling of an autonomous cleaning robot.
- **Section** 7 concludes the article and suggests future directions, including extensions to other formalisms such as timed automata and DEVS.

2 Related Work

The modeling of discrete event systems (DES) relies on various formalisms, each offering a specific perspective and dedicated analysis tools. The three main ones, finite automata, Petri nets (RDP), and DEVS models (Discrete Event System Specification), have been extensively studied for their ability to represent, simulate, or transform discrete behaviors.

This section first reviews the main modeling formalisms used in Discrete Event Systems (DES), then discusses the transformation methods that enable interoperability between these heterogeneous models.

2.1 DES Formalisms

Regarding automata, the foundational work of Kleene on regular expressions [10], followed by that of Rabin and Scott [12], established the basis for regular language recognition and sequential behavior modeling. Extensions such as timed automata [1] now allow modeling of time-constrained dynamic systems. Their efficiency and formal rigor make them essential tools in formal verification, compilation, and embedded systems. In parallel, Petri nets introduced by Carl Adam Petri were further developed by Murata [11], highlighting key structural properties such as liveness and coverability. These works positioned RDP as a reference model for concurrency and synchronization. Extensions to hybrid and timed systems have been described in [4]. The DEVS formalism, introduced by Zeigler in the 1970s [15], provides a hierarchical modeling framework based on event and time management. Thanks to its modularity, DEVS has become a powerful simulation framework for complex systems.

2.2 Transformation Methods

Transformation between these formalisms is a major challenge for interoperability. Research has been conducted by Haddouche et al. to transform automata into RDP [7] using the Triple Graph Grammar (TGG) formalism [9]. Zhu et al. [16] proposed an integer linear programming based approach to derive RDP structures from automata.

Other studies focus on translating timed Petri nets (TPN) into timed automata such as Cassez and Roux [2] developed a method preserving the behavioural semantics. EL TOUATI et al. [5] explore the extended timed Petri net towards linear hybrid automata for system analysis.

The transformation from timed automata to DEVS was addressed by Giambiasi [6], through encapsulating behaviors in atomic DEVS blocks.

Finally, several authors emphasized the value of combining approaches to improve diagnosis, simulation, and verification. Tolbi et al. [14] proposed a structural modelling approach using Hybrid Petri Nets (HPNs) to describe and analyse faults in continuous flow hybrid systems without rebuilding the original model. It introduces a hierarchical translation method from an Elementary HPN to a Hybrid Automaton (HA), preserving behavioural semantics and timed behaviour through Timed Transition Systems (TTS).

3 Modeling Formalisms and Methods Transformation

3.1 Formalization of Main Modeling Formalisms

a- Finite Automata. A finite automaton is a mathematical model used to represent a system with a finite number of states, evolving based on events or inputs. This model describes the transition logic between system states in response to external stimuli [8].

A finite automaton defined over the alphabet E is a system :

$$G = (X, \delta, x_0, X_f) \tag{1}$$

- X is a **finite set** of states.
- $\delta : X \times E \rightarrow X$ is a **transition function**, which determines the transition from one state to another based on an input symbol.
- $x_0 \in X$ is the **initial state**, where the execution of the automaton begins.
- $X_f \subseteq X$ is a **set of final states** (or marked states).

b - Petri Nets. A Petri Net is a mathematical formalism widely used for modeling and analyzing discrete event systems, particularly those involving concurrency, synchronization, and event causality [11].

A Petri Net is formally defined as:

$$PN = (P, T, Pre, Post, M_0)$$

where:

- $P = \{p_1, p_2, \ldots, p_m\}$ is a finite set of **places**,
- $T = \{t_1, t_2, \ldots, t_n\}$ is a finite set of **transitions**,
- $Pre : P \times T \rightarrow \mathbb{N}$ is the **input function** (arc weights from places to transitions),
- $Post : P \times T \rightarrow \mathbb{N}$ is the **output function** (arc weights from transitions to places),
- M_0 is the **initial marking**.

c - Discrete Event System Specification (DEVS). The *DEVS* (Discrete Event System Specification) formalism is a rigorous framework for modeling and simulating discrete event systems. It was introduced by Zeigler in the 1970s to represent complex systems in a modular, hierarchical, and event-driven manner.

An atomic **DEVS** model is formally defined as a 7-tuple [15]:

$$M = (X, S, Y, \delta_{\text{int}}, \delta_{\text{ext}}, \lambda, D)$$

where:

- X: set of input events,
- S: set of states,
- Y: set of output events,

- δ_{int}: internal transition function,
- δ_{ext}: external transition function,
- λ: output function,
- D: For a given state, s, D(s) represents the time interval during which the model will remain in the state s if no external event occurs.

d - Comparison Between the Main Modeling Formalisms. Finite automata, Petri nets, and the DEVS formalism are three major formalisms for modeling discrete event dynamic systems. Each formalism offers specific advantages depending on the nature of the system to be modeled.

Finite automata are particularly well suited for simple sequential systems, where states and transitions are clearly defined. However, they present notable limitations when it comes to modeling concurrency or handling simultaneous events.

Petri nets, on the other hand, allow for effective modeling of systems involving parallel behaviors and complex synchronizations. Their ability to represent concurrency makes them particularly useful for production systems, workflows, or complex industrial processes.

The DEVS formalism stands out for its modular and hierarchical nature, as well as its ability to explicitly manage time. It is particularly suitable for complex, hybrid, or distributed systems and allows a clear separation between the model structure and the simulation engine. This approach makes DEVS highly powerful for multi-level, scalable, and temporally precise simulations.

In the following, we describe four existing transformation approaches between commonly used discrete-event system modeling formalisms. These transformations include: (a) from a finite automaton to Petri net, (b) from timed Petri nets (TPN) to timed automata (TA), (c) from timed automata to DEVS models, and (d) from Petri nets to DEVS models.

3.2 Existing Transformation Methods

a - Transformation from Automaton to Petri Net. The transformation of finite automata into Petri Nets relies on the *Triple Graph Grammars* (TGG) formalism [7], which formalizes correspondences between entities of the two formalisms. It involves two main steps: (1) defining the **meta-models** of both formalisms (automaton and Petri Net), and (2) specifying the **TGG rules** to perform the transformation.

The first step is structured around three core elements:

- **Source Metamodel:** representing the structure of the automaton (states, transitions, events, actions).
- **Target Metamodel:** defining the components of a Petri net (places, transitions, tokens).
- **Correspondence Metamodel:** formally linking each element of the two models.

The transformation rules include:

- **Global Anchoring Rule:** `diagEtatTransition2RDPetri`
  This rule serves as the starting point of the transformation. It establishes a correspondence between the source model (state-transition diagram) and the target model (Petri net), initializing the global transformation structure. From this rule, the specific transformation rules are triggered.
- **Specific Rules:**
  - `InitialState2RTransition`: transforms an initial state of the automaton into a transition in the Petri net. This transition injects a token into the place corresponding to the initial state to simulate the start of the system.
  - `State2Place`: associates each automaton state with a place in the Petri net. This rule ensures the basic structural correspondence between the two formalisms.
  - `Transition2RTransition`: transforms a transition of the automaton into a transition in the Petri net, connected by arcs to the places representing the source and target states.
  - `FinalState2RTransition`: converts a final state of the automaton into a special transition in the Petri net, marking the end of the process execution.

Each rule formally defines a link between an element of the source model (LHS) and its equivalent in the target model (RHS), with explicit traceability ensured throughout the transformation process.

b - Transformation from Timed Petri Nets to Timed Automata. The transformation of Timed Petri Nets (TPN) into Timed Automata (TA) leverages the formal analysis capabilities of TA while modeling the concurrency inherent in TPN.

Several works have proposed systematic approaches to transform a TPN into a TA in *three* main steps, the fourth step related to optimization is optional [3]:

- **TPN dechronization:** removing timing constraints to obtain a standard Petri Net (PN).
- **Construction of the Marking Class Graph (MCG)**: extending the marking graph to integrate clock evolution associated with transitions.
- **Generation of the Timed Automaton:** each class becomes a TA state, with transitions featuring guards ($[\alpha, \beta]$), clock resets, and state invariants.

To improve the effectiveness of the proposed approach, reduction techniques - which make up the final optimization step shown in Fig. 1—are applied to limit the size of the generated automaton:

- Removing inaccessible states due to timing constraints.
- Merging similar classes based on clock similarities.
- Using P-invariants (P-semiflows) to bound unbounded places.

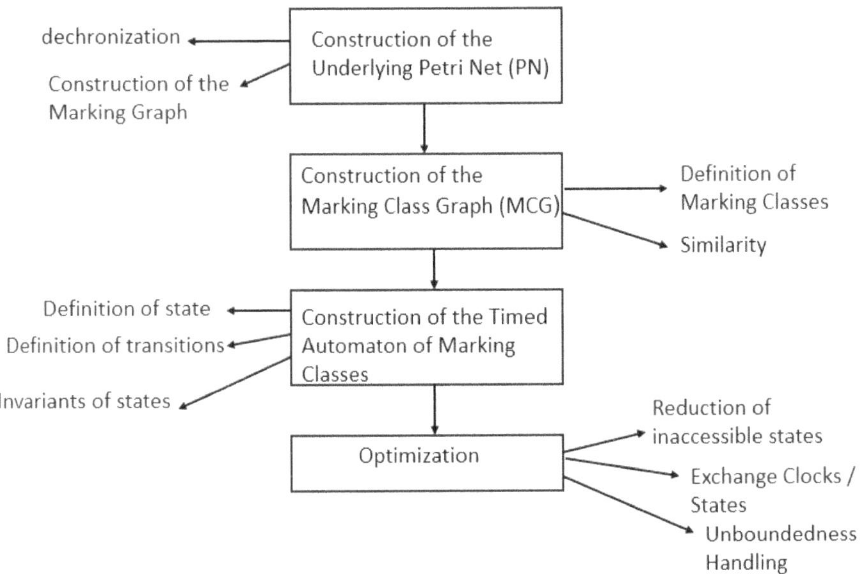

Fig. 1. Steps for transforming a Timed Petri Net (TPN) into a Timed Automaton (TA)

c - Transformation from Timed Automata to DEVS Models. Transforming a **Timed Input Output Automaton (TIOA)** into a **DEVS** model aims to exploit the formal analysis power of timed automata and the simulation capabilities of the DEVS formalism. This approach was formalized by Giambiasi and Mostefaoui [6].

For this transformation, Giambiasi and Mostefaoui make two hypotheses:

- Each output event is associated with a unique emission timestamp.
- Concurrent transitions triggered by the same event must be associated with different clocks to ensure determinism.

The approach is based on three main steps:

1. **Syntactic Transformation (Timeless):** TIOA states, input and output events are mapped to DEVS elements states (S), inputs (X), outputs (Y). Input transitions are mapped to function δ_{ext}. Output transitions are mapped to functions δ_{int} and λ.
2. **Lifetime Function—D:** Introduce temporal state variables to capture the time spent in each state. It defines a lifetime function D(s) based on the guards and invariants of the source automaton.
3. **Operational Semantics:** Each DEVS model state is represented as a triplet (s, v, e), where: s: current logical state, v: valuation of temporal variables (clocks), and e: elapsed time since entering s.
   The system respects the condition $0 \leq e \leq D(s)$ for each state.

d - Transformation from Petri Nets to DEVS Models. The automatic transformation of a Petri Net (PN) into a DEVS model combines the structural rigor of PNs with the simulation power of DEVS [13]. The transformation steps are:

1. **Generated Model Structure:** Create atomic models for each place (P_i) and transition (T_j). Each place becomes a *PDEVS* component managing tokens, and each transition becomes a *TDEVS* handling transition firing.
2. **Model Dynamics:**
   - Assign specific ports for initialization, token control, and message exchanges (for *PDEVS*, `InitPi`, `OutPi`, and for *TDEVS* `InitTi`, `OutTi`, `CPiTi`, and `CPiTi`). The initial marking (M_0) is sent to PDEVS via `InitPi` ports, while TDEVS are activated through the `InitTi` port, ensuring correct synchronization at startup.
   - Connect components based on *Pre* and *Post* matrices representing network arcs.
   - Final assembly into a coupled DEVS model with all components and ports. PDEVS respond to requests, manage reservations, and update marking via decrements/increments. TDEVS follow a state cycle: `checking`, `reserving`, `validated`, `firing`, `canceling`, modeling transition firing logic.

This method ensures the preservation of essential PN properties (concurrency, conflicts, parallelism) in a DEVS-based simulation environment [13].

4 Comparison of Transformation Rules from Finite Automata to Petri Nets: Literature Vs Generative AI

In this section, we focus on comparing the transformation rules from a finite automaton to a Petri net, contrasting approaches from scientific literature with those proposed by generative AI tools using prompts.

4.1 Rules Proposed by Mistral AI

Mistral AI proposed an intuitive and synthetic transformation method, centered on a direct correspondence between the automaton and the Petri Net elements:

- Each state of the automaton is transformed into a place.
- The initial marking places one token on the place corresponding to the initial state.
- Each transition of the automaton becomes a transition in the Petri net, consuming a token from the source place and producing a token in the target place.
- Events are preserved as transition labels.
- Final states become final places.
- Concurrency or synchronization is modeled through parallel or shared structures .

4.2 Rules Proposed by DeepSeek

The approach proposed by DeepSeek for transforming an automaton into a Petri Net relies on a direct correspondence between the core components of both models. The main rules are as follows:

- Each state q_i of the automaton becomes a place p_i in the Petri net.
- The place corresponding to the initial state q_0 receives one token in the initial marking.
- Each transition $\delta(q_i, a) = q_j$ becomes a transition t in the net, with: an incoming arc from place p_i (source state), an outgoing arc to place p_j (target state).
- Transitions ε (without external events) are also represented by unlabeled Petri transitions.
- Final States can be modeled either with specific markings or special places.

4.3 Rules Proposed by ChatGPT

ChatGPT proposes a structured and accessible method for transforming an automaton into a Petri Net, with a pragmatic orientation. The rules are:

- Each automaton state becomes a place in the Petri net.
- Each transition becomes a Petri transition connected to its origin and destination places.
- The Petri net starts with a token in the place corresponding to the initial state.
- Final states may be represented as "terminal" places
- In the case of synchronized automata or interactions with other components, ChatGPT recommends using classical Petri net synchronization mechanisms (shared or synchronized transitions).
- If the automaton contains internal actions or events, these can be translated into conditions or annotations on Petri transitions.

4.4 Recall of the Scientific Approach (TGG)

The detailed presentation of this approach is described in Sect. 3.2. It relies on a more complex and rigorous framework "the **Triple Graph Grammars (TGG)**" formalism. Here we recall only the main rules.

TGG transformation rules, to generate a Petri Net from a state diagram, include:

`diagEtatTransition2RDPetri`: anchoring rule (transformation axiom),
- `InitialState2RTransition` and `FinalState2RTransition`: transform initial and final states,
- `State2Place`: converts simple states to places,
- `transition2RTransition`: transforms transitions into Petri transitions.

4.5 Critical Analysis

The transformation rules proposed by generative AI models are generally simple and intuitive, and they overlap significantly with those defined in the scientific literature. The first three rules proposed by Mistral AI, DeepSeek, and ChatGPT—which map states to places, transitions to Petri net transitions, and the initial state to initial marking places—are well-defined and align with the scientific rules `State2Place`, `Transition2RTransition`, and *InitialState2RTransition*. However, the handling of final states differs. Specifically, Mistral AI suggests representing final states as final places in Petri nets, DeepSeek proposes modeling them as specific marking or specific places. ChatGPT recommends using "terminal" places. However, the concept of a final or terminal place does not exist in classical Petri nets. This undermines the structural rigor of these transformations. Moreover, rules concerning concurrency and synchronization—which are fundamental aspects of Petri nets—are not adequately addressed by these AI-generated transformations, making them unsuitable for complex or safety-critical applications.

By contrast, the scientific approach maintains a strict correspondence that respects the formal principles of each modeling formalism. However, the introduction of a specific transition for the final state can prevent the correct representation of cyclic behaviors that may exist in timed automata. This point will be revisited in the implementation of the hybrid approach presented in the next section.

5 Hybrid Transformation Method

In this work, we present a hybrid method for transforming a finite automaton into a Labelled Petri Net. This method combines transformation rules generated by artificial intelligence tools with additional rules derived from the scientific literature. In this section, we first define the transformation rules and then describe the implementation of the hybrid approach in Python.

5.1 Definition of Transformation Rules

The rules underlying our hybrid transformation method are defined as follows:

1. Each state of the automaton is mapped to a place in the Labelled Petri Net (IA & Literature [7]).
2. The initial is represented by a place containing an initial token (IA & Literature [7]).
3. Each transition of the automaton is translated into a transition in the Labelled Petri Net (IA & Literature [7]).
4. Final states are associated with end transitions connected to the corresponding places (Literature [7]).
5. Each Petri transition is connected by arcs to the source place (original state) and the target place (destination state).

6. The event associated with the automaton transition is preserved as a label on the corresponding Labelled Petri Net transition (added by us).

These rules ensure a consistent and automatable correspondence between the two formalisms. In the next subsection, we provide an implementation of the hybrid approach in Python.

5.2 Implementation of the Hybrid Approach

To implement the proposed hybrid transformation method, we developed a Python algorithm that systematically applies the defined rules.

Algorithm 1. Hybrid Method for Transforming a Finite Automaton into a Labelled Petri Net

---

1: **Define the structure of the automaton A using the following classes:**
   - `State`: name, boolean flags for initial or final state
   - `Event` : event label
   - `AutomatonTransition` : (source, event, target)
   - `Automaton`: stores lists of states, events, and transitions

2: **Define the structure of the labeled Petri net `LabeledPetriNet` using the following classes:**
   - `Place` : place name and initial number of tokens
   - `PetriTransition`: name, list of input places, list of output places, label
   - `LabeledPetriNet`: stores `places`, `transitions`, and matrices `Pre` and `Post`

3: **Define the function `TransformAutomatonToLabeledPetriNet` according to the following rules:**
   - Initialize an empty labeled Petri net `rdp`
   - For each state in the automaton:
     - Create a place with the name of the state
     - Add a token if it is the initial state
     - Store the mapping state → place
     - If it is a final state, create a special transition labeled `"final"`
   - For each transition in the automaton:
     - Create a labled Petri net transition connecting the corresponding places
     - Label the transition with the event name
   - Return the constructed labeled Petri net

4: DisplayAutomaton(A)

5: DisplayLabeledPetriNet(R)

First, the automaton and the Labelled Petri Net are modeled using dedicated Python classes. The **Finite Automaton** is represented by the following classes:

- `State`: represents a state X (cf. Formula 1), with attributes indicating whether it is initial or final.
- `Event`: corresponds to the alphabet E (cf. Formula 1).

- `AutomatonTransition`: represents a transition δ (cf. Formula 1), as a triplet $(\text{source}, \text{event}, \text{target})$.
- `Automaton`: aggregates the states, events, and transitions.

The **Labelled Petri Net** is structured around the following classes:

- `Place`: represents a place P and stores its name and initial marking.
- `PetriTransition`: represents a transition T, with its input and output places and an associated label.
- `LabeledPetriNet`: stores the places, transitions, and the incidence matrices `Pre` and `Post`.

The core transformation which applies the hybrid rules, is implemented in the function `TransformAutomatonToLabeledPetriNet`, as follows:

- For each state in the automaton, a corresponding place is created. If the state is initial, the place is marked with a token. If the state is final, a dedicated end transition is added.
- For each automaton transition, a corresponding Petri Net transition is created, connecting the source and target places. The event label is assigned to the Petri Net transition.

Algorithm 1 summarizes the main steps of the transformation process.

Visualization tools (`graphviz`) and `Pre`/`Post` matrix calculation tools have also been integrated to display results (*DisplayAutomaton*(A), *DisplayLabeledPetriNet*(R)).

In the following section, a concrete case study, which is the modeling of an autonomous cleaning robot, is presented.

6 Case Study: Cleaning Robot

We present a case study illustrating the concrete application of the hybrid method for transforming a finite automaton into a Labelled Petri Net. The chosen system is an autonomous cleaning robot, initially modeled as an automaton, then automatically converted into a Labelled Petri Net using a Python script. Behavioral consistency between the two representations is also verified.

6.1 Description of the Case Study

The robot starts in an idle state that simulates a passive mode of the system. It waits for a start command. Once initiated, the robot performs a scan of the room to identify the areas to clean.

It then proceeds to carry out the cleaning task. During this phase, it may encounter different events. If an obstacle is detected, it temporarily interrupts its path to execute an avoidance maneuver, then resumes cleaning once the obstacle is cleared. Additionally, if the battery becomes low, it automatically returns to its charging station, recharges, and then resumes the mission where it left off.

Modeling this behavior with a **Deterministic Finite Automaton (DFA)** provides a rigorous and structured way to represent the different states the robot can occupy and the events that trigger transitions between these states. The resulting model is detailed below.

6.2 Modeling of the Case Study

Identified States in the Model

- **Idle:** initial passive waiting state.
- **Room analysis:** scanning and mapping the environment.
- **Cleaning in progress** active cleaning phase.
- **Obstacle avoidance:** maneuvering around detected obstacles.
- **Low battery:** energy level is critically low.
- **Returning to base:** navigating back to charging station.
- **Charging:** battery recharging phase.
- **Cleaning completed:** final state, mission complete.

Triggering Events

- `start`
- `analysis_done`
- `obstacle_detected`
- `obstacle_cleared`
- `low_battery`
- `return_to_base`
- `arrived_at_base`
- `battery_charged`
- `cleaning_done`

Detailed Description of Transitions Each event causes a specific state transition:

- The event `start` transitions the system from **Idle** to **Room analysis**, signaling the beginning of the mission.
- Once the analysis is complete, `analysis_done` triggers a transition to **Cleaning in progress**, which marks the start of active work.

- If an obstacle is detected, `obstacle_detected` causes a switch to **Obstacle avoidance**. Once cleared, `obstacle_cleared` returns the system to **Cleaning in progress**.
- When the battery level is critical, `low_battery` moves the robot to the **Low battery** state.
- The robot then initiates its return with the event `return_to_base`, transitioning to **Returning to base**.
- Upon arrival (`arrived_at_base`), it enters the **Charging** state.
- When fully recharged (`battery_charged`), it resumes cleaning from the **Cleaning in progress** state.
- Finally, when cleaning is completed, `cleaning_done` triggers the transition to the terminal state **Cleaning completed**.

6.3 Automatic Transformation Into a Labelled Petri Net Using the Hybrid Method

The hybrid method uses a set of formal transformation rules to convert the DFA into a structurally equivalent Labelled Petri Net (LPN, denoted R) that faithfully preserves the original system's behavioral logic.

The transformation procedure, detailed in Algorithm 2, proceeds as follows: First, the DFA A is constructed according to the description provided in Subsect. 6.2 (states, events, transitions). Next, the Python function applied to A to generate the corresponding LPN R is `TransformAutomatonToLabeledPetriNet(A)`. Finally, both the DFA and the resulting LPN are visualized, with the generated diagrams included in the appendix.

Algorithm 2. Implementation of Hybrid Method to concrete case of the cleaning robot

1: Create a new automaton A representing the cleaning robot
2: Add states and transitions, and define the initial and final states
3: **Define the structure of the labeled Petri net `LabeledPetriNet` using the following classes:**
   - `Place` : place name and initial number of tokens
   - `PetriTransition` : name, list of input places, list of output places, label
   - `LabeledPetriNet` : stores `places`, `transitions`, and matrices `Pre` and `Post`
4: TransformAutomatonToLabeledPetriNet(A) $\rightarrow R$
5: DisplayAutomaton(A)
6: DisplayLabeledPetriNet(R)

6.4 Behavioral Consistency Verification

After the transformation, consistency verification was conducted:

- **Structural:** each state has been correctly transformed into a place, each transition has been preserved, and arcs are accurately defined.
- **Behavioral:** transition sequences in the Labelled Petri Net faithfully reproduce the automaton sequences (paths, alternatives, return to initial state, etc.).
- **Simulational:** tokens evolve in the network according to the same logic observed in the automaton (e.g., recharging after low battery).

The hybrid method, implemented in this concrete case, therefore enables a faithful and usable transformation for simulation purposes while facilitating structured analysis of the modeled behaviors.

7 Conclusion and Perspectives

This work has led to proposing a hybrid method for transforming discrete-event system modeling formalisms, combining rules from the literature with rules generated by artificial intelligence. Applied to an automaton representing a cleaning robot, this method was implemented in Python and demonstrated its effectiveness in producing a coherent Labelled Petri Net.

A short-term perspective is to test the method on more complex scenarios and to check formal property preservation. A mid-term perspective is to extend this approach to transformations between Labelled Petri Nets and DEVS models, as well as between timed automata and DEVS models, with the goal of achieving full automation that integrates formal verification mechanisms.

A Automaton and Labeled Petri Net Representing the Cleaning Robot

This appendix illustrates two representations of the robot's behavior. The first figure (Fig. 2) shows the finite automaton that models the robot's operation. The second figure (Fig. 3) presents the labeled Petri net obtained after transformation, following the defined conversion rules.

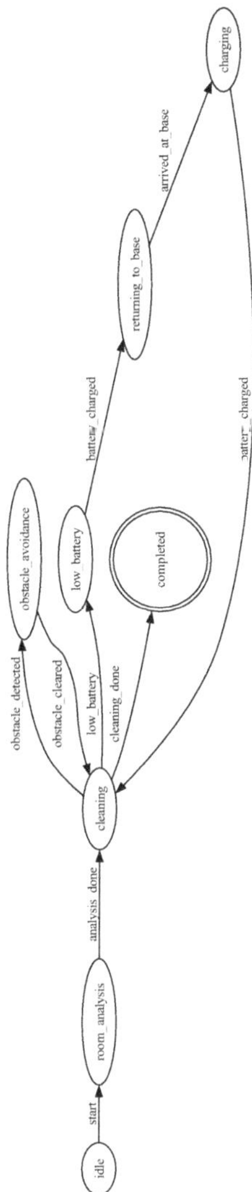

Fig. 2. The finite automaton.

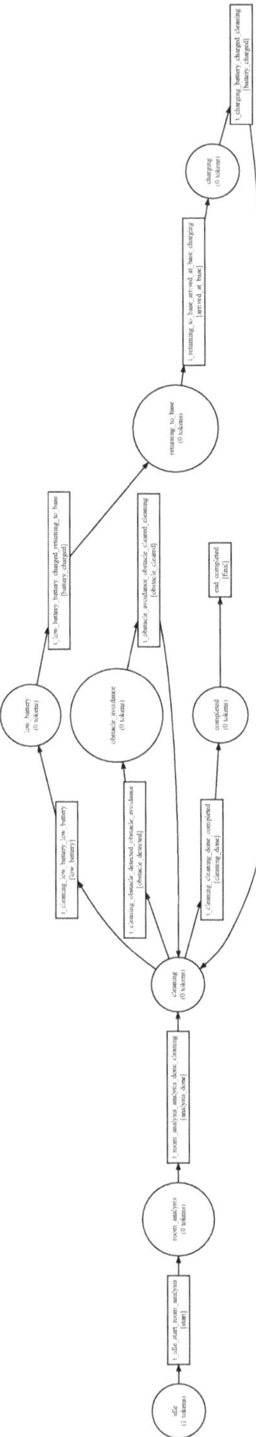

Fig. 3. The labeled Petri net.

References

1. Alur, R., Dill, D.L.: A theory of timed automata. Theoret. Comput. Sci. **126**(2), 183–235 (1994)
2. Cassez, F., Roux, O.H.: Traduction structurelle des réseaux de petri temporels vers les automates temporisés. In: Hermès Science, éditeur: 4ème Colloque Francophone sur la modélisation des Systèmes Réactifs (MSR 2003), vol. 54 (2003)
3. D'Aprile, D., Donatelli, S., Sangnier, A., Sproston, J.: From time petri nets to timed automata: an untimed approach. In: Proceedings of the 12th International Conference on Application of Concurrency to System Design (ACSD), pp. 1–10. IEEE (2012). https://doi.org/10.1109/ACSD.2012.13
4. David, R., Alla, H.: Discrete, Continuous, and Hybrid Petri Nets. Springer Series in Advanced Manufacturing, 2nd edn. Springer (2015)
5. Etouati, Y., Yeddes, M., Alouane, N.H., Alla, H.: Du réseau de petri temporel étendu vers les automates hybrides linéaires pour l'analyse des systèmes. In: CIFA 2009-IEEE Conférence Internationale Francophone d'Automatique (2009)
6. Giambiasi, N., Mostefaoui, G.: From timed automata to DEVS models. Simul. Model. Pract. Theory **11**(3–4), 157–176 (2003)
7. Haddouche, Y., Bourekkache, S., Sadeg, B.: Transformation automatique des automates vers les réseaux de petri en utilisant le formalisme triple graph grammar. Rev. Sci. Technol. **54**, 53–61 (2022)
8. Hopcroft, J.E., Motwani, R., Ullman, J.D.: Introduction to Automata Theory, Languages, and Computation. Addison-Wesley (2001)
9. Kindler, E., Wagner, R.: Triple graph grammars: concepts, extensions, implementations, and application scenarios. Technical report (2007)
10. Kleene, S.C.: Representation of events in nerve nets and finite automata. Autom. Stud. **3**, 3–42 (1951)
11. Murata, T.: Petri nets: properties, analysis and applications. Proc. IEEE **77**(4), 541–580 (1989). https://doi.org/10.1109/5.24143
12. Rabin, M.O., Scott, D.: Finite automata and their decision problems. IBM J. Res. Dev. **3**(2), 114–125 (1959)
13. Redjimi, M., Boukelkoul, S.: Algorithmic tools for the transformation of petri nets to DEVS. Informatica **37**(4), 411–418 (2013)
14. Tolbi, B., Tebbikh, H., Alla, H.: Fault-tolerant continuous flow systems modelling. Ph.D. thesis (2017)
15. Zeigler, B.P., Kim, T.G., Praehofer, H.: Theory of Modeling and Simulation, 2nd edn. Academic Press (2000)
16. Zhu, G., Yin, L., Li, Y., Li, Z., Wu, N.: Identification of labeled petri nets from finite automata. Inf. Sci. **667**, 120488 (2024)

Intelligent Path Planning for UAV Swarms via Deep Reinforcement Learning

Hafedh Jouini[1(✉)], Hamza Gharsellaoui[2], and Mohamed Khalgui[3]

[1] Polytechnic School of Tunisia (EPT), University of Carthage, Tunis 1054, Tunisia
jouinihafedh@gmail.com

[2] National School of Computer Science (ENSI), University of Manouba, Manouba 2010, Tunisia
hamza.gharsellaoui@ensi-uma.tn

[3] National Institute of Applied Sciences and Technology (INSAT), University of Carthage, Tunis 1054, Tunisia
khalgui.mohamed@gmail.com

Abstract. The rapid advancement of Deep Reinforcement Learning (DRL) has opened new opportunities for improving the autonomy and energy efficiency of Unmanned Aerial Vehicles (UAVs) in collaborative missions. In this paper, we propose **E-MAPPO-CTDE** (Energy-aware Multi-Agent Proximal Policy Optimization with Centralized Training and Decentralized Execution), a novel trajectory optimization framework designed for UAV swarms operating in constrained environments. Unlike existing approaches, E-MAPPO-CTDE integrates a realistic energy consumption model based on displacement, acceleration, and flight time into a centralized learning process that yields decentralized, real-time decision policies. Each UAV learns to generate collision-free, communication-aware, and energy efficient trajectories using a multi objective reward function. Through extensive simulations involving static obstacles and multiple agents, E-MAPPO-CTDE demonstrates significant energy savings and improved path coordination. These results confirm the potential of our framework for scalable deployment in real-world scenarios such as surveillance, search and rescue, and logistics.

Keywords: Multi-UAV Systems · Deep Reinforcement Learning DRL · CTDE · MAPPO · Trajectory Efficiency · Energy Optimization

1 Introduction

Unmanned Aerial Vehicles (UAVs), commonly known as drones, are increasingly deployed across military [1], industrial [2], and civilian domains [3], including applications such as surveillance [4], search and rescue, delivery, and environmental monitoring. Their autonomous capabilities [5], rapid deployment, and high mobility make them well suited for complex and dynamic missions. However, optimizing UAV trajectories remains a critical challenge due to limited

B. Ben Hedia et al. (Eds.): VECoS 2025, LNCS 16263, pp. 66–81, 2026.
https://doi.org/10.1007/978-3-032-20440-0_5

battery life [6,7], dynamic environmental conditions, and the need for real-time decision making [8].

In collaborative multi-agent environments, UAVs must perform accurate trajectory planning to minimize energy consumption while ensuring mission success. Classical methods such as A* and Dijkstra [9], Rapidly-exploring Random Trees (RRT) [10], and convex optimization approaches [11] have been widely applied to UAV path planning. While effective in structured environments, these methods face major limitations in dynamic scenarios: they lack adaptability, require high computational resources when scaled to multi-agent systems, and struggle to jointly optimize multiple objectives such as energy efficiency, safety, and communication reliability. These shortcomings make it difficult to detect truly optimal paths and support real-time decision-making, which highlights the need for more flexible and scalable learning-based solutions.

Artificial Intelligence (AI) encompasses a broad set of techniques aimed at creating systems capable of tasks that typically require human intelligence [12]. Within AI, Machine Learning (ML) focuses on learning patterns from data to make decisions or predictions. Deep Reinforcement Learning (DRL), a subfield of ML, extends reinforcement learning to handle high-dimensional state and action spaces, and has shown strong potential for solving complex sequential decision-making problems under uncertainty [13,14]. This work focuses specifically on DRL methods to address UAV trajectory optimization challenges.

We propose **E-MAPPO-CTDE** (Energy-aware Multi-Agent Proximal Policy Optimization with Centralized Training and Decentralized Execution), a novel framework leveraging the MAPPO algorithm to enable UAVs to learn energy-efficient, collision-free, and coordinated flight paths [15]. E-MAPPO-CTDE incorporates a realistic energy consumption model accounting for displacement, acceleration, and flight duration, integrated within a centralized training scheme that produces decentralized policies executable in real time by each UAV.

Our approach allows UAVs to adapt dynamically to environmental changes, avoid obstacles, and coordinate with other agents or ground control stations (GCS), enhancing overall autonomy and mission effectiveness. The primary contributions of this paper are:

- Development of a DRL-based model that enables UAVs to autonomously optimize flight trajectories with minimized energy consumption.
- Proposal of an AI-driven trajectory planning framework based on MAPPO and CTDE principles, ensuring real-time adaptation to dynamic environments and efficient multi-agent collaboration.
- Comprehensive simulation studies demonstrating significant improvements in energy efficiency and mission endurance compared to conventional approaches.

The remainder of this paper is organized as follows: Sect. 2 reviews related work in UAV communication and reinforcement learning applications. Section 3 details the system model and problem formulation. Section 4 presents the proposed DRL algorithm, including training methodology and reward function design. Section 5 describes the simulation setup, results, and discussion of key insights. Finally, Sect. 6 concludes the paper and outlines future research directions.

2 Related Work

The deployment of UAVs in communication networks has received growing attention in recent years, particularly regarding trajectory optimization and energy management [16]. Classical approaches such as A* and Dijkstra graph search algorithms [17], Rapidly-exploring Random Trees (RRT) [18], and convex optimization-based methods [19] have been widely adopted for UAV path planning. While these methods provide deterministic guarantees and perform well in structured or static environments, they exhibit several shortcomings: they lack adaptability in highly dynamic or uncertain scenarios, incur significant computational costs when scaled to multi-UAV systems, and struggle to jointly optimize multiple objectives such as energy efficiency, collision avoidance, and communication reliability.

To overcome these limitations, recent studies have increasingly turned toward learning-based methods, particularly reinforcement learning (RL). Qiu et al. (2024) [20], for example, developed a DRL optimization model based on MAPPO for UAV communication missions, demonstrating significant improvements in energy efficiency and mission effectiveness. However, their approach suffers from computational overhead that limits its scalability in real-time scenarios. Similarly, Rezwan and Choi (2022) [21] applied multi-agent reinforcement learning (MARL) combined with convolutional neural networks (CNNs) to enhance navigation and obstacle avoidance. While effective in improving UAV coordination, their method remains energy-intensive and vulnerable to unpredictable environmental changes. Tlili et al. (2024) [22] investigated RL for UAV security, integrating CNNs for real-time anomaly detection. Their work enhances UAV resilience against cyber threats but is hindered by processing complexity and sensitivity to false alarms, reducing reliability in long-duration missions.

Other contributions adopt broader AI techniques to improve UAV autonomy. Umashankar and Geethanjali (2024) [23] explored machine learning algorithms, optimization methods, and image processing for autonomous navigation and decision-making, though their approach is constrained by real-time computational limits. Caballero-Martin et al. (2024) [24] emphasized transfer learning and sensor fusion to improve UAV adaptability across environments, but the reliance on large datasets and sensor limitations reduces generalizability. Genetic algorithms and swarm intelligence have also been studied, as in the work of Puente-Castro et al. (2022) [25], where optimized path planning and swarm coordination improved fuel efficiency. Nevertheless, their scalability strongly depends on reliable inter-UAV communication, which remains a bottleneck in large-scale deployments.

Our proposed approach addresses these research gaps by introducing an energy-aware Multi-Agent Proximal Policy Optimization framework within a Centralized Training and Decentralized Execution (E-MAPPO-CTDE) paradigm. Unlike earlier works, our method explicitly integrates a realistic energy consumption model while simultaneously ensuring collision avoidance and communication reliability. Furthermore, the CTDE architecture enables scalable and decentralized real-time execution, allowing UAVs to operate autonomously in dynamic and partially observable environments. This combination provides a more comprehensive solution to the core challenges of multi-UAV trajectory planning, bridging the gap between theoretical optimization and practical deployment.

Table 1. Comparative summary of recent multi-UAV path planning approaches.

Work / Category	Method Used	Energy Optimization	Multi-UAV Coordination	Real-Time Adaptation
A*, Dijkstra , RRT [17], Convex optimization [19]	Graph search/sampling	✗ no energy model/optimization	Limited pairwise only	✗ offline computation
Qiu et al. (2024) [20]	MAPPO-based DRL	Partial energy-focused	Limited	✗ high complexity
Rezwan and Choi (2022) [21]	MARL + CNN	✗ energy-consuming	✓ coordination improved	✗ processing overhead
Tlili et al. (2024) [22]	RL + CNN security focus	✗ not targeted	Partial resilience	✗ limited real-time
Umashankar et al. (2024) [23]	ML-based planning and optimization	Theoretical only	Limited	imited real-time
Caballero-Martin et al. (2024) [24]	Transfer learning + sensor fusion	no energy mode	Limited sensor-based	Partial fast adaptation
Puente-Castro et al. (2022) [25]	Genetic algorithms + swarm intelligence	✓ fuel/energy efficiency	✓ swarm-based	✗ no reactivity
This Work	**E-MAPPO-CTDE (DRL)**	**✓ realistic energy model**	**✓ collision avoidance + coordination**	**✓ real-time decentralized execution**

3 Problem Formulation

In multi-UAV systems for mission-critical tasks (e.g., surveillance, logistics, disaster response), the core challenge is to generate trajectories that satisfy multiple, often conflicting objectives: energy efficiency, safety, communication robustness, and adaptability. Traditional optimization-based methods struggle to jointly capture these objectives under dynamic conditions. Motivated by recent advances in multi-agent deep reinforcement learning (MADRL), we reformulate this task as a constrained multi-objective learning problem, solvable via our proposed E-MAPPO-CTDE approach.

3.1 Objective Function

The main objective is to minimize the cumulative energy usage while ensuring that UAV trajectories remain safe, efficient, and communication-aware. The overall objective function is defined as:

$$\min_{\text{path}_i} \sum_{i=1}^{N} (E_i(t) + \lambda \cdot D_i(t)) \tag{1}$$

where:

- $E_i(t)$ is the energy consumed by UAV i at time t,
- $D_i(t)$ is the distance traveled by UAV i at time t,
- λ is a weighting coefficient balancing energy and distance for efficiency and smoothness.

This formulation guides UAVs to follow smoother, shorter paths that reduce energy waste and unnecessary motion.

3.2 Constraints

The optimization problem is governed by the following constraints:

Energy Constraint:

$$E_i(t) \leq E_{\text{max}}, \quad \forall i \tag{2}$$

Collision Avoidance Constraint:

$$\text{dist}(P_i(t), P_j(t)) \geq \delta, \quad \forall i \neq j \tag{3}$$

Trajectory Constraint (Operational Zone):

$$\text{path}_i \subseteq \text{valid\_area}, \quad \forall i \tag{4}$$

Communication Constraint:

$$\text{signal\_strength}(i, j, t) \geq \gamma, \quad \forall i, j \tag{5}$$

Adaptation Constraint:

$$\text{trajectory\_adjustment}(t) \leq \text{time\_limit}, \quad \forall t \tag{6}$$

3.3 Integration with E-MAPPO-CTDE: From Optimization to DRL

To address this complex optimization problem, we propose **E-MAPPO-CTDE** approach. This reinforcement learning-based solution transforms the constrained optimization problem into a learning problem where each UAV agent learns an optimal policy through interaction with the environment.
Mapping Constraints to Rewards: The constraints (2)–(6) are incorporated implicitly through the reward design, providing learning signals to guide the agents toward feasible and efficient solutions:

- **Energy constraint (2):** Penalize excessive $E_i(t)$ to enforce energy budgets.
- **Collision avoidance (3):** Apply strong negative rewards when $\text{dist}(P_i, P_j) < \delta$.
- **Trajectory constraint (4):** Penalize UAVs that exit the mission area.
- **Communication (5):** Reward agents for maintaining $\text{signal\_strength} \geq \gamma$.
- **Adaptation (6):** Reward smooth and responsive trajectory adjustments within the allowed time limit.

CTDE Framework: Under centralized training, a shared critic network has access to the global state $S = \{s_1, s_2, ..., s_N\}$, including all UAVs' positions, energy, and communication data. This allows the critic to learn value functions that reflect system-wide objectives. During decentralized execution, each UAV relies only on its local observation o_i and its actor policy π_i to make real-time decisions. This ensures scalability and resilience without requiring continuous global communication.

4 Proposed Approach

To address the challenges formulated in Sect. 3, we propose an optimization-based solution leveraging Deep Reinforcement Learning (DRL) within a multi-agent framework using Multi-Agent Proximal Policy Optimization (MAPPO). The objective is to optimize UAV trajectories while minimizing energy consumption, avoiding obstacles, and ensuring reliable communication with both the Ground Control Station (GCS) and peer UAVs.

Our method follows a **Centralized Training and Decentralized Execution (CTDE)** paradigm. During training, all UAV agents share experiences with a centralized critic that evaluates the joint state-action space. Once trained, each UAV independently selects actions based on local observations, enabling scalability and real-time responsiveness.

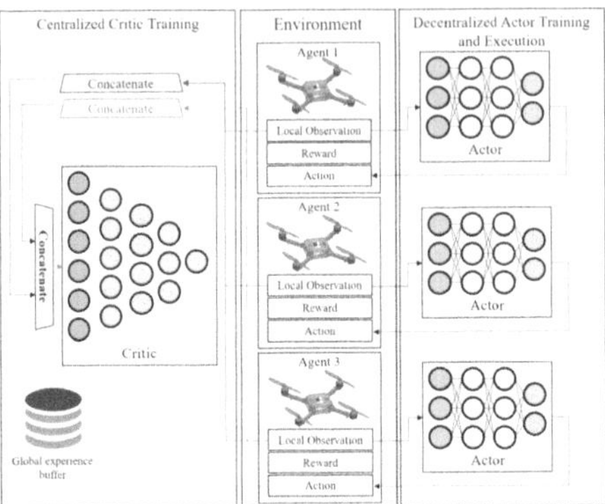

Fig. 1. CTDE architecture with centralized critic and decentralized actors for UAV coordination.

4.1 Optimization Algorithm (MAPPO)

We utilize MAPPO, suitable for continuous action spaces and cooperative multi-agent environments. Each UAV is modeled as an agent with its own actor network π_i, responsible for selecting actions (e.g., velocity or heading adjustments). A centralized critic network V_c evaluates the value of the global state using joint observations.

- **Actor Network:** Learns the local policy $\pi_i(o_i)$ for UAV i.
- **Centralized Critic:** Evaluates joint state $S = \{s_1, s_2, ..., s_N\}$ to estimate the advantage function.

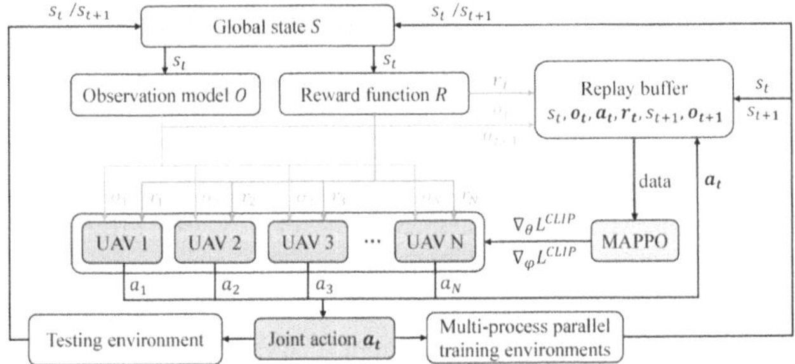

Fig. 2. Training and execution framework of E-MAPPO-CTDE based on MAPPO with centralized critic and decentralized actors.

As shown in Fig. 2, the E-MAPPO-CTDE framework relies on parallelized environments to collect experience tuples $(s_t, o_t, a_t, r_t, s_{t+1}, o_{t+1})$ during the training stage. The joint policy π generates actions based on local observations, while the centralized critic uses the global state to compute value estimates. Experiences are stored in a shared replay buffer and used to update both actor and critic networks once sufficient data is collected.

During testing, only decentralized actor policies are deployed. Each UAV receives its local observation o_i and selects an action $a_i = \pi_i(o_i)$ without access to the centralized state or other agents' observations.

Learning Procedure (CTDE with Experience Replay)

Algorithm 1: Multi-UAV Actor-Critic Training

1: Initialize actor networks π_i for each UAV i
2: Initialize a centralized critic network V_c
3: Initialize replay buffer B
4: Set hyperparameters: `learning_rate`, γ, `epsilon_clip`, `batch_size`, etc.
break;
5: **foreach** *episode* **do**
  6: Reset environment; obtain initial states $S = \{s_1, ..., s_N\}$;
  7: Initialize `total_rewards` $\leftarrow 0$;
  8: **foreach** *timestep in episode* **do**
    9: **foreach** *UAV i* **do**
      10: Observe o_i;
      11: Select action $a_i = \pi_i(o_i)$;
    end
    12: Execute joint action $A = \{a_1, ..., a_N\}$;
    13: Receive next states S', rewards R, and done flags;
    14: Store $(S, A, R, S', \texttt{done})$ in buffer B;
    15: Accumulate `total_rewards`;
    16: Update $S \leftarrow S'$;
    17: **if** *done* **then**
    end
    break;
  end
end
18: **if** *buffer B is full* **then**
  19: Sample mini-batches from B;
  20: **foreach** *mini-batch* **do**
    21: Compute advantage $A_i(t)$ using V_c;
    22: Calculate actor and critic losses;
    23: Update π_i and V_c using gradient descent;
  end
  24: Clear buffer B;
end
25: Log: `"Episode {episode}, Total Rewards: {total_rewards}"`;

Where:

- π_i: Actor policy network for UAV i, responsible for selecting actions based on local observations.
- V_c: Centralized critic network estimating global value based on full state information.
- B: Replay buffer used to store agent transitions for off-policy training.
- $S = \{s_1, ..., s_N\}$: Set of initial states for all N UAVs.
- o_i: Local observation of UAV i at a given timestep.
- a_i: Action selected by UAV i from its policy π_i.
- $A = \{a_1, ..., a_N\}$: Joint action executed by all UAVs.
- R: Reward signal returned by the environment based on joint actions.
- γ: Discount factor that balances short-term and long-term rewards.
- $A_i(t)$: Estimated advantage function used to guide policy updates.
- ϵ_{clip}: Clipping factor to stabilize training (used in PPO-based methods).
- `total_rewards`: Accumulated reward over one episode, used for monitoring performance.

4.2 Reward Function Design

In our proposed E-MAPPO-CTDE framework, each UAV agent learns to optimize its trajectory through a multi-objective reward function that balances energy efficiency, safety, communication reliability, and trajectory smoothness. The instantaneous reward received by UAV i at timestep t is defined as:

$$r_i(t) = \alpha_1 \cdot r_i^{\text{energy}}(t) + \alpha_2 \cdot r_i^{\text{collision}}(t) + \alpha_3 \cdot r_i^{\text{comm}}(t) + \alpha_4 \cdot r_i^{\text{smooth}}(t)$$

where α_1, α_2, α_3, and α_4 are non-negative weighting factors with $\sum_{k=1}^{4} \alpha_k = 1$.

Energy Efficiency Term:

$$r_i^{\text{energy}}(t) = -\left(\eta_1 \cdot \|v_i(t)\|^2 + \eta_2 \cdot \|a_i(t)\|^2\right)$$

This penalizes high velocities and accelerations to reduce propulsion-related energy consumption, where $v_i(t)$ and $a_i(t)$ denote the velocity and acceleration of UAV i at time t, and η_1, η_2 are scaling factors.

Collision Avoidance Term:

$$r_i^{\text{collision}}(t) = \begin{cases} -1 & \text{if } \exists j \neq i \text{ with } \text{dist}(i,j) < \delta \\ 0 & \text{otherwise} \end{cases}$$

This penalizes UAVs for breaching the minimum safety distance δ from other agents or static obstacles.

Communication Maintenance Term:

$$r_i^{\text{comm}}(t) = \begin{cases} +1 & \text{if } \text{RSSI}(i, \text{GCS}) \geq \gamma \\ -0.5 & \text{otherwise} \end{cases}$$

Rewards agents for maintaining sufficient signal strength (RSSI) with the Ground Control Station, with a threshold γ.

Trajectory Smoothness Term:

$$r_i^{\text{smooth}}(t) = -\|a_i(t) - a_i(t-1)\|^2$$

This penalizes abrupt changes in acceleration, encouraging smooth and stable trajectories.

5 Simulation Results and Analysis

This section evaluates the effectiveness of our proposed trajectory optimization framework, which integrates Deep Reinforcement Learning (DRL) with the Multi-Agent Proximal Policy Optimization (MAPPO) algorithm, implemented under the Centralized Training and Decentralized Execution (CTDE) paradigm. The simulation results demonstrate improvements in energy efficiency, collision avoidance, and coordination across both single and multi-agent UAV scenarios.

5.1 Objective of the Simulation

The main objective is for each UAV to reach its assigned destination while avoiding both static (e.g., buildings) and dynamic obstacles (e.g., birds, other UAVs) and maintaining safe inter-agent distances. Static obstacles remain fixed, whereas dynamic ones are randomly repositioned at each iteration to emulate realistic disturbances.

Unlike classical shortest-path planners, our approach integrates multi-agent interactions, dynamic obstacle layouts, and energy-aware decision-making. Although the figures are presented in 2D for clarity, altitude is explicitly modeled: each UAV operates at a distinct flight layer, and vertical movement is embedded in the state and reward design to ensure safe 3D navigation.

The CTDE framework enables joint training through a centralized critic, while execution relies on decentralized actor policies using only local observations. This ensures both cooperative behavior during training and scalable real-time decision-making during deployment, reflecting practical UAV applications in surveillance, logistics, and rescue missions.

5.2 Simulation Parameters

The environment spans a 100 m × 100 m area populated with randomly placed circular obstacles of variable radii. Four UAVs are initialized from different locations and tasked with reaching designated goal areas.

For evaluation, we considered three types of trajectories:

- **A*:** Classical grid-based planner used as a deterministic baseline.
- **Dijkstra:** Another standard baseline offering slightly smoother paths than A* but longer trajectories.
- **Optimized (E-MAPPO-CTDE):** A trajectory generated by a trained actor network using the CTDE strategy.

This choice of baselines highlights the contrast between deterministic algorithms and our learning-based adaptive approach.

Training hyperparameters were empirically tuned for stable convergence: learning rate 3×10^{-4}, discount factor $\gamma = 0.99$, GAE parameter $\lambda = 0.95$, clipping parameter $\epsilon = 0.2$, centralized critic hidden layers [256, 256], and batch size 128. These values ensured a balance between stability and responsiveness to dynamic changes.

Single-Agent Analysis. Figure 3 illustrates a typical baseline trajectory (A*) followed by a single UAV. The path exhibits oscillatory movement and inefficient detours around obstacles, leading to elevated energy consumption.

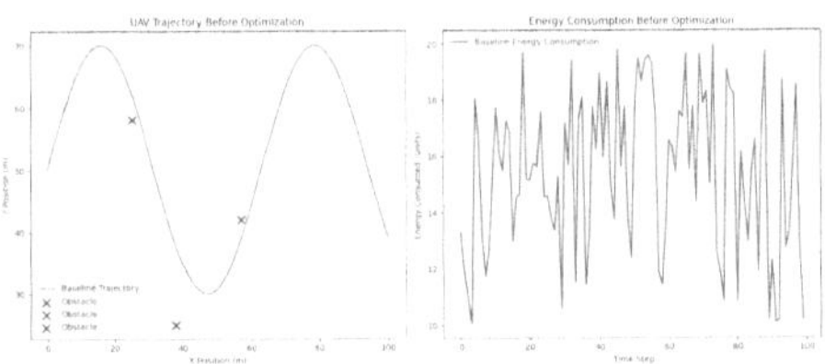

Fig. 3. UAV trajectory and energy consumption with a classical baseline.

After training with MAPPO, the UAV produces a smoother, more direct path (Fig. 4). The agent learns energy-efficient policies through centralized training, while its decisions during inference are made autonomously via the actor network using only its local state.

Multi-Agent Analysis and Coordination. To validate scalability, we extended the simulation to a multi-agent setup with four UAVs. Initially, baseline trajectories generated by A* and Dijkstra exhibit large overlaps, indirect paths, and no mutual awareness (Fig. 5).

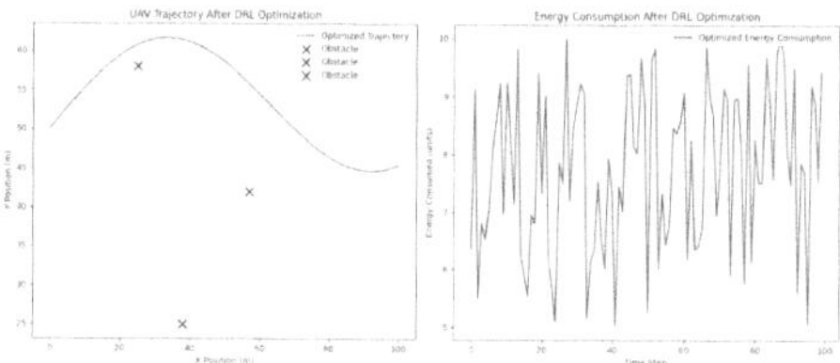

Fig. 4. UAV trajectory and energy consumption after DRL optimization (E-MAPPO-CTDE).

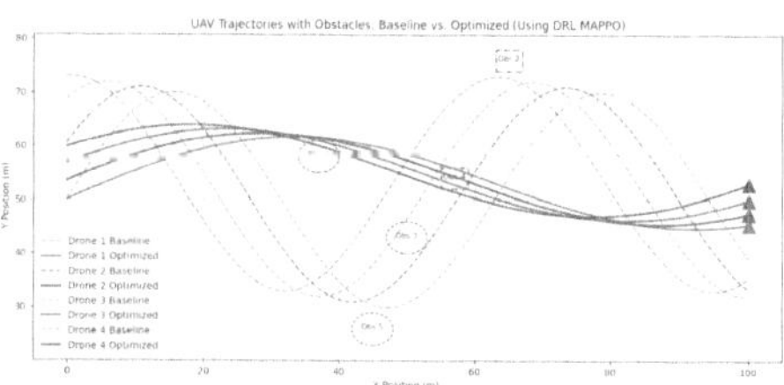

Fig. 5. UAV Trajectories with Obstacles: Baselines vs. E-MAPPO-CTDE.

After applying E-MAPPO-CTDE, the UAVs demonstrate streamlined paths and distributed coordination. Each agent independently selects actions using its trained actor policy while implicitly respecting other agents. The centralized critic, used during training, promotes conflict avoidance and energy minimization.

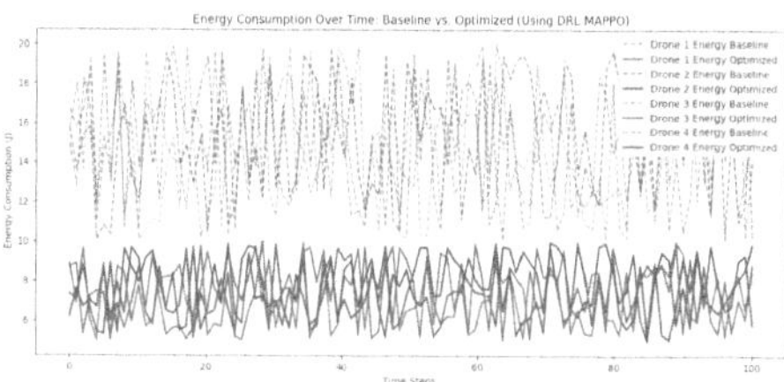

Fig. 6. Energy Consumption Over Time: Baselines vs. E-MAPPO-CTDE.

Although the figures show 2D projections, UAVs maintain separate flight altitudes to guarantee collision-free navigation in 3D.

5.3 Energy Consumption Comparison and Optimization Analysis

We compare the total energy consumption of four UAVs under three trajectory planning methods: A*, Dijkstra, and the proposed DRL-based E-MAPPO-

CTDE. The environment includes static obstacles, distinct start and goal positions, and 2D projections for visualization (altitude considered during training).

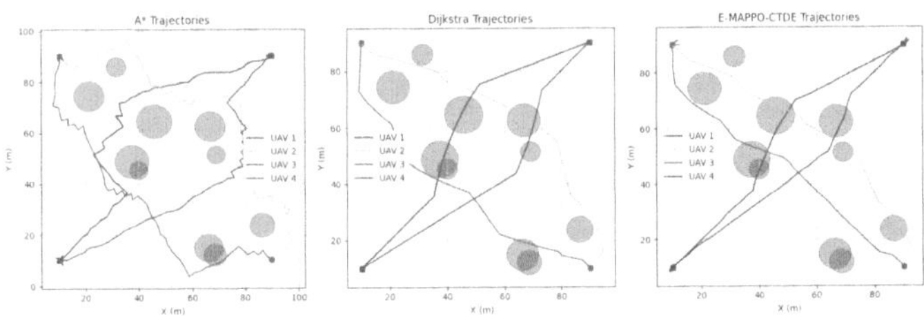

Fig. 7. Comparison of UAV Trajectories: A*, Dijkstra, and E-MAPPO-CTDE.

Figure 7 shows that A* and Dijkstra generate longer, oscillatory paths with frequent overlaps, whereas E-MAPPO-CTDE yields smoother and more direct trajectories. This demonstrates implicit inter-agent coordination and energy-aware decision-making at each timestep.

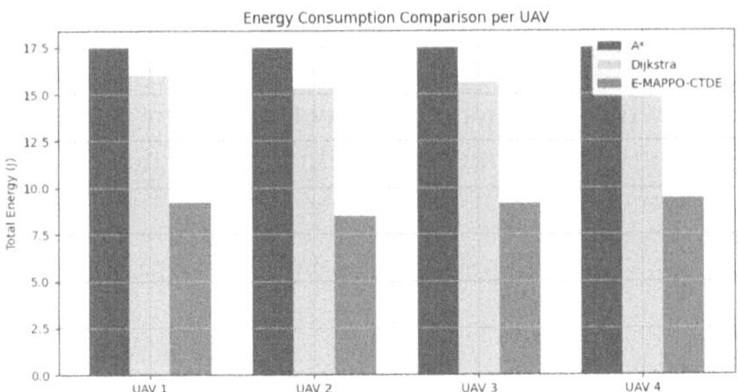

Fig. 8. Total Energy Consumption per UAV for A*, Dijkstra, and E-MAPPO-CTDE.

As shown in Table 2, E-MAPPO-CTDE reduces energy use by nearly 50% compared to A* and 44–46% compared to Dijkstra. These gains result from: smoother trajectories minimizing detours, energy-aware local policies, implicit coordination reducing conflicts and altitude integration ensuring safe 3D navigation.

These improvements directly enhance mission endurance, safety, and scalability. Unlike deterministic baselines, E-MAPPO-CTDE adapts to dynamic constraints in real time, achieving a robust balance between energy efficiency, obstacle avoidance, and distributed coordination.

Table 2. Total Energy Consumption and Energy Savings (%) per UAV

UAV	A* (J)	Dijkstra (J)	E-MAPPO-CTDE (J)	Savings vs A* (%)
UAV 1	17.75	15.13	8.44	52.4%
UAV 2	17.75	15.68	8.89	50.0%
UAV 3	17.75	15.01	8.35	53.0%
UAV 4	17.75	15.49	8.56	51.8%

5.4 Discussion

The simulation results demonstrate the clear advantages of our DRL-based E-MAPPO CTDE framework over classical methods such as A* and Dijkstra. By leveraging deep reinforcement learning, UAVs adapt trajectories dynamically, achieving smoother paths, reduced overlaps, and nearly 50% energy savings, which improves both individual efficiency and multi-agent coordination.

The DRL framework ensures implicit coordination: UAVs maintain safe distances, distribute efficiently, and avoid redundant maneuvers without explicit communication. CTDE enables cooperative strategies during training while allowing decentralized execution, ensuring scalability and real-time adaptability.

Additionally, energy- and altitude-aware optimization addresses both lateral and vertical dimensions, enhancing mission reliability, obstacle avoidance, and overall operational performance. These results confirm that DRL-based E-MAPPO-CTDE effectively meets the objectives of energy efficiency, safety, and decentralized multi-UAV coordination.

6 Conclusion

This work presented **E-MAPPO-CTDE**, a Deep Reinforcement Learning (DRL) framework for multi-UAV trajectory optimization, enabling energy-efficient, collision-free, and coordinated swarm navigation. The approach enhances mission endurance and operational efficiency, making it highly relevant for energy-aware UAV swarm applications. It can be further integrated with terrestrial cobots to enable complementary multi-agent operations, where coordinated decision-making optimizes both task execution and operational costs. Future work will focus on multi-UAV data processing, including image analysis using deep learning, to extend the system's intelligence and adaptiveness while maintaining synergy with the current framework.

References

1. Mohsan, S.A.H., Khan, M.A., Noor, F., Ullah, I., Alsharif, M.H.: Towards the unmanned aerial vehicles (UAVs): a comprehensive review. Drones **6**(6), 147 (2022). https://doi.org/10.3390/drones6060147

2. Cheikhrouhou, O., Khoufi, I.: A comprehensive survey on the multiple traveling salesman problem: applications, approaches and taxonomy. Comput. Sci. Rev. **40**, 100369 (2021). https://doi.org/10.1016/j.cosrev.2021.100369
3. AL-Dosari, K., Hunaiti, Z., Balachandran, W.: Systematic review on civilian drones in safety and security applications. Drones **7**(3), 210 (2023). https://doi.org/10.3390/drones7030210
4. Sliusar, N., Filkin, T., Huber-Humer, M., Ritzkowski, M.: Drone technology in municipal solid waste management and landfilling: a comprehensive review. Waste Manage. **139**, 1–16 (2022). https://doi.org/10.1016/j.wasman.2021.12.006
5. Eskandaripour, H., Boldsaikhan, E.: Last-mile drone delivery: past, present, and future. Drones **7**(2), 77 (2023). https://doi.org/10.3390/drones7020077
6. Shukla, P., Shukla, S., Singh, A.K.: Trajectory-prediction techniques for unmanned aerial vehicles (UAVs): a comprehensive survey (2024). IEEE Commun. Surv. Tutor. https://doi.org/10.1109/COMST.2024.3471671
7. Li, F., Luo, J., Sun, P., Teng, S.: Energy-efficient UAV-based data collection 3D trajectory optimization with wireless power transfer for forest monitoring. IEEE Internet Things J. (2025). https://doi.org/10.1109/JIOT.2025.3555415
8. Sorbelli, F.: UAV-based delivery systems: a systematic review, current trends, and research challenges. ACM J. Auton. Transport. Syst. **1**(3), 12 (2024). https://doi.org/10.1145/3649224
9. Li, J., et al.: The improved A* algorithm for quadrotor UAVs under forest obstacle avoidance path planning. Appl. Sci. **13**, 4290 (2023). https://doi.org/10.3390/app13074290
10. Huang, T., Fan, K., Sun, W., Li, W., Guo, H.: Potential-field-RRT: a path-planning algorithm for UAVs based on potential-field-oriented greedy strategy to extend random tree. Drones **7**, 331 (2023). https://doi.org/10.3390/drones7050331
11. Liu, H.: Distributed constrained optimization algorithms for drones. Drones **9**, 36 (2025). https://doi.org/10.3390/drones9010036
12. Kurunathan, H., Huang, H., Li, K., Ni, W., Hossain, E.: Machine learning-aided operations and communications of unmanned aerial vehicles: a contemporary survey. IEEE Commun. Surv. Tutor., **26**(1), 496–533 (2024). https://doi.org/10.1109/COMST.2023.3312221
13. Bao, Z., Tang, C., Yu, X., Lin, F., Wen, G., Zheng, Z.: Cost-effective power delivery via deep reinforcement learning-based dynamic electric vehicle transportation. IEEE Internet Things J. (2025). https://doi.org/10.1109/JIOT.2025.3552823
14. Chung, K.T., Lee, C.K.M., Tsang, Y.P.: Neural combinatorial optimization with reinforcement learning in industrial engineering: a survey. Artif. Intell. Rev. **58**, 130 (2025). https://doi.org/10.1007/s10462-024-11045-1
15. Liu, Y., Li, X., Wang, J., Wei, F., Yang, J.: Reinforcement-learning-based Multi-UAV cooperative search for moving targets in 3D scenarios. Drones **8**(8), 378 (2024). https://doi.org/10.3390/drones8080378
16. Javaid, S., et al.: Communication and control in collaborative UAVs: recent advances and future trends. IEEE Trans. Intell. Transp. Syst. **24**, 5719–5739 (2023)
17. Cheriet, H., Khellat Kihel, B., Chouraqui, S.: Comparative analysis of UAV path planning algorithms for efficient navigation in urban 3D environments. In: Proceedings of the 2024 Afro-European Conference for Industrial Advancement (AFROS), Algiers, Algeria, 13–15 November (2024). https://doi.org/10.1109/AFROS62115.2024.11037069
18. Khuat, T.H., Bui, D.-N., Nguyen, H.T.T., Trinh, M.L., Nguyen, M.T., Phung, M.D.: Multi-goal rapidly exploring random tree with safety and dynamic con-

straints for UAV cooperative path planning. arXiv preprint arXiv:2504.11823 (2025). https://doi.org/10.48550/arXiv.2504.11823
19. Zhang, N.: Collision risk modeling and resolution path planning for UAV conflict management in dynamic environments. Doctoral thesis, Nanyang Technological University, Singapore (2024). https://hdl.handle.net/10356/180915
20. Qiu, W., Shao, X., Masui, H., Liu, W.: Optimizing drone energy use for emergency communications in disasters via deep reinforcement learning. Future Internet **16**(7), 245 (2024). https://doi.org/10.3390/fi16070245
21. Rezwan, S., Choi, W.: Artificial intelligence approaches for UAV navigation: recent advances and future challenges. IEEE Access **10**, 26320–26339 (2022). https://doi.org/10.1109/ACCESS.2022.3157626
22. Tlili, F., Ayed, S., Fourati, L.C.: Advancing UAV security with artificial intelligence: a comprehensive survey of techniques and future directions. Internet Things, **27** (2024). https://doi.org/10.1016/j.iot.2024.101281
23. Umashankar, N., Geethanjali, K.: A comprehensive study of artificial intelligence applications of drone (2024). https://doi.org/10.31224/4194
24. Caballero-Martin, D., Lopez-Guede, J.M., Estevez, J., Graña, M.: Artificial intelligence applied to drone control: a state of the art. Drones **8**(7), 296 (2024). https://doi.org/10.3390/drones8070296
25. Puente-Castro, A., Rivero, D., Pazos, A., Fernandez-Blanco, E.: A review of artificial intelligence applied to path planning in UAV swarms. Neural Comput. Appl. **34**(1), 153–170 (2021). https://doi.org/10.1007/s00521-021-06569-4
26. Çinar, H., Ignatyev, D., Zolotas, A.: A comprehensive review and future challenges of energy-aware path planning for small unmanned aerial vehicles with hydrogen-powered hybrid propulsion. Aeronautical J., 1–26 (2025). https://doi.org/10.1017/aer.2025.11

Partially Aggregatable Distributed Multi-Key Generation Protocol

Rym Kalai[1](✉), Wafa Neji[2], and Narjes Ben Rajeb[3]

[1] LIPSIC Laboratory, Faculty of Sciences of Tunis, University of Tunis El Manar, Tunis, Tunisia
Rym.Kalai@gmail.com
[2] LIPSIC Laboratory, Higher Institute of Management of Bizerte (ISG Bizerte), University of Carthage, Bizerte, Tunisia
wafa.neji@gmail.com
[3] EPITA Research Lab (LRE), EPITA, Le Kremlin-Bicêtre, France
narjes.ben-rajeb@epita.fr

Abstract. In Publicly Verifiable Secret Sharing (PVSS) schemes, any participant can verify the validity of the shares distributed among the participants as well as the correctness of the recovered secret. Thus, the corrupted shares and misbehaving participants can be identified and there is no need for complaint management phase. Since there are less communication rounds, this contribution offers a positive impact in distributed protocols that are based on PVSS to decrease communication's complexity. An aggregatable PVSS permit to homomorphically combine several transcripts into a single transcript relative to the sum of their individual secrets.

In this paper, we propose a Distributed Multi-Key Generation (DMKG) protocol with partially aggregatable and publicly verifiable transcripts. The proposed protocol benefits from the efficiency of the complaint management strategy introduced by Kalai et al. in [20] and from the contribution of the publicly verifiable secret sharing (PVSS) scheme based on the enhanced SCRAPE PVSS presented by Gurkan et al. in [18].

Keywords: Publicly Verifiable Secret Sharing (PVSS) · Aggreagation · Distributed Multi-Key Generation (DMKG) protocol

1 Introduction

Secret Sharing (SS) is a cryptographic technique that has been introduced by Shamir [31] and Blakley [6] in 1979. It enables one trusted party called dealer to split a secret into multiple shares and to distribute them among n participants. Individual shares are of no use on their own [21]. Furthermore, in threshold schemes, only a subgroup of the participants of size no less than t members such that $(2 \leq t < n)$ can combine their shares together to recover the secret. Publicly Verifiable Secret Sharing (PVSS) is a cryptographic primitive proposed in [32] to overcome the weakness of threshold SS and to achieve security against cheating participants. Verifiability is the property of verifying the validity of the shares or the correctness of the recovered secret when the shares

B. Ben Hedia et al. (Eds.): VECoS 2025, LNCS 16263, pp. 82–96, 2026.
https://doi.org/10.1007/978-3-032-20440-0_6

and the secret are not compromised. Stadler [32] designed the first PVSS. It enables a secret s to be shared between n participants through a publicly verifiable transcript of encrypted shares with a proof. This parameter allows any participant to check the validity of the shares or the correctness of the recovered secret and to check that the dealer has behaved honestly. Even better, any third party can do this verification [3]. So, there is no need for complaint management phase to expose misbehaving participants. Indeed, this contribution has a positive and an outstanding impact in PVSS based protocols [13] especially distributed protocols to decrease communication's cost and complexity since fewer communication rounds are required. Aggregable PVSS makes it possible to homomorphically join several transcripts into a single aggregated transcript relative to the sum of their individual secrets.

In cryptographic system with SS scheme, the dealer is the unique participant that holds the secret and distributes the shares and whose corruption will break the security of the entire system. DKG protocols offer the solution to avoid this problem. The idea is to have many participants that cooperate together to generate and share a secret key without using a unique trusted party such that all honest participants will have valid shares of the unique secret key. It is equivalent to having n parallel secret sharing processes: Each participant is a dealer on a single sharing process. DKG protocol is an outstanding building block for many threshold cryptosystems such as data archive systems [35], public randomness beacons [16,33] and Byzantine consensus [2,36].

The term Distributed Multi-Key Generation (DMKG) protocol was presented in 2020 by Ma et al. in [22]. This is the same principle applied in DKG protocols, except that in DMKG protocols the participants handle l several secrets at the same time. It is equivalent to a distributed and parallel executions of a multi secret sharing (MSS) scheme where all the participants cooperate together and share several secrets in order to generate a public-private key pair.

In this article, we present a new DMKG protocol with an aggregatable PVSS scheme that benefits from the contributions of Gurkan et al. [18] which introduced an enhanced version of SCRAPE PVSS and applied it in a DKG protocol without disputation. Our contribution considerably reduces the communication complexity of our DMKG, simplifies the complaint management strategy previously defined in [20] and offers a public verification of the aggregated transcripts.

This paper is organized as follows: We start by presenting a state of art of DKG and DMKG protocols. Afterwards, we describe the important building block of our research which is the aggregatable DKG with the enhanced variant of SCRAPE PVSS introduced in [18]. After that, we present our new partially aggregatable DMKG with a simplified complaint management strategy. Then, we prove the security of the proposed contribution. Finally, we end this paper with a brief comparison of our proposed DMKG and some of the related works.

2 State of Art

DKG protocol is an outstanding building block for many threshold cryptosystems. The first DKG without trusted party was presented in 1991 by Pedersen [28] for discrete log-based cryptosystems. It is based on Feldman VSS [12]. It was considered for many years as a central component to build a lot of cryptographic protocols such as threshold ElGamal cryptosystem, Digital Signature Standard (DSS), and electronic voting. However, in 1999, Gennaro et al. [17] proved that in the presence of an adversary, the Pedersen's DKG does not guarantee a uniformly random distribution of generated keys. Gennaro et al. proposed a secure protocol based on Pedersen's VSS protocol [27] and Feldman's VSS protocol [12] but at the cost of lower efficiency. It uses private channels that hide malicious participants and requires an extra communication round to manage complaints. Despite that, several recent contributions used this protocol to construct threshold cryptosystems [14,26,34,37]. Canetti et al. [7] improved the solution of Gennaro et al. to handle adaptive corruptions, but they also used private channels. Fouque and Stern [13] presented in 2001, a one-round DKG protocol without private channels. Instead of a VSS, it is based on a PVSS and publicly verifiable encryption and uses Paillier cryptosystem [25] to encrypt the shares. However, this leads to a more challenging key management process under different mathematical assumptions, to a slow key management and to a high communication costs. Neji et al. [24] proposed a more efficient DKG protocol as an extended version of Joint-Feldman DKG that guarantees a uniformly random distribution of generated keys. It removes the bias without using an additional secret sharing round. They also use public channels and introduced the disputation phase, a new strategy to manage the complaint among participants. However, this strategy requires additional consensus invocation. In PVSS schemes the main idea is that the dealer randomly and uniformly samples a t degree polynomial $f \in \mathbb{Z}_p$, commits to it via Feldman commitments [12] then computes encryptions of shares with Shamir threshold secret sharing. The other participants compute commitments to the shares $f(i)$ using Feldman commitments. Zero-knowledge proofs are used to prove that these commitments correspond to the encrypted received shares. Stadler [32] used the Fiat-Shamir heuristics in the random oracle model [3]. A variant of Stadler's PVSS is proposed by Schoenmakers [30] that improves the scheme's security and reduces it from the computational Diffie-Hellman assumption. Jhanwar [19] introduced a new PVSS that is based on pairing in the plain model that assures security under the Decisional Bilinear Square assumption and the multi-sequence of exponents Diffie-Hellman assumption. However, this results on quadratic computation cost. PVSS are used in distributed randomness beacons [4,5,10,29] and DKG [1,13,18]. Over the years, several improved schemes have been presented. Cascudo et al. [8] designed SCRAPE PVSS scheme to overcome the problem of quadratic computation cost. The dealer commits to the polynomial evaluations $f(i)$ instead of the coefficients of the polynomial f and then publishes $g^{f(i)}$. Participants can verify that these commitments actually correspond to a t degree polynomial. Thus, the complexity reduces to $O(n)$.

Gurkan et al. [18] proposed an enhancement of the SCRAPE PVSS scheme to design a DKG protocol that requires from each participant P_i to broadcast n messages of $O(1)$ size and $log n$ messages of size $O(n)$ where n is the number of participants cooperating in the DKG protocol. As mentioned in [3,10,11], the PVSS scheme proposed by Gurkan et al. [18] assumes hardness of the Symmetric External Diffie-Hellman (SXDH) problem for Type 3 pairing groups.

DMKG protocols apply the same idea proposed in DKG protocols except that they handle l several secrets at the same time. They solve the problem of the single trusted party in MSS schemes as each participant can be the dealer and all participants cooperate together to share multiple secrets to generate a public-private key pair. In 2020 Ma et al. [22] introduced the first DMKG protocol to design BTSOF : a Blockchain Traceable Scheme with Oversight Function. It implements identity tracing to over come the flaws related to privacy protection in Blockchain applications. A regulator needs to trace the users' identities of the Blockchain data and needs the consent of the committee which is formed by n participants that cooperate together to generate the traceable public-private key pair $(sk, pk) = ((x_1, x_2, y_1, y_2, z), (C_1, C_2, C_3)) = ((x_1, x_2, y_1, y_2, z), (g_1{}^{x_1} g_2{}^{x_2}, g_1{}^{y_1} g_2{}^{y_2}, g_1{}^{z}))$. After that, the secret key is sent to the regulator to enable tracing. This protocol is built on the Gennaro's DKG protocol [17] to assure uniform distribution of generated keys. It uses private channels between participants who are not all honest. Some can distribute invalid shares and others may lie and claim to have received invalid shares. The use of private channels hides dishonest participants and leads to additional communications to manage the conflicts between participants and to difficulties to identify dishonest ones. In addition, whenever there is a complaint, the protocol requires participants to reveal their shares to prove their honesty which can lead a cheater to claim to have received an invalid share in order to disqualify the honest participant. Ma et al. [23] presented in 2021, a traceable scheme suitable for consortium Blockchain with leverage of [22].

Kalai et al. [20] introduced a new DMKG protocol built on the DMKG protocol of BTSOF presented in [22]. It focused on the generation of the traceable secret key with a MSS scheme based on the Pedersen-VSS scheme [27] to distribute z_i and leverage the Franklin-Yung MSS scheme [15] to distribute (x_1, x_2, y_1, y_2). The challenge is to prove the honesty of participants without revealing their shares and also to identify malicious ones. This DMKG protocol uses only public channels. There are no private channels between participants and all the shares of secrets are encrypted and sent over the public channel. In addition, the DMKG protocol presents a new strategy to manage complaints between participants that needs the contribution of all the participants. Thanks to this new strategy and to the use of public channels the protocol offers a precise and effective detection of malicious participants and avoids the honest ones to publicly reveal their shares of secrets. In fact, the protocol is able to eliminate participants that falsely pretend receiving invalid shares and participants that send invalid ones. In another hand, in this protocol there is no need to verify all broadcasted information of all participants. Each participant verifies his received shares and the complaint management strategy is executed whenever there is at least one complaint between two participants. But it turned out that this strategy leads to a considerable increase in the complexity and time of the protocol, particularly with the multi-secret context. For each complaint between 2 participants, all the participants cooperate together and each of the n participants verify the information received from all the other to finally be able to judge who is the dishonest one among the 2 participants in the conflict. The verification complexity is estimated to $O(kn^2)$ such that k is a security parameter.

In this paper, we propose a new DMKG protocol that leverage the efficient complaint management strategy proposed in [20] and benefits from the contribution of the enhanced version of SCRAPE PVSS introduced by Gurkan et al. in [18] to aggregate transcripts exchanged among participants. This contribution makes the transcripts publicly verifiable, considerably simplifies the disputation phase and leads to a significant decrease in communication costs.

3 Aggregatable DKG Protocol of Gurkan Et Al

This section describe the DKG protocol of Gurkan et al. [18] build on an enhanced SCRAPE PVSS that is a variant of the pairing-based SCRAPE [8] that supports aggregation. As mentioned in [3], it is secure under the Symmetric External Diffie Hellman (SXDH) assumption for Type 3 pairings and it uses signatures of knowledge to efficiently aggregate PVSS transcripts. We note $bp = (p, \mathbb{G}_1, \mathbb{G}_2, \mathbb{G}_T, e, g_1, \hat{h}_1)$ a bilinear group description such that $\mathbb{G}_1$, $\mathbb{G}_2$ and $\mathbb{G}_T$ are groups with order divisible by the prime $p \in \mathbb{G}$, g_1 respectively $\hat{h}_1$ generates $\mathbb{G}_1$ respectively $\mathbb{G}_2$ and $e : \mathbb{G}_1 \times \mathbb{G}_2 \rightarrow \mathbb{G}_T$ is a (non-degenerate) bilinear map. All the participants use the same common reference string (CRS) that combine the following elements : bp a bilinear group description, $enc_i \in \mathbb{G}_2$ encryption keys with $i \in [1,n]$, $dec_i \in \mathbb{F}$ decryption keys where $enc_i = \hat{h}_1^{dec_i}$ with $i \in [1,n]$, vk_i verification keys with $i \in [1,n]$, nth roots of unity ω_i in $\mathbb{F}$ with $i \in [1,n]$, $\hat{u}_1 \in \mathbb{G}_2$ a random group element such that nobody knows $log_{\hat{h}_1}(\hat{u}_1)$. Each participant deals a secret using the enhanced SCRAPE PVSS. In this DKG, to avoid the $O(n^2)$ verification complexity per participant as with other DKG, Gurkan et al. [18] leverage aggregation of SCRAPE PVSS transcripts : Each participant that verified more than one transcript can aggregate them to obtain a single verified transcript and sends it to another participant that will act in a similar way. In this way, it decreases the verification complexity per participant to $O(n \log^2 n)$. It should be noted that the aggregation can be achieved gradually and executed by any participant and that participant's contribution c_i can be integrated several times noted w_i in the final secret. Gurkan et al. [18] uses a signature of knowledge to permit to each participant P_i at the same time to sign its contribution and to prove knowledge of it to the final secret. P_i signs C_i using its secret key sk_i with corresponding verification key $verif_i = g_1^{sk_i}$ as $\sigma_i = (\sigma_{i,1}, \sigma_{i,2}) = (Hash_{\mathbb{G}_2}(C_i)^{c_i}, Hash_{\mathbb{G}_2}(verif_i, C_i)^{sk_i})$ such that $Hash_{\mathbb{G}_2}$ is a hash function that maps to $\mathbb{G}_2$. Then any verifier that has $verif_i$ can verify σ_i as $e(C_i, Hash_{\mathbb{G}_2}(C_i) = e(g_1, \sigma_{i,1})) \wedge e(verif_i, Hash_{\mathbb{G}_2}(verif_i, C_i)) = e(g_1, \sigma_{i,2})$.

The different phases of the enhanced variant of SCRAPE PVSS are described in the following.

- **Distribution phase** A dealer share a secret $\hat{u}_1^{a_0} \in \mathbb{G}_2$ such that $a_0 \in \mathbb{F}$ then randomly chooses a polynomial $f(x) = a_0 + a_1 x + \ldots + a_t x^t$ such that $f(0) = a_0$, after that commits to it via Feldman [12] $F_i = {g_1}^{a_i}$ for $i = 0, \ldots, t$. Next, the dealer computes the PVSS transcript that consists of : the shares such that $\hat{h}_1^{f(\omega_i)}$, the Feldman commitments such that $A_i = {g_1}^{f(\omega_i)}$ and the shares' encryptions $enc_i^{f(\omega_i)}$.
- **Verification phase** P_i verifies, via Lagrange interpolation in the exponent, if the Feldman commitments A_i to the shares $f(\omega_i)$ are compatible with the Feldman commitments to $f(x)$. Next, P_i verifies their encryption of $f(\omega_i)$ against A_i. This phase enables the participant to check whether the PVSS transcript is a correct sharing of $\hat{u}_1^{a_0}$ and to guarantees that encrypted shares are the evaluations of the committed polynomial f.
- **Aggregation phase** This is the most important phase in the PVSS of Gurkan et al. [18]. The aggregation benefits from the homomorphism of Feldman commitments and

of the encryption scheme. The scheme consider as input 2 PVSS transcripts $pvss_1$ for polynomial f_1 and $pvss_2$ for polynomial f_2 and outputs an aggregated transcript for their sum $f_1 + f_2$ as follows : for $b \in \{1,2\}$ and $i \in [0,t]$ $F_{b,i} = g_1^{a_{b,i}}$ will be aggregated such that $F_i = F_{1,i}F_{2,i} = g^{a_{1,i}+a_{2,i}}$ is an Feldman commitment to $f_1 + f_2$. In the same way, $A_i = A_{1,i}A_{2,i} = g^{(f_1+f_2)(\omega_i)}$ as the share commitments. Then, the encryptions $enc_i^{(f_1+f_2)(\omega_i)} = enc_i^{f_1(\omega_i)} enc_i^{f_2(\omega_i)}$.

- **Reconstruction phase** Note that S is the set of honest participants. First, P_i decrypt its share $\hat{A}_i = \hat{Y}_i^{dec_i^{-1}} = (enc_i^{f(\omega_i)})^{dk_i^{-1}} = \hat{h}_1^{f(\omega_i)}$ for $i \in [1,n]$. If there is no supplied share from P_i, then P_i is disqualified. Then, each supplied decrypted share is checked as $e(A_i, \hat{h}_1) \stackrel{?}{=} e(g_1, \hat{A}_i)$. If it fails, then P_i is disqualified. The secret $sk = \prod_{i \in S} \hat{A}_i^{\mathcal{L}_{S,i}(0)}$ can be recovered by any set S of size at least t where $\mathcal{L}_{S,i}(X)$ is a Lagrange polynomial that is equal to 1 at ω_i and equal to 0 at $\omega_j \in S$ for $i \neq j$.

4 Proposed Partially Agregatable DMKG Protocol

The traceable public-private key pair $(sk, pk) = ((x_1, x_2, y_1, y_2, z), (C_1, C_2, C_3)) = ((x_1, x_2, y_1, y_2, z), (g_1{}^{x_1} g_2{}^{x_2}, g_1{}^{y_1} g_2{}^{y_2}, g_1{}^{z}))$ is generated by the committee through the DMKG protocol. In [20], for the traceable secret key generation, the VMSS scheme is based on the Pedersen-VSS scheme to distribute z and leverage the Franklin-Yung MSS scheme to distribute (x_1, x_2, y_1, y_2). In this present contribution, we use the enhanced SCRAPE PVSS presented by Gurkan et al. [18] to distribute z. Since any third party can perform the verification, so there is no need for complaint management phase. Thus, this improvement leads to a considerable simplification in the complaint management strategy introduced in [20].

4.1 Communication And Adversary Model

We suppose that there are n probabilistic polynomial time participants $P_1, \cdots, P_n$, a common broadcast channel between them in a fully synchronous network and a static adversary that chooses the corrupted participants at the beginning of the protocol and can corrupt at most $(t-1)$ participants such that $(t-1) < \frac{n}{2}$.

4.2 Generation of Z

In this section, we describe our contribution based on the enhanced SCRAPE PVSS presented by Gurkan et al. [18] to distribute z component for the traceable secret key generation. In addition, we construct the set Q_{agg} a set of dishonest participants that have been reported whenever a participant P_i encounters non-compliance and inconsistency in the verification phase. At the end, Q_{agg} is made up of all dishonest participants that have been identified in the generation of the component z. This set will be taken into consideration during the simplified complaints management phase of the VMSS described in the next section.

Phase 1 : Initialisation Phase. All the participants use the same SCRAPE Common Reference String (CRS) described in details in 3. Each participant P_i has a decryption key $dec_i \in \mathbb{F}$ for enc_i where $enc_i = \hat{h}_1^{dec_i}$ and a secret key sk_i for $verif_i$ where $verif_i = g_1^{sk_i}$

Phase 2 : Distribution Phase. This phase is carried out in several steps as follows:
Step 2.a Participant P_i chooses at random $z_i \in \mathbb{F}$
Step 2.b Participant P_i randomly chooses a polynomial $h_i(x)$ of degree t such that $h_i(x) = a''_{i0} + a''_{i1}x + ... + a''_{it}x^t$ where $h_i(0) = z_i = a''_{i0}$,
Step 2.c Participant P_i computes $Z_i = {g_1}^{z_i}$, commits to it via Feldman and broadcast it to other participants.
Step 2.d Participant P_i computes the shares $h_i(\omega_j)$ for $j \in [1,n]$
Step 2.e Participant P_i computes a $pvss\_T$ that includes $H_{ik} = {g_1}^{a''_{ik}}$ for $k \in [0,t]$, $\hat{u}_{i2} = \hat{u}_1^{z_i}$, a vector w_i where $w_{ij} = 1$ if $i = j$, otherwise $w_{ij} = 0$, $A_{ij} = {g_1}^{h_i(\omega_j)}$ Feldman commitments, $Y_{ij} = {enc_j}^{h_i(\omega_j)}$ encryption of each share, a vector σ_i where $\sigma_{ij} = (Hash_{\mathbb{G}_2}(Z_i)^{z_i}, Hash_{\mathbb{G}_2}(verif_i, Z_i)^{sk_i})$ if $i = j$, otherwise $\perp$.
Step 2.f As mentioned in [18], each transcript $pvss\_T$ is linked with the information related to the public-verifiability to obtain the transcript $T = ((Z_1, ..., Z_n), (w_1, ..., w_n), (\sigma_1, ..., \sigma_n), pvss\_T)$ that includes: $Z_i = {g_1}^{z_i}$ the commitment to each participant's contribution z_i, the weights w_i of z_i, the signature of knowledge σ_i of z_i and a PVSS transcript for $z = \sum_{i=1}^{n} w_i z_i$.
Step 2.g Participant P_i gossips its transcript according to the gossip phase described in [18].

Phase 3 : Verification Phase. In this phase, each participant P_i verifies the received transcripts T according to the description below. In case that two transcripts verify then the participant P_i aggregate these transcripts according to the description in *Step 4*. First of all, each participant P_i checks if the received $pvss\_T$ is a correct sharing of the secret. It checks if the Feldman commitments A_{ij} to the shares $h_j(\omega_i)$ is in accordance with the Feldman commitment to $h_j(x)$ via Lagrange interpolation in the exponent. After that P_i checks the Feldman commitments A_{ij} against $enc^{h_j(\omega_i)}$ the encryption of $h_j(\omega_i)$. Next, we can checks the signature of knowledge σ_i of each z_i that has $w_i \neq 0$ in T. Then, we verify that $\prod_{i=1}^{n} {Z_i}^{w_i} = H_0$. So, if all checks verify, we consider that every participant P_i that has $w_i \neq 0$ in T is a honest participant else we consider that it is dishonest and added to Q_{agg} the set of reported dishonest participants.

Phase 4 : Aggregation Phase. In this step, the main idea is aggregating two transcripts T_1 and T_2 such that $T_1 = ((Z_{11}, ..., Z_{1n}), (w_{11}, ..., w_{1n}), (\sigma_{11}, ..., \sigma_{1n}), pvss\_T_1)$, $T_2 = ((Z_{21}, ..., Z_{2n}), (w_{21}, ..., w_{2n}), (\sigma_{21}, ..., \sigma_{2n}), pvss\_T_2)$ into a unique transcript $T = ((Z_1, ..., Z_n), (w_1, ..., w_n), (\sigma_1, ..., \sigma_n), pvss\_T)$
Step 4.a We aggregate $pvss\_T_1$ for polynomial h_1 and $pvss\_T_2$ for polynomial h_2 into a unique transcript $pvss\_T$ for $h_1 + h_2$. It exploits the homomorphism of encryption scheme and of Feldman commitments such that $H_i = H_{1i}H_{2i}$ a Feldman commitments to $h_1 + h_2$ for $i = 1, ..., t$; then for $i = 1, ..., n$, $A_i = A_{1i}A_{2i} = g^{(h_1+h_2)(\omega_i)}$ a share commitments ; $\hat{Y}_i = \hat{Y}_{1i}\hat{Y}_{2i} = {enc_i}^{(h_1+h_2)(\omega_i)} = {enc_i}^{h_1(\omega_i)}{enc_i}^{h_2(\omega_i)}$ the encryptions. Next, we aggregate $\hat{u}_i = \hat{u}_{12}\hat{u}_{22}$; $w_i = w_{1i} + w_{2i}$; $\sigma_i = \sigma_{1i}$ if $\sigma_{1i} \neq \perp$ otherwise $\sigma_i = \sigma_{2i}$; $Z_i = Z_{1i}$ if $Z_{1i} \neq \perp$ otherwise $Z_i = Z_{2i}$.
Step 4.b P_i gossips the aggregated transcript T.
Step 4.c In each transcript $(w_1, ..., w_n)$ indicates the number of contributions of every

participant. When P_i gets a complete transcript, meaning transcript with a size $k \geq t$ of $w_j \neq 0$, then P_i broadcast it as a candidate final transcript and the Aggregation ends here for the participant P_i.

Step 4.d This step is executed whenever there is a complete transcript that has been broadcast by a participant. If there are many candidate transcripts, we select the one with the lowest bit count in $(\prod_{i=1}^{n} Z_i^{\omega_i}, \prod_{i=1}^{n} \hat{u}_{i2}^{\omega_i})$ as the final transcript.

Phase 5 : Reconstruction Phase. Since the selected transcript T is actually an extended SCRAPE PVSS transcript as described by Gurkan et al. [18], we use the same reconstruction phase of Sect. 3.

4.3 Simplified DMKG Protocol

Our previous DMKG protocol [20] introduced an efficient complaint management strategy to avoid the participants from publicly revealing their shares of secrets whenever there is a conflict between them. It is true that disputation was an effective way of managing conflicts between participants, identifying malicious participants and eliminating them, but this strategy added an extra complexity to the protocol. Indeed, each of the two participants in conflict must prove his innocence to all the other participants by regenerating information related to all the components of the private key. Since the z component of the private key has been aggregated and generated in a publicly verifiable way, we no longer need to use a complaint management strategy for this part. As a result, the complaint management phase is simplified to eliminate the whole complaint management part concerning z which considerably reduces the number of exchanged messages between participants and communication time. We focus only on exposing misbehaving participants for (x_1, x_2, y_1, y_2) generation. In addition, we take into consideration the set Q_{agg} of dishonest participants already identified in Sect. 4.2. Let denote p and q two large prime numbers where $q|(p-1)$; $\mathbb{Z}_p$ a group of order p and $\mathbb{Z}_q$ a group of order q. The exponential operation performs modulo p operation such that g^x refers to $g^x mod p$, where $g \in \mathbb{Z}_p$ and $x \in \mathbb{Z}_q$. The simplified DMKG protocol is done as follows:

Phase 1 : Distribution Phase. As a dealer P_i randomly chooses $x_{1i}, x_{2i}, y_{1i}, y_{2i} \in \mathbb{Z}_q$; $\beta_{0i}, \beta_{1i}, \beta_{2i}, \beta_{3i}, \beta_{4i} \in \mathbb{Z}_q$ and 4 polynomials $f(x), f'(x), g(x)$ and $g'(x)$ of degree t such that $f_i(x) = a_{i0} + a_{i1}x + ... + a_{it}x^t$ where $f_i(-1) = x_{1i}$, $f_i(-2) = y_{1i}$, $f_i'(x) = b_{i0} + b_{i1}x + ... + b_{it}x^t$ where $f_i'(-1) = \beta_{1i}$, $f_i'(-2) = \beta_{2i}$, $g_i(x) = a_{i0}' + a_{i1}'x + ... + a_{it}'x^t$ where $g_i(-1) = x_{2i}$, $g_i(-2) = y_{2i}$, $g_i'(x) = b_{i0}' + b_{i1}'x + ... + b_{it}'x^t$ where $g_i'(-1) = \beta_{3i}$, $g_i'(-2) = \beta_{4i}$. Next, P_i broadcasts $CM_{ik} = {g_1}^{a_{ik}}.{h_1}^{b_{ik}}\ {g_2}^{a_{ik}'}.{h_2}^{b_{ik}'}$ for $k \in [0,t]$. After that, P_i computes the shares $sf_{ij} = f_i(j)$, $sf_{ij}' = f_i'(j)$, $sg_{ij} = g_i(j)$, $sg_{ij}' = g_i'(j)$ for $j \in [1,n]$. Note that, each participant P_i has a public-private key pair (sk_{P_i}, pk_{P_i}) to encrypt and decrypt the shares. So, P_i computes for $j \in [1,n]$: $enc_{sf_{ij}} = sf_{ij}(pk_{P_j})^{sf_{ij}} = sf_{ij}(g^{sk_{P_j}})^{sf_{ij}}$, $enc_{sf_{ij}'} = sf_{ij}'(pk_{P_j})^{sf_{ij}'} = sf_{ij}'(g^{sk_{P_j}})^{sf_{ij}'}$, $enc_{sg_{ij}} = sg_{ij}(pk_{P_j})^{sg_{ij}} = sg_{ij}(g^{sk_{P_j}})^{sg_{ij}}$, $enc_{sg_{ij}'} = sg_{ij}'(pk_{P_j})^{sg_{ij}'} = sg_{ij}'(g^{sk_{P_j}})^{sg_{ij}'}$.

Finally, P_i sends publicly the encrypted shares $(enc_{sf_{ij}}, enc_{sf_{ij}'}, enc_{sg_{ij}}, enc_{sg_{ij}'})$ to P_j for $j \in [1,n]$.

Phase 2 : Verification Phase. This phase is executed as follows:
Step 2.a To decrypt the received shares from P_i, each participant P_j uses his private key sk_{P_j} as follows $sf_{ij} = enc_{sf_{ij}}[(g^{sf_{ij}})^{sk_{P_j}}]^{-1}$, $sf'_{ij} = enc_{sf'_{ij}}[(g^{sf'_{ij}})^{sk_{P_j}}]^{-1}$, $sg_{ij} = enc_{sg_{ij}}[(g^{sg_{ij}})^{sk_{P_j}}]^{-1}$, $sg'_{ij} = enc_{sg'_{ij}}[(g^{sg'_{ij}})^{sk_{P_j}}]^{-1}$.
Step 2.b Each participant P_j verify Eq. 1 to validate the set of received shares. If it verify, then P_j accepts the shares. Otherwise, P_j complaints against P_i.

$$g_1{}^{sf_{ij}}.h_1{}^{sf'_{ij}}.g_2{}^{sg_{ij}}.h_2{}^{sg'_{ij}} \stackrel{?}{=} \prod_{k=0}^{t}(CM_{ik})^{j^k} \tag{1}$$

Phase 3 : Simplified Complaint Management Phase. It should be noted that the disputation is only executed if there is a complaint from a participant P_j against a participant P_i. First of all, we check whether P_i is present in Q_{agg} the set of dishonest participants reported during aggregation. If this is the case, then P_i is disqualified. Otherwise, we verify if the number of complaints against P_i is $> (t-1)$ in the *Step 2.b* then we consider P_i as disqualified. After that, each participant that is not disqualified and is not present in Q_{agg} will be added to Q_{temp} the set of temporarily qualified participants. At the end, we accept all the complaints against a participant P_i that is already disqualified. Otherwise, both P_i and P_j have to demonstrate their honesty to all the other participants. Let's consider the set $Q = \{Q_{temp} \setminus \{P_i, P_j\}\}$.
Step 3.a P_j randomly chooses $S'_j = \{a_j, b_j, a'_j, b'_j\}$ and publishes $S''_j = \{g_1{}^{a_j}, g_2{}^{a'_j}, h_1{}^{b_j}, h_2{}^{b'_j}\}$
Step 3.b Each $P_k \in Q$ randomly chooses $S'_k = \{a_k, b_k, a'_k, b'_k\}$ and publishes $S''_k = \{g_1{}^{a_k}, g_2{}^{a'_k}, h_1{}^{b_k}, h_2{}^{b'_k}\}$.
Step 3.c P_i computes and publishes $\lambda_1 = sf_{ij}[g_1{}^{a_j}.\prod_{k=1;P_k\in Q}^{n} g_1{}^{a_k}]^{sf_{ij}}$, $\lambda_2 = sf_{ij}(g_1{}^{a_j})^{sf_{ij}}$, $\lambda'_1 = sg_{ij}[g_2{}^{a'_j}.\prod_{k=1;P_k\in Q}^{n} g_2{}^{a'_k}]^{sg_{ij}}$, $\lambda'_2 = sg_{ij}(g_2{}^{a'_j})^{sg_{ij}}$, $\gamma 1 = sf'_{ij}[h_1{}^{b_j}.\prod_{k=1;P_k\in Q}^{n} h_1{}^{b_k}]^{sf'_{ij}}, \gamma 2 = sf'_{ij}(h_1{}^{b_j})^{sf'_{ij}}$, $\gamma' 1 = sg'_{ij}[h_2{}^{b'_j}.\prod_{k=1;P_k\in Q}^{n} h_2{}^{b'_k}]^{sg'_{ij}}$, $\gamma' 2 = sg'_{ij}(h_2{}^{b'_j})^{sg'_{ij}}$.
Step 3.d Each $P_k \in Q$ publishes his set S'_k. If it not coherent with his set S''_k, then it will be disqualified and removed from Q, and the process resumes at *Step 3.b*.
Step 3.e Each $P_k \in Q$ computes $\alpha = \frac{\lambda_1}{\lambda_2}$, $\alpha' = \frac{\lambda'_1}{\lambda'_2}$, $\beta = \frac{\gamma_1}{\gamma_2}$, $\beta' = \frac{\gamma'_1}{\gamma'_2}$ and $r = \sum_{k=1}^{n} a_k$, $r' = \sum_{k=1}^{n} a'_k$, $t = \sum_{k=1}^{n} b_k$, $t' = \sum_{k=1}^{n} b'_k$. Next, P_k computes: $\alpha^{\frac{1}{r}} = g_1{}^{sf_{ij}}$, $\alpha'^{\frac{1}{r'}} = g_2{}^{sg_{ij}}$ and $\beta^{\frac{1}{t}} = h_1{}^{sf'_{ij}}$, $\beta'^{\frac{1}{t'}} = h_2{}^{sg'_{ij}}$. P_k verifies Eq. 2. If it checks, then the protocol continues. Otherwise, $(sf_{ij}, sf'_{ij}, sg_{ij}, sg'_{ij})$ is not accepted and P_k identifies P_i as dishonest and the protocols ends.

$$\alpha^{\frac{1}{r}}.\beta^{\frac{1}{t}}.\alpha'^{\frac{1}{r'}}.\beta'^{\frac{1}{t'}} \stackrel{?}{=} \prod_{k=0}^{t}(CM_{ik})^{j^k} \tag{2}$$

Step 3.f Participant P_j computes: $sf_{ij} = \frac{\lambda_2}{(g_1{}^{sf_{ij}})^{a_j}}$, $sg_{ij} = \frac{\lambda'_2}{(g_2{}^{sg_{ij}})^{a'_j}}$ and $sf'_{ij} = \frac{\gamma_2}{(h_1{}^{sf'_{ij}})^{b_j}}$, $sg'_{ij} = \frac{\gamma'_2}{(h_2{}^{sg'_{ij}})^{b'_j}}$ then verifies if they check Eq. 1. If it fails, P_j sends S'_j to all participants in Q. Else, P_j confirms to all participants in Q that it has a valid shares and the protocol

ends.
Step 3.g Each $P_k \in Q$ verifies the validity of the set S'_j sent by P_j by checking the coherence between the values $({g_1}^{a_j}, {g_2}^{a'_j}, {h_1}^{b_j}, {h_2}^{b'_j})$ published by P_j in *step 3.a* and the values of S'_j published by P_j in *step 3.f*. If it fails, P_k identifies P_j as dishonest and the protocol ends. Else, the protocol continues.
Step 3.h Each $P_k \in Q$ computes $({g_1}^{sf_{ij}})^{a_j}$, $({g_2}^{sg_{ij}})^{a'_j}$, $({h_1}^{sf'_{ij}})^{b_j}$, $({h_2}^{sg'_{ij}})^{b'_j}$ and $e_1 = \frac{\lambda_2}{({g_1}^{sf_{ij}})^{a_j}}$, $e'_1 = \frac{\lambda'_2}{({g_2}^{sg_{ij}})^{a'_j}}$, $e_2 = \frac{\gamma_2}{({h_1}^{sf'_{ij}})^{b_j}}$, $e'_2 = \frac{\gamma'_2}{({h_2}^{sg'_{ij}})^{b'_j}}$. Then, P_k verifies if the equations in *Step 3.c* are correct with the values $e_1 = sf_{ij}$, $e'_1 = sg_{ij}$, $e_2 = sf'_{ij}$, $e'_2 = sg'_{ij}$. If it checks, then P_k identifies that P_j is dishonest, else, P_i is dishonest. Finally P_k broadcasts the vote about the identified dishonest participant : P_i or P_j.
Step 3.i From the votes sent by each participants P_k, we can determine the dishonest participant between P_i and P_j. Thus, all dishonest participants are identified and eliminated.

Phase 4 : Recovery Phase. We consider $QUAL$ as the set of non disqualified participants. Each participant $P_i \in QUAL$ computes the shares: $sf_i = \sum_{j \in QUAL} sf_{ji} mod q$, $sf'_i = \sum_{j \in QUAL} sf'_{ji} mod q$, $sg_i = \sum_{j \in QUAL} sg_{ji} mod q$, $sg'_i = \sum_{j \in QUAL} sg'_{ji} mod q$.

5 Security

We rely on the security requirements for DMKG protocols defined in [9] in the presence of an adversary that can corrupts at most $t-1$ participants such that $t-1 < \frac{n}{2}$. These requirements are correctness and secrecy.

5.1 Security Requirements

Correctness. The correctness of the protocol consists of the following elements:
C1. The same unique secret key $sk = (x_1, x_2, y_1, y_2, z)$ is defined by any set of t shares supplied by honest participants.
C2. There is an efficient algorithm that takes on input the public information generated by the DMKG protocol and the n shares submitted by participants and that outputs the unique secret key sk even if up to $t-1$ invalid shares are submitted by malicious participants.
C3. All honest participants have the same public key $pk = (c_1, c_2, c_3) = ({g_1}^{x_1}{g_2}^{x_2}, {g_1}^{y_1}{g_2}^{y_2}, {g_1}^{z})$, such that (x_1, x_2, y_1, y_2, z) is the unique secret key guaranteed by (C1).
C4. The values of the secret key components $sk = (x_1, x_2, y_1, y_2, z)$ are uniformly distributed in $\mathbb{Z}_q$.

Secrecy. The DMKG protocol verifies the secrecy requirement if the adversary cannot get sk, or any information on sk except for the pubic key pk. The shared private key sk is a confidential information that should not be found by any party that is unauthorized to get it. The secrecy of the DMKG can be formally expressed by a simulator. We keep the same simulation as in [22]. It proves that an adversary that influences and corrupts a certain number of participants without exceeding $(t-1)$, cannot compute the value of a secret key sk. As input, the simulator gets the public key pk and outputs a distribution that generates pk and that is indistinguishable from the adversary's view of a real execution of the DMKG protocol. Thus, the adversary cannot compute the value of the secret key sk.

5.2 Security Proofs

In this section, we show that our DMKG protocol satisfies the security requirements defined in Sect. 5.1. First of all, we need to present the following lemmas about the the VMSS scheme in [22].

Lemma 1. *Any t shares of the honest participants can reconstruct the secret s in the presence of an adversary that corrupts at most $t-1$ participants. If the dealer is honest, then all shares held by honest participants can interpolate to a unique polynomial of degree t.*

Lemma 2. *Any t shares of the honest participants can reconstruct the secret set $S = s_1,...,s_l$ in the presence of an adversary that corrupts at most $t-l$ participants. If the dealer is honest, then all shares held by honest participants can interpolate to a unique polynomial of degree t.*

Correctness Proof.

Theorem 1. *Our DMKG protocol satisfies the security requirement (C1). All shares submitted by a set of honest participants define the same private key sk.*

Proof. At the end of the *Complaint Management* phase, if the participant P_i is not disqualified, which means that $P_i \in QUAL$ and that as a dealer, he has correctly performed the VMSS scheme. We rely on Lemma 1 and Lemma 2. Then, all honest participants have valid shares of P_i that they use to compute the polynomials $f_i(x)$, $g_i(x)$ and $h_i(x)$ where $f_i(-1) = x_{1i}$, $f_i(-2) = y_{1i}$, $g_i(-1) = x_{2i}$ and $g_i(-2) = y_{2i}$. For this purpose, for a set Q of t valid shares, a unique value x_{1i} (respectively x_{2i}, y_{1i}, y_{2i}) is computed with the Lagrange interpolation as $x_{1i} = \sum_{j\in Q}\lambda_{1j}sf_{ij}$, $x_{2i} = \sum_{j\in Q}\lambda_{1j}sg_{ij}$, $y_{1i} = \sum_{j\in Q}\lambda_{2j}sf_{ij}$, $y_{2i} = \sum_{j\in Q}\lambda_{2j}sg_{ij}$ where $\lambda_{1j} = \prod_{k\in Q,k\neq j}\frac{-1-k}{j-k}$, $\lambda_{2j} = \prod_{k\in Q,k\neq j}\frac{-2-k}{j-k}$ are the coefficient of Lagrange. Thus, from these shares x_1 (respectively x_2, y_1, y_2) can be generated as $x_1 = \sum_{i\in QUAL}x_{1i} = \sum_{i\in QUAL}\sum_{j\in Q}\lambda_{1j}sf_{ij} = \sum_{j\in Q}\lambda_{1j}\sum_{i\in QUAL}sf_{ij} = \sum_{j\in Q}\lambda_{1j}sf_j$ (respectively $x_2 = \sum_{j\in Q}\lambda_{1j}sg_j$, $y_1 = \sum_{j\in Q}\lambda_{2j}sf_j$, $y_2 = \sum_{j\in Q}\lambda_{2j}sg_j$). For any authorized set Q of participants, the private key $sk = (x_1, x_2, y_1, y_2, z)$ is unique.

Theorem 2. *Our DMKG protocol satisfies the security requirement (C2). Only valid shares of honest participants who check successfully the shares verification are used to reconstruct the private key sk.*

Proof. The validity of the shares (sf_i, sg_i) submitted by the participant P_i with $i \in QUAL$ can be checked as follows: $g_1^{sf_i}g_2^{sg_i} = g_1^{\sum_{i\in QUAL}sf_{ij}}g_2^{\sum_{i\in QUAL}sg_{ij}} = \prod_{i\in QUAL}g_1^{sf_{ij}}g_2^{sg_{ij}}$ $= \prod_{i\in QUAL}\prod_{k=0}^{t}(A_{ik})^{j^k}$. Therefore, only valid shares (sf_i, sg_i) submitted by honest participants who passed successfully the check are used.

Theorem 3. *Our DMKG protocol satisfies the security requirement (C3). After the Complaint Management phase, all qualified participants compute the same value of the public key* $pk = (c_1, c_2, c_3) = g_1{}^{x_1} g_2{}^{x_2}, g_1{}^{y_1} g_2{}^{y_2}, g_1{}^{z})$, *where* $sk = (x_1, x_2, y_1, y_2, z)$ *is the unique secret key guaranteed by Theorem 1.*

Proof. Since we did not modify the generation of the public key used in [22], we use the same proof of *Theorem 3* to prove that all qualified participants from the *Complaint Management* phase compute the same value of the public key pk. More details in [22].

Theorem 4. *Our DMKG protocol satisfies the security requirement (C4). The values* x_1, x_2, y_1 *and* y_2 *of the secret key sk are uniformly distributed in* $\mathbb{Z}_q$.

Proof. At the end of the *Complaint Management* phase, only honest participants are in the set *QUAL*. Each participant P_i, $i \in QUAL$ has already selected a secret value x_{1i} (respectively x_{2i}, y_{1i}, y_{2i}) randomly in $\mathbb{Z}_q$. As x_1 (respectively x_2, y_1, y_2) is defined as the sum of all x_{1i} (respectively x_{2i}, y_{1i}, y_{2i}) then it can be guaranteed that x_1 (respectively x_2, y_1, y_2) is randomly chosen in $\mathbb{Z}_q$. At the end of the *Distribution* phase of our DMKG protocol, these values are already chosen and uniformly distributed via VMSS protocol. Neither the values x_{1i} (respectively x_{2i}, y_{1i}, y_{2i}) nor the set *QUAL* change later. Thereby, as $x_1 = \sum_{i \in QUAL} x_{1i}$, then x_1 is uniformly distributed in $\mathbb{Z}_q$. In the same way, x_2, y_1 and y_2 are also uniformly distributed.

Secrecy Proof. The secrecy of the DMKG is formally expressed by a simulator. Since we have kept the same simulator used in [22], we also keep the same proof of secrecy. We hence refer the reader to the aforementioned publication for further details.

6 Comparison and Discussion

The comparison of our aggregatable DMKG protocol with the related works is reviewed in Table 1. It is based on the following criteria: first, the communication model: private or public channels, second, the verification complexity, third, the complaint management efficiency based on the fact that honest participants are not forced to divulge their shares and on the fact that dishonest participants are identified and disqualified, fourth, the public verifiability of the secret sharing scheme, fifth, whether the transcript is aggregatable or not and finally the context of secret sharing : multi-key generation or not.

BTSOF's DMKG uses private channels to send shares to participants and a broadcast channel. As a result, each participant will have to check the received shares of the secret as well as the proof of verifiability of these shares. The complexity is therefore $O(n^2)$ per participant. On the other hand, this DMKG uses an interactive and non-publicly verifiable secret sharing scheme which requires significant communication time and a complaint management strategy to identify dishonest participants. However, the used strategy forces conflicting participants to reveal their shares, which creates a major security flaw and makes the complaints management strategy ineffective and unable to identify all dishonest participants.

In [20], Kalai et al. used only public channels. Each participant checks its received shares of the secret, which implies a complexity $O(kn)$ per participant. But, if there is a complaint between two participants, each participant in the conflict management will check all the data sent by all the participants which results in a quadratic complexity for the verifications carried out during the complaint management strategy. This complexity increases with the number of complaints to manage.

In our proposed DMKG protocol, the idea is to simplify the complaint management strategy and reduce the probability of its execution. Indeed, we used a PVSS which makes it possible to publicly verify the shares and not have to resort to complaint management. Furthermore, when distributing the component z, we identified a set of dishonest participants and constructed Q_{agg}. This set is taken into consideration before executing the complaints management phase. Indeed, all complaints against participants in Q_{agg} are accepted, thus avoiding any unnecessary additional complaints management. On the other hand, for the distribution of the component z, the use of the improved version of SCRAPE PVSS made it possible to reduce the cost of verification to $O(nlogn)$.

Table 1. Comparison of our Aggregatable DMKG protocol with related work.

Criteria	Communication model	Verification complexity	Complaint management efficiency	Publicly verifiable	Aggregatable	Multi-key generation
BTSOF [23]	public + private	$O(kn^2)$	no	no	no	yes
Kalai et al. [20]	public	$O(kn^2)$	yes	no	no	yes
Gurkan et al. [18]	public	$O(kn\log n)$	no need	yes	yes	no
our DMKG	public	$O(kn\log n)$	yes	partially	partially	yes

7 Conclusion

In this paper, we presented our partially aggregatable DMKG protocol with a simplified complaint management strategy based on our previous DMKG introduced in [20]. We leverage the enhanced SCRAPE PVSS scheme described by Gurkan et al. [18] that allows to share a secret among n participants through a publicly verifiable transcript and moreover to homomorphically combine several transcripts into a single aggregate transcript result of their sum. Indeed, the participants cooperate together to generate, verify and aggregate shares in order to avoid the use of a complaint management strategy that increases the complexity of the protocol. The implementation of our contribution will be the subject of a new article which will be supported by experimental results. We also plan to expand the use of aggregation in our DMKG to design a totally aggregatable publicly verifiable multi-secret sharing scheme to benefit from the contribution of aggregation in the entire sk component. The proposed DMKG protocol can be seen as a basic contribution that can be extended and applied in other contexts such as identity-based cryptography and electronic voting.

References

1. Abraham, I., Jovanovic, P., Maller, M., Meiklejohn, S., Stern, G., Tomescu, A.: Reaching consensus for asynchronous distributed key generation. In: Proceedings of the 2021 ACM Symposium on Principles of Distributed Computing, pp. 363–373 (2021)
2. Abraham, I., Malkhi, D., Spiegelman, A.: Asymptotically optimal validated asynchronous byzantine agreement. In: Proceedings of the 2019 ACM Symposium on Principles of Distributed Computing, pp. 337–346 (2019)
3. Bacho, R., Loss, J.: Adaptively secure (aggregatable) PVSS and application to distributed randomness beacons. In: Proceedings of the 2023 ACM SIGSAC Conference on Computer and Communications Security, pp. 1791–1804 (2023)
4. Bhat, A., Shrestha, N., Kate, A., Nayak, K.: Optrand: optimistically responsive distributed random beacons. Cryptology ePrint Archive (2022)
5. Bhat, A., Shrestha, N., Luo, Z., Kate, A., Nayak, K.: Randpiper–reconfiguration-friendly random beacons with quadratic communication. In: Proceedings of the 2021 ACM SIGSAC Conference on Computer and Communications Security, pp. 3502–3524 (2021)
6. Blakley, G.R.: Safeguarding cryptographic keys. In: Managing Requirements Knowledge, International Workshop on, pp. 313–313. IEEE Computer Society (1979)
7. Canetti, R., Gennaro, R., Jarecki, S., Krawczyk, H., Rabin, T.: Adaptive security for threshold cryptosystems. In: Wiener, M. (ed.) CRYPTO 1999. LNCS, vol. 1666, pp. 98–116. Springer, Heidelberg (1999). https://doi.org/10.1007/3-540-48405-1_7
8. Cascudo, I., David, B.: Scrape: scalable randomness attested by public entities. In: International Conference on Applied Cryptography and Network Security, pp. 537–556. Springer (2017)
9. Cramer, R., Shoup, V.: A practical public key cryptosystem provably secure against adaptive chosen ciphertext attack. In: Annual International Cryptology Conference, pp. 13–25. Springer (1998)
10. Das, S., Krishnan, V., Isaac, I.M., Ren, L.: Spurt: scalable distributed randomness beacon with transparent setup. In: 2022 IEEE Symposium on Security and Privacy (SP), pp. 2502–2517. IEEE (2022)
11. Das, S., Yurek, T., Xiang, Z., Miller, A., Kokoris-Kogias, L., Ren, L.: Practical asynchronous distributed key generation. In: 2022 IEEE Symposium on Security and Privacy (SP), pp. 2518–2534. IEEE (2022)
12. Feldman, P.: A practical scheme for non-interactive verifiable secret sharing. In: 28th Annual Symposium on Foundations of Computer Science (SFCS 1987), pp. 427–438. IEEE (1987)
13. Fouque, P.-A., Stern, J.: One round threshold discrete-log key generation without private channels. In: Kim, K. (ed.) PKC 2001. LNCS, vol. 1992, pp. 300–316. Springer, Heidelberg (2001). https://doi.org/10.1007/3-540-44586-2_22
14. Fournaris, A.P.: A distributed approach of a threshold certificate-based encryption scheme with no trusted entities. Inf. Secur. J. Global Persp. **22**(3), 126–139 (2013)
15. Franklin, M., Yung, M.: Communication complexity of secure computation. In: Proceedings of the Twenty-fourth Annual ACM Symposium on Theory Of Computing, pp. 699–710 (1992)
16. Galindo, D., Liu, J., Ordean, M., Wong, J.M.: Fully distributed verifiable random functions and their application to decentralised random beacons. In: 2021 IEEE European Symposium on Security and Privacy (EuroS&P), pp. 88–102. IEEE (2021)
17. Gennaro, R., Jarecki, S., Krawczyk, H., Rabin, T.: Secure distributed key generation for discrete-log based cryptosystems. In: International Conference on the Theory and Applications of Cryptographic Techniques, pp. 295–310. Springer (1999)

18. Gurkan, K., Jovanovic, P., Maller, M., Meiklejohn, S., Stern, G., Tomescu, A.: Aggregatable distributed key generation. In: Annual International Conference on the Theory and Applications of Cryptographic Techniques, pp. 147–176. Springer (2021)
19. Jhanwar, M.P.: A practical (non-interactive) publicly verifiable secret sharing scheme. In: Bao, F., Weng, J. (eds.) ISPEC 2011. LNCS, vol. 6672, pp. 273–287. Springer, Heidelberg (2011). https://doi.org/10.1007/978-3-642-21031-0_21
20. Kalai, R., Neji, W., Ben Rajeb, N.: A distributed multi-key generation protocol with a new complaint management strategy. In: European, Mediterranean, and Middle Eastern Conference on Information Systems, pp. 150–164. Springer (2022)
21. Kalai, R., Neji, W., Ben Rajeb, N.: Reviewing the role of secret sharing schemes in electronic payment protocols. In: European, Mediterranean, and Middle Eastern Conference on Information Systems, pp. 52–60. Springer (2023)
22. Ma, T., Xu, H., Li, P.: A blockchain traceable scheme with oversight function. In: International Conference on Information and Communications Security, pp. 164–182. Springer (2020)
23. Ma, T., Xu, H., Li, P.: A traceable scheme for consortium blockchain. In: 2021 IEEE 9th International Conference on Smart City and Informatization (iSCI), pp. 39–46. IEEE (2021)
24. Neji, W., Blibech, K., Ben Rajeb, N.: Distributed key generation protocol with a new complaint management strategy. Secur. Commun. Netw. **9**(17), 4585–4595 (2016)
25. Paillier, P.: Public-key cryptosystems based on composite degree residuosity classes. In: International Conference on the Theory and Applications of Cryptographic Techniques, pp. 223–238. Springer (1999)
26. Pakniat, N., Noroozi, M., Eslami, Z.: Distributed key generation protocol with hierarchical threshold access structure. IET Inf. Secur. **9**(4), 248–255 (2015)
27. Pedersen, T.P.: Non-interactive and information-theoretic secure verifiable secret sharing. In: Annual International Cryptology Conference, pp. 129–140. Springer (1991)
28. Pedersen, T.P.: A threshold cryptosystem without a trusted party. In: Workshop on the Theory and Application of of Cryptographic Techniques, pp. 522–526. Springer (1991)
29. Schindler, P., Judmayer, A., Stifter, N., Weippl, E.: Hydrand: efficient continuous distributed randomness. In: 2020 IEEE Symposium on Security and Privacy (SP), pp. 73–89. IEEE (2020)
30. Schoenmakers, B.: A simple publicly verifiable secret sharing scheme and its application to electronic voting. In: Annual International Cryptology Conference, pp. 148–164. Springer (1999)
31. Shamir, A.: How to share a secret. Commun. ACM **22**(11), 612–613 (1979)
32. Stadler, M.: Publicly verifiable secret sharing. In: International Conference on the Theory and Applications of Cryptographic Techniques, pp. 190–199. Springer (1996)
33. Syta, E., et al.: Scalable bias-resistant distributed randomness. In: 2017 IEEE Symposium on Security and Privacy (SP), pp. 444–460. IEEE (2017)
34. Wang, F., Chang, C.C., Harn, L.: Simulatable and secure certificate-based threshold signature without pairings. Secur. Commun. Netw. **7**(11), 2094–2103 (2014)
35. Wong, T.M., Wang, C., Wing, J.M.: Verifiable secret redistribution for archive systems. In: First International IEEE Security in Storage Workshop, 2002. Proceedings, pp. 94–105. IEEE (2002)
36. Yin, M., Malkhi, D., Reiter, M.K., Gueta, G.G., Abraham, I.: Hotstuff: BFT consensus with linearity and responsiveness. In: Proceedings of the 2019 ACM Symposium on Principles of Distributed Computing, pp. 347–356 (2019)
37. Yuan, H., Zhang, F., Huang, X., Mu, Y., Susilo, W., Zhang, L.: Certificateless threshold signature scheme from bilinear maps. Inf. Sci. **180**(23), 4714–4728 (2010)

On the Formalization of Pseudoinverse of the Laplacian Matrix in HOL

Kubra Aksoy(✉), Adnan Rashid, and Sofiene Tahar

Department of Electrical and Computer Engineering, Concordia University, Montréal, QC, Canada
k_aksoy@encs.concordia.ca, {rashid,tahar}@ece.concordia.ca

Abstract. Laplacian matrices are essential algebraic representations of network systems, which facilitate the description of topological characteristics, such as connectivity and symmetry. However, a critical issue emerges when the Laplacian matrix of a network is inherently singular, i.e., its inverse does not exist. In this case, it is crucial to use the generalized inverse of the matrix, known as pseudoinverse. In this paper, we provide a rigorous formalization of the pseudoinverse of the Laplacian matrix representing a weighted graph within higher-order logic theorem proving. Particularly, we formalize in Isabelle/HOL the generic concept of a matrix pseudoinverse that is applicable for both singular and non-singular matrices. We then formalize the pseudoinverse of a Laplacian matrix and verify its classical properties. As an application, we formally verify the Kirchhoff index of a two-horizontal bridge circuit network.

Keywords: Laplacian Matrix · Pseudoinverse · Kirchhoff Index · Higher-Order Logic · Isabelle/HOL

1 Introduction

Laplacian matrices [1] are fundamental algebraic constructs that encapsulate the topological characteristics of networks represented as graphs. They offer a compact and structured representation of systems of equations governed by physical laws, such as Newton's [2] and Kirchhoff's [3] laws, enabling systematic solutions of these equations through algebraic methods. These matrices are widely used in modeling and analysis of networks across various disciplines, including engineering, computer science, physics and chemistry. For instance, in mechanical systems, spring networks, encountered in safety-critical applications and composed of many rigid bodies interconnected by springs, can be effectively modeled using Laplacian matrices. These allow for the analysis of oscillation dynamics and equilibrium displacements by establishing force balance equations [4]. Similarly, in wireless communication systems, Laplacian matrices are employed to analyze energy efficiency in wireless sensor networks, aiding in strategies aimed at extending network lifetime [5]. Thus, these matrices inherently bridge graph

B. Ben Hedia et al. (Eds.): VECoS 2025, LNCS 16263, pp. 97–113, 2026.
https://doi.org/10.1007/978-3-032-20440-0_7

theory, spectral theory, and linear and matrix algebra, making them essential tools for the modeling and analysis of complex networked systems.

The analysis of systems modeled by Laplacian matrices primarily involves solving matrix equations that concisely represent the underlying physical or network dynamics. However, a key challenge arises when the Laplacian matrix is *singular*, making it non-invertible. In such cases, the generalized inverse concept, particularly the *pseudoinverse* [6], also known as Moore-Penrose pseudoinverse, becomes essential. The pseudoinverse extends the concept of matrix inversion to singular or non-square matrices and coincides with the standard inverse for non-singular matrices. In many applications involving Laplacian matrices, such as dynamical flow networks, electrical resistive circuits and multi-agent networks, the pseudoinverse of the Laplacian matrix plays a crucial role in characterizing system behavior. Moreover, in disciplines like chemistry and electrical engineering, this concept is widely used to describe topological indices, such as Wiener [7] and Kirchhoff [8] indices, that quantify structural properties of molecular graphs and electrical networks. Given its broad applicability across safety-critical domains, the pseudoinverse of Laplacian matrix-based analysis is fundamental to obtain a comprehensive understanding of complex network systems.

Conventionally, the analysis of networks based on pseudoinverse of Laplacian matrices has been performed using paper-and-pencil [8] and computer-based simulations [9]. The major limitation of the former approach is human-error proneness. On the other hand, computer-based simulations often rely on approximation techniques and unverified numerical algorithms, which may compromise the accuracy and precision of results, especially when analyzing large-scale or complex networks. In contrary, higher-order-logic (HOL) theorem proving [10] is a formal methods approach that offers mathematically sound and reliable results with the rigor necessary for critical system analysis. HOL theorem provers provide the expressiveness required to accurately formalize and reason about sophisticated mathematical constructs, including matrix-algebra, graph theory, and integral calculus.

Several notable formalizations of graph-associated matrices have been developed within interactive theorem provers. For instance, Heras et al. [11] used the Coq theorem prover to analyze 2D digital image processing systems by formalizing the incidence matrix of undirected graphs. Similarly, Edmonds et al. [12] employed Isabelle/HOL to formalize incidence matrices for verifying the Fisher's inequality in combinatorial design theory. More recently, Aksoy et al. [13] formalized both incidence and loop matrices of directed graphs in Isabelle/HOL to support the formal analysis of electrical network topologies, including the implementation of Kirchhoff's current and voltage laws. However, to the best of our knowledge, no formalization exists for the pseudoinverse of Laplacian matrices associated with weighted graphs in any HOL-based theorem prover. For instance, the Lean 4 mathlib library[1] only consists of basic formalizations of adjacency,

[1] https://github.com/leanprover-community/mathlib4/tree/master/Mathlib/Combinatorics/SimpleGraph.

incidence and Laplacian matrices for simple graphs. Addressing this gap, our proposed formalization contributes a foundational formalization that not only extends the state-of-the-art in formal methods but also supports a rigorous reasoning about a wide range of safety-critical systems. In this paper, we propose to use the Isabelle/HOL theorem prover [14] to formally analyze the pseudoinverse of the Laplacian matrix. The novelty of our contribution is reflected in the following outcomes:

- We formalize the pseudoinverse for general $m \times n$ matrices, whether singular or non-singular, and verify its core properties such as uniqueness and the transpose characterization.
- We formalize the pseudoinverse of Laplacian matrices and verify its various properties, such as symmetry and row/column linear independence.
- We utilize these formalizations to define and verify the Kirchhoff index for weighted graphs representing electrical resistive networks.
- We formally verify the Kirchhoff index of a two-horizontal bridge circuit network.

The remainder of the paper is outlined as follows: Sect. 2 presents an overview of the Isabelle/HOL theorem prover and introduces some preliminary definitions of matrix theory. We provide the formalization of weighted directed graphs and their corresponding Laplacian matrices in Sect. 3. In Sect. 4, we formalize the pseudoinverse of Laplacian matrices, starting with a general case for arbitrary matrices. Section 5 demonstrates the application of the formalized pseudoinverse of the Laplacian matrix, and Sect. 6 concludes the paper.

2 Preliminaries

2.1 Isabelle/HOL Theorem Prover

Isabelle/HOL is an interactive proof assistant extensively used for the formalization of mathematics and the verification of physical and engineering systems. It allows the precise modeling of systems through formal mathematical definitions and supports the verification of system properties, expressed as lemmas and theorems. A fundamental design principle of Isabelle/HOL is its small trusted logical core, which consists of a minimal set of axioms and inference rules. All new theorems must be proven based either directly on this core or by building on previously verified results, ensuring a high degree of soundness and reliability. Isabelle/HOL integrates various external automated theorem provers and SMT solvers to assist with proof development. A prominent component is Sledgehammer [15], which bridges Isabelle/HOL with external tools such as Z3 [16] and CVC4 [17] to automatically suggest proof strategies. Similarly, users can employ counterexample generator tools such as Nitpick [18] to check whether the statement to be proven is correct or not. Isabelle also features a declarative proof language, known as Isabelle/Isar, which significantly enhances the readability of goals (theorem/lemma statements) and proofs. Additionally, Isabelle/HOL provides a powerful module system known as *locales*, which encapsulates a collection of parameters, assumptions, and definitions. Locales are particularly useful for expressing algebraic and mathematical concepts concisely. A key advantage of locales is their extensibility, allowing new assumptions, parameters, or definitions can be added, promoting reusability and structural clarity in formal developments.

2.2 Formalization of Matrix Theory in Isabelle/HOL

We provide some commonly used Isabelle/HOL definitions and lemmas that are encountered in the proposed formalization. This formalization relies on the Jordan Normal Form (JNF) matrix library and its extension libraries available on Archive of Formal Proofs (AFP)[2]. Therefore, we leverage existing matrix concepts and extend the current library by incorporating new formalizations that are essential for our work. In the JNF matrix library, the type of matrices `'a mat` is represented as a triple `(nr,nc,f)`:

```
typedef 'a mat = {(nr,nc,mk_mat nr nc f) | nr nc f :: nat × nat ⇒ 'a. True}
```

where `mk_mat` is a function that takes 3 inputs: `nr`, representing the number of rows of the matrix; `nc`, the number of columns; and `f`, the characteristic function of the matrix, i.e., `f(i,j)` = f_{ij} = `f_ ij` providing the individual entries. As the dimensions of a matrix are not encoded in its type, they are explicitly specified in the following definition:

```
definition carrier_mat :: nat ⇒ nat ⇒ 'a mat set
        where carrier_mat nr nc = { m. dim_row m = nr ∧ dim_col m = nc}
```

where the function `dim_row` represents the dimension of the matrix row and `dim_col` extracts the dimension of the matrix column. Next, we provide the formalization of an invertible matrix as follows:

```
definition invertible_mat :: 'a :: semiring_1 mat ⇒ bool where
  invertible_mat A ≡ square_mat A ∧ (∃B. inverts_mat A B ∧ inverts_mat B A)
```

Here, `square_mat` is a function that ensures the matrix has equal row and column dimensions. Furthermore, the predicate `inverse_mat` is formalized as follows:

```
definition inverts_mat :: 'a :: semiring_1 mat ⇒ 'a mat ⇒ bool
     where inverts_mat A B ≡ A * B = 1m (dim_row A)
```

where 1_m represents the identity matrix whose size matches the row dimension of `A`. The following definition ensures that a set of vectors satisfies the solution of a matrix equation, and it is formalized in Isabelle/HOL as follows:

[2] https://www.isa-afp.org/.

```
definition mat_kernel :: 'a :: comm_ring_1 mat ⇒ 'a vec set
  where mat_kernel A = {v. v ∈ carrier_vec (dim_col A) ∧ A *v v = 0v}
```

where `carrier_vec` is the set of vectors whose dimensions match to the column size of the matrix `A`, and $*_{\mathtt{v}}$ is the operator used for the matrix-vector multiplication. More details about the formalization of matrix theory can be found in the JNF matrix library available at Isabelle's AFP[3].

3 Formalization of Laplacian Matrix

The Laplacian matrix is a central network topology matrix, widely used for modeling and analyzing both static and dynamic behavior of systems based on their structural properties. This algebraic representation is typically associated with weighted directed graphs to study topological and spectral properties, such as connectivity, symmetry and graph partitioning. A weighted graph is defined as a triple $WG = (N, E, w)$, where N is the set of nodes, E represents the set of edges and w is a weight function $w : E \rightarrow \mathbb{R}$ that assigns a real-values weight to each edge in the graph. A symmetric directed graph satisfies the condition $w(i,j) = w(j,i)$, ensuring that edge weights are equal in both directions between any two nodes. This symmetry facilitates the verification of several classical properties of pseudoinverse of the Laplacian matrix, which are presented in the subsequent sections.

For a weighted directed graph, the corresponding Laplacian matrix is mathematically defined as follows:

Definition 1. *Laplacian Matrix of a Weighted Directed Graph [19]*
The Laplacian matrix $L = [\ell_{ij}]$ of a weighted directed graph with m nodes is defined by an $m \times m$ matrix, such that

$$L = D_{out} - A \tag{1}$$

where $A = [a_{ij}]$ represents the adjacency matrix and $D_{out} = [d_{ij}^{out}]$ is the out-degree matrix of the given network. Each (i,j)-th entry of the adjacency matrix is defined as:

$$a_{ij} = \begin{cases} w(i,j) & \text{if there is an edge directed from node } i \text{ to node } j \\ 0 & \text{otherwise} \end{cases} \tag{2}$$

Similarly, the out-degree matrix D_{out} is a diagonal matrix of size $m \times m$, and it can be mathematically defined as:

$$D_{out} = diag(AJ_{\mathtt{m}}) \tag{3}$$

where $J_{\mathtt{m}}$ denotes an $m \times m$ matrix with all elements equal to 1.

Figure 1 depicts a 4-port bridge resistive electrical network and its corresponding symmetric weighted directed graph representation. The graph consists

[3] https://www.isa-afp.org/entries/Jordan_Normal_Form.html.

of four nodes, each representing a port labeled from 1 to 4, and five edges that correspond to the resistive connections between the ports. The edge weights are defined as $\mathtt{w}_{ij} = \frac{1}{\mathtt{R}_{ij}}$ for all $i, j \in \{1, 2, 3, 4\}$, where $\mathtt{R}_{ij}$ denotes the resistance between nodes i and j. For instance, *node* 1 is adjacent to *node* 2, and their mutual resistance is represented by edge $(1, 2)$ with weight $\mathtt{w}_{12}$, or equivalently, by the edge $(2, 1)$ with weight $\mathtt{w}_{21}$. Since the graph is symmetric (bidirectional), we have $\mathtt{w}_{12} = \mathtt{w}_{21}$, which reflects the physical symmetry of resistive electrical networks.

Figure 2 demonstrates that the Laplacian matrix of the bridge electrical network depicted in Fig. 1 is a 4×4 symmetric matrix, constructed according to Definition 1. It can be observed that the rows and columns of this matrix are linearly dependent, and hence, the matrix is non-invertible.

To formalize the Laplacian matrix, we first model the structure of a weighted directed graph using the locale `wdg_sys` in Isabelle/HOL, as follows:

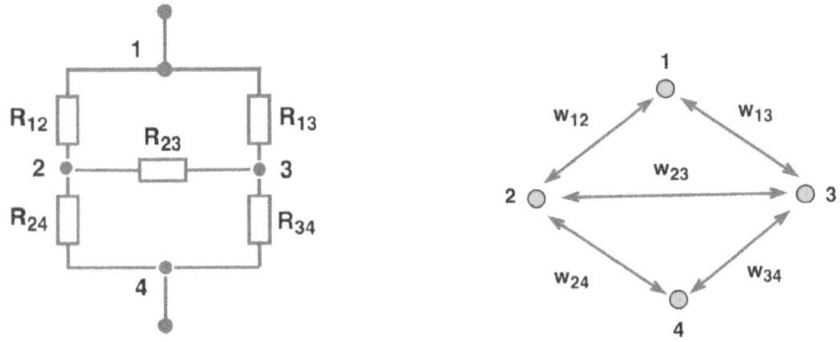

Fig. 1. A Bridge Electrical Network and its Graph Representation.

$$\begin{bmatrix} w_{12} + w_{13} & -w_{12} & -w_{13} & 0 \\ -w_{12} & w_{12} + w_{23} + w_{24} & -w_{23} & -w_{24} \\ -w_{13} & -w_{23} & w_{13} + w_{23} + w_{34} & -w_{34} \\ 0 & -w_{24} & -w_{34} & w_{24} + w_{34} \end{bmatrix}$$

Fig. 2. Laplacian Matrix of Fig. 1.

```
locale wdg_sys = nomulti_netw_sys +
 fixes weight :: 'b weig ("wei")
 assumes positive: ∀e ∈ ℰ. wei e > 0
 and zero: ∀ x y. (x,y) ∉ ℰ ⟷ wei (x,y) = 0
```

The locale `wdg_sys` is built upon `nomulti_netw_sys`, which defines a network system with nonempty and distinct nodes and directed edges (pair of nodes). Throughout the paper, the lists of nodes and edges are denoted as $\mathcal{N}$s and $\mathcal{E}$s, respectively, while the sets of nodes and edges are represented by $\mathcal{N}$ and $\mathcal{E}$, respectively. The fixed parameter `'bweig` represents the embedded type of the weight function `wei`, defined as `'b weig = edge ⇒ real`, where `edge = nat × nat`. The assumption `positive` ensures that all weights are positive, while the assumption `zero` assigns a weight of zero to edges that are not present in the network. Furthermore, we formalize a symmetric weighted directed graph by extending the locales `wdg_sys` and `sym_netw_sys`. Here, `sym_netw_sys` represents a network system with nonempty nodes and edges, which is characterized by the property that for all $e \in \mathcal{E}$, the reverse edge also belongs to $\mathcal{E}$, i.e., $\forall e \in \mathcal{E}.(\text{snd}\,e, \text{fst}\,e) \in \mathcal{E}$.

```
locale sym_wdg_sys = wdg_sys + sym_netw_sys +
 assumes sym_weight: ⋀ i j. wei(𝒩s!i, 𝒩s!j) = wei(𝒩s!j, 𝒩s!i)
```

where the assumption `sym_weight` ensures that edge weights are symmetric for all node pairs (`𝒩s!i`,`𝒩s!j`). We now formalize Definition 1 within the locale `wdg_sys` as follows:

```
definition laplacian_mat where laplacian_mat ≡ out_degree_mat - 𝒜
```

Here, the adjacency matrix, denoted as $\mathcal{A}$, is formalized as follows:

```
definition adjacency_matrix :: real mat where
   adjacency_matrix ≡ mat m m (λ(i,j). wei (𝒩s!i, 𝒩s!j))
```

where `m` represents the number of nodes in the graph. Note that the formalization of aforementioned matrices and their various properties are available at [20].

4 Formalization of Pseudoinverse of the Laplacian Matrix

This section provides the formalization of pseudoinverse of a general matrix and its core properties. We then formalize the pseudoinverse of the Laplacian matrix of a weighted directed graph and verify its classical properties in Isabelle/HOL.

4.1 Pseudoinverse of a Matrix

Definition 2. *Pseudoinverse of a Matrix [21]*
Let P be an $m \times n$ matrix over a field (either $\mathbb{R}$ or $\mathbb{C}$). An $n \times m$ matrix P' is called the pseudoinverse of P if it satisfies the following conditions:

$$P\,P' = (P\,P')^T \tag{4}$$

$$P'\,P = (P'\,P)^T \tag{5}$$

$$P\,P'\,P = P \tag{6}$$

$$P'\,P\,P' = P' \tag{7}$$

We formalize pseudoinverse (Definition 2) in Isabelle/HOL as follows:

```
definition pseudoinverse :: 'a :: field mat ⇒ 'a mat ⇒ bool
  where pseudoinverse P P′ ≡ (P ∗ P′)^T = P ∗ P′ ∧ (P′ ∗ P)^T = P′ ∗ P
                               ∧ P ∗ P′ ∗ P = P ∧ P′ ∗ P ∗ P′ = P′
```

The pseudoinverse is uniquely defined for any matrix, whether square or non-square. More precisely, if two matrices both satisfy the defining conditions of the pseudoinverse for a given matrix P, then these matrices must be equal. To formally verify the uniqueness of the pseudoinverse of a given matrix P, we establish the following lemma in Isabelle/HOL:

```
lemma uniqueness_pseudo:
    assumes A1: P′ ∈ carrier_mat (dim_col P) (dim_row P)
    assumes A2: B ∈ carrier_mat (dim_col P) (dim_row P)
    assumes A3: pseudoinverse P P′
    assumes A4: pseudoinverse P B
    shows P′ = B
```

Here, we assume that two matrices P′ and B are both pseudoinverses of the matrix P with same dimensions, as specified in Assumptions A1-A4. The goal is to prove that P′= B, thereby establishing the uniqueness of the pseudoinverse. To achieve this, we define two auxiliary matrices: $P{*}B\text{-}P^2$ and B*P-P'*P. We proceed with the proof by utilizing the symmetry of these expressions, applying the pseudoinverse conditions (Equations (4)-(7)), and performing algebraic reasoning using matrix identities to conclude the equality. We also verified the existence property, which states that for any given matrix P, there is always at least one matrix P' satisfying the pseudoinverse conditions. The proof of this property can be found in our proof script [22].

We formally verify some core properties of pseudoinverse of a matrix, as presented in Table 1, and their verification in Isabelle/HOL establishes the correctness of our model. The verification of these properties in Isabelle/HOL provides the correctness of our model, which is an extension of the inverse concept. For example, the first entry, i.e., the self-pseudoinverse property, demonstrates that the pseudoinverse of the pseudoinverse of a matrix is equal to the matrix itself. The second property establishes the scalability, i.e., the pseudoinverse of $c.P$ is scaled by $\frac{1}{c}$. The final entry confirms the transpose commutativity of the pseudoinverse, showing that the pseudoinverse of P satisfies $(\mathrm{P}')^T = (\mathrm{P}^T)'$. The proofs of these properties relies on the verification of pseudoinverse conditions, using the formal definition of the pseudoinverse and applying matrix algebraic reasoning.

Table 1. Some Fundamental Properties of Pseudoinverse of a Matrix

Mathematical Descriptions	Isabelle/HOL Formalization

$(P')' = P$	`lemma self_pseudoinv:`
	`assumes pseudoinverse P P′`
	`shows pseudoinverse P′ P`

$(cP)' = (\frac{1}{c})P'$	`lemma scalar_mult_pseudoinv:`
	`fixes c :: real`
	`assumes P′ ∈ carrier_mat (dim_col P) (dim_row P)`
	`assumes pseudoinverse P P′`
	`shows pseudoinverse (c ·m P) ((1/c) ·m P′)`

$(P')^T = (P^T)'$	`lemma transp_pseudoinv:`
	`assumes P′ ∈ carrier_mat (dim_col P) (dim_row P)`
	`assumes pseudoinverse P P′`
	`shows pseudoinverse PT (P′)T`

4.2 Pseudoinverse of Laplacian Matrix

Definition 3. *Pseudoinverse of the Laplacian Matrix [23]*
Let L be a Laplacian matrix of a graph with m nodes. Then, the pseudoinverse L^+ is defined as:

$$L^+ = (L + \frac{J}{m})^{-1} - \frac{J}{m} \tag{8}$$

where $(L + \frac{J}{m})$ is invertible and J is an $m \times m$ matrix with elements equal to 1.

As an example, we assume that all resistances in the network shown in Fig. 1 are unit-valued. The corresponding Laplacian matrix and its pseudoinverse, computed using Equation (8), are illustrated in Fig. 3, where $m = 4$ and J is 4×4 matrix of all ones.

We formalize the pseudoinverse of the Laplacian matrix (Equation (8)) in Isabelle/HOL as follows:

```
definition psinv_mat :: real mat ⇒ real mat
  where psinv_mat L ≡ (inverse_mat (L + (1/(dim_row L)) ·m (Jm (dim_row L)))
                        - (1/(dim_row L)) ·m (Jm (dim_row L)))
```

$$\begin{bmatrix} 2 & -1 & -1 & 0 \\ -1 & 3 & -1 & -1 \\ -1 & -1 & 3 & -1 \\ 0 & -1 & -1 & 2 \end{bmatrix}$$

(a) Laplacian Matrix

$$\begin{bmatrix} 5/16 & -1/16 & -1/16 & -3/16 \\ -1/16 & 3/16 & -1/16 & -1/16 \\ -1/16 & -1/16 & 3/16 & -1/16 \\ -3/16 & -1/16 & -1/16 & 5/16 \end{bmatrix}$$

(b) Pseudoinverse of the Laplacian Matrix

Fig. 3. Example Matrix Instances for the Graph in Fig. 1.

We now present the core properties of the pseudoinverse of the Laplacian matrix for a connected weighted graph[4]. The connectedness of a graph can be characterized by the kernel of its Laplacian matrix, which has a zero eigenvalue [24]. Given our focus on electrical network applications, we restrict our attention to graphs with a single connected component. For instance, as shown in Fig. 1, the graph corresponding to the bridge electrical network is connected. This implies that the associated Laplacian matrix is singular. The singularity of the Laplacian matrix can also be understood in terms of its structure: the sum of each row (or column) is zero. This property is formally verified in Isabelle/HOL:

```
lemma laplacian_singular:
  shows ¬ invertible_mat ℒ
```

Here, the real matrix $\mathcal{L}$ is the abbreviation of `laplacian_mat`, which is used throughout this paper. The verification of the above lemma relies on the auxiliary result `laplacian_allones_right` (presented in Table 2), along with the properties of invertible matrices and reasoning about the matrix kernel. To ensure that Definition 2 is well-defined, we first verify that for connected symmetric graphs, the matrix $L + \frac{J}{m}$ is nonsingular, i.e., it is invertible.

```
lemma invertible_lap_all:
  assumes connect1_ntw
  shows invertible_mat (ℒ + (1/m) ·m (Jm m))
```

Here the assumption `connect1_ntw` ensures that the graph is connected, i.e., the corresponding Laplacian matrix has a simple zero eigenvalue. This is formalized as follows:

```
definition connect1_ntw where
  connect1_ntw ≡ mat_kernel ℒ = {k ·v (uv m) | k. k ≠ 0 ∧ k ∈ real}
```

where $\mathtt{u_v}$ represents a vector with all entries equal to one. The verification of the lemma `invertible_lap_all` is performed using proof by contradiction. The proof begins by assuming that $\mathcal{L} + \mathtt{(1/m)}\cdot_{\mathtt{m}}(\mathtt{J_m\ m})$ is not invertible. Using the connectedness assumption, we establish the relationship between the matrix kernel and invertibility. Then, we apply relevant lemmas regarding the linear dependency of the rows and columns of the Laplacian matrix $\mathcal{L}$ and the all-ones matrix $\mathtt{J_m}$. The contradiction is derived by showing that this assumption leads to two different values for the sum of the elements of an eigenvector, thus violating the uniqueness of eigenvalues in the connected case. This proof relies on several auxiliary lemmas, as listed in Table 2. The first two lemmas verify that the sum of elements in every row or column of the Laplacian matrix is zero, which confirms that the rows and columns are linearly dependent. The third lemma demonstrates that if the matrix M has a non-trivial kernel, there exists non-zero eigenvectors in the kernel. These lemmas are verified using the definitions L, J, the matrix kernel alongside some matrix algebraic reasoning.

[4] Going forward, we consider weighted graphs to be symmetric.

Table 2. Some Auxiliary Properties

Mathematical Descriptions	Isabelle/HOL Formalization
$LJ = \mathbf{0}$	`lemma laplacian_allones_right:` `shows ℒ * J_m m = 0_m m m`
$JL = \mathbf{0}$	`lemma laplacian_allones_left:` `shows (J_m m) * ℒ = 0_m m m`

For any $M \in \mathbb{R}^{n\times n}$,
$ker\ M \neq \{\vec{0}\} \implies$
$\exists v.v \neq \vec{0} \wedge Mv = \vec{0}$
	`lemma non_zero_kernel:`
	`fixes M :: real mat assumes square_mat M`
	`assumes mat_kernel M ≠ {0_v (dim_row M)}`
	`obtains v where v ≠ 0_v (dim_row M) ∧`
	`M *_v v = 0_v (dim_row M)`

The following lemma verifies the symmetry property of the pseudoinverse of the Laplacian matrix in Isabelle/HOL:

```
lemma psinv_lap_mat_sym:
  assumes connect1_ntw
  shows symmetric_matrix (psinv_mat ℒ)
```

We now mathematically demonstrate the row and column linear dependence property of the pseudoinverse of the Laplacian matrix, expressed by the following identities:

$$L^{+}J = \mathbf{0} \tag{9}$$

$$JL^{+} = \mathbf{0} \tag{10}$$

The following lemmas verify Equations (9) and (10) in Isabelle/HOL as follows:

```
lemma psinv_lap_one_right:
  assumes connect1_ntw
  shows (psinv_mat (ℒ)) * (J_m m) = 0_m m m
```

```
lemma psinv_lap_one_left:
  assumes connect1_ntw
  shows (J_m m) * (psinv_mat (ℒ)) = 0_m m m
```

Next, the relationship between the Laplacian matrix and its pseudoinverse can be mathematically presented as:

$$L^{+}L = I - (\frac{1}{m})J \tag{11}$$

where I denotes the identity matrix of the same dimensions as the Laplacian matrix, and m represents the number of nodes in the corresponding graph. We formally verify Eq. (11) in Isabelle/HOL as the following lemma:

```
lemma eq_mult_psinv_lap:
  assumes connect1_ntw
  shows (psinv_mat (ℒ)) * ℒ = 1m m - (1/m) ·m (Jm m))
```

To prove the above lemma, we first simplify the left-hand side of Eq. (11) as $(L + \frac{J}{m})^{-1}L$. This is verified by using the definition of the pseudoinverse of the Laplacian matrix, `invertible_lap_all`, `laplacian_allones_left` (presented in Table 2), along with manipulations on dimension and matrix identities. Then, we establish the subgoal $(L + \frac{J}{m})(I - \frac{J}{m}) = L$ to complete the verification by utilizing the definitions L, J, the column linear dependency of L, alongside some matrix algebraic reasoning. We now verify that Eq. (8) satisfies the pseudoinverse conditions in Isabelle/HOL as the following lemma:

```
lemma ver_psinv_lap:
  assumes connect1_ntw
  shows pseudoinverse ℒ (psinv_mat (ℒ))
```

Next, we verify the well-established property, ensuring that the Laplacian matrix of a connected graph with symmetry commutes with its pseudoinverse. This is mathematically presented as:

$$L^+L = LL^+ \tag{12}$$

We establish the following Isabelle/HOL lemma to verify (Equation (12)):

```
lemma mult_lap_psinv_lap:
  assumes connect1_ntw
  shows (psinv_mat (ℒ)) * ℒ = ℒ * (psinv_mat (ℒ))
```

5 Application: Kirchhoff Index

The Kirchhoff index is a graph-theoretic metric that captures topological structures of a network and evaluates its impact on overall network performance. This index has been extensively investigated in electrical engineering because of its broad applicability in analyzing structural efficiency and connectivity. Fundamentally, the Kirchhoff index is based on the notion of resistance distance, a concept originating from electrical network theory. The pseudoinverse of the Laplacian matrix serves as the classical approach for computing the Kirchhoff index of a connected graph. It is mathematically defined as follows:

Definition 4. *Kirchhoff Index [25]*
Consider the Laplacian matrix L of a connected graph with m nodes, whose pseudoinverse is denoted by $L^+ = [\ell^+_{ij}]$ for $i, j \in \{1, \ldots, m\}$. The Kirchhoff index $\mathcal{KI}$ of the graph is defined as the sum of resistance distances between all distinct pairs of nodes in the graph:

$$\mathcal{KI} = \sum_{i<j} r_{ij} \tag{13}$$

where r_{ij} denotes the resistance between nodes i and j, and is defined as

$$r_{ij} = \ell^{+}_{ii} + \ell^{+}_{jj} - 2\ell^{+}_{ij} \tag{14}$$

A more compact formulation of the Kirchhoff index can be expressed it in terms of the trace of the pseudoinverse of the Laplacian matrix:

$$\mathcal{KI} = \sum_{i<j} \ell^{+}_{ii} + \ell^{+}_{jj} - 2\ell^{+}_{ij} = m\,\mathtt{tr}(L^{+}) \tag{15}$$

For instance, in the case of the bridge electrical network, shown in Fig. 1, the Kirchhoff index is obtained via its pseudoinverse matrix (Fig. 3), yielding $\mathcal{KI} = 4$. In Isabelle/HOL, we need to express $\mathcal{KI}$ as a double summation over all indices i and j separately, i.e., $\mathcal{KI} = \frac{1}{2}\sum_{i=0}^{m-1}\sum_{j=0}^{m-1} \ell^{+}_{ii} + \ell^{+}_{jj} - 2\ell^{+}_{ij}$, as shown in the following definition:

```
definition Kirchh_index :: real mat ⇒ real where
  Kirchh_index L ≡ (1/2) * (∑ i ∈ {0..< dim_row L}. ∑ j ∈ {0..< dim_row L}.
   (psinv_mat L) $$ (i,i) + (psinv_mat L) $$ (j,j) - 2 * (psinv_mat L) $$ (i,j))
```

Subsequently, we formally verify Equation (15) to establish the equivalence between the double-sum form and the compact trace-based expression of the Kirchhoff index.

```
lemma KI_compact:
   assumes connect1_ntw
   shows Kirchh_index (ℒ) = m * trace (psinv_mat ℒ)
```

5.1 Two-Horizontal Bridge Circuit Network

To build upon the preceding formalization, we now present a two-horizontal bridge circuit network and its corresponding graph representation depicted in Fig. 4. This bridge circuit network exemplifies a cascaded electrical resistance configuration, comprising two distinct horizontal bridge circuits. The associated graph is composed of 10 nodes and 17 edges, where each edge represents a resistor with weight 1. Nodes are labeled from 1 to 10, and edges are denoted as ordered pairs indicating the connection between node pairs. For instance, $\mathtt{R}_{12}$ is the resistor between nodes 1 and 2, and $\mathtt{w}_{12}$ represents the corresponding weight in the graph. Such complex networks cannot be simplified using conventional series-parallel reduction techniques, thereby necessitating more robust analysis methods. In this context, the pseudoinverse of the Laplacian matrix is used to compute global metrics such as effective resistance or Kirchhoff index [23]. We formalize the graph model of this network in Isabelle/HOL and compute its Kirchhoff index accordingly.

For the construction of the pseudoinverse of the Laplacian matrix of the network in Isabelle/HOL, we first establish the network's adjacency matrix as the following lemma:

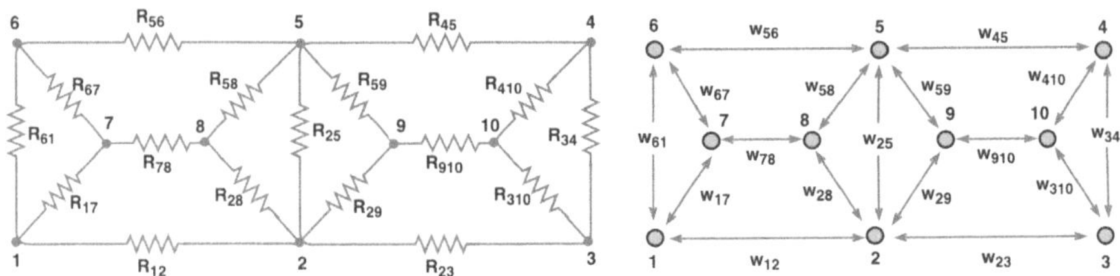

Fig. 4. Two-horizontal Bridge Circuit Network and its Graph Representation.

```
lemma ver_adj_mat:
  assumes two_bridge_netw
  shows 𝒜 = mat_of_rows_list 10 [[0,1,0,0,0,1,1,0,0,0],
        [1,0,1,0,1,0,0,1,1,0],[0,1,0,1,0,0,0,0,0,1],[0,0,1,0,1,0,0,0,0,1],
        [0,1,0,1,0,1,0,1,1,0],[1,0,0,0,1,0,1,0,0,0],[1,0,0,0,0,1,0,1,0,0],
        [0,1,0,0,1,0,1,0,0,0],[0,1,0,0,1,0,0,0,0,1],[0,0,1,1,0,0,0,0,1,0]]
```

Here, assumption `two_bridge_netw` represents the specification of the graph (depicted in Fig. 4) by indicating the list of nodes and edges and the weight function. We then derive the Laplacian matrix from the network by verifying the following Isabelle/HOL lemma:

```
lemma ver_lap_mat:
  assumes two_bridge_netw
  shows ℒ = mat_of_rows_list 10 [[3,-1,0,0,0,-1,-1,0,0,0],
              [-1,5,-1,0,-1,0,0,-1,-1,0],[0,-1,3,-1,0,0,0,0,0,-1],
              [0,0,-1,3,-1,0,0,0,0,-1],[0,-1,0,-1,5,-1,0,-1,-1,0],
              [-1,0,0,0,-1,3,-1,0,0,0],[-1,0,0,0,0,-1,3,-1,0,0],
              [0,-1,0,0,-1,0,-1,3,0,0],[0,-1,0,0,-1,0,0,0,3,-1],
              [0,0,-1,-1,0,0,0,0,-1,3::real]]
```

To prove this lemma, we first verify the degree matrix of the network, given by $\mathcal{D}_{\text{out}} = diag(3, 5, 3, 3, 5, 3, 3, 3, 3, 3)$. The definition of the Laplacian matrix is then used to conclude the proof. The verification is carried out in Isabelle/HOL by applying the matrix equivalence rule. This step formally validates the network model and ensures the correctness of its structural connectivity. Subsequently, we compute the inverse of the matrix $\mathcal{L} + \frac{J}{10}$, denoted as $\texttt{M}_{\texttt{inv}}$, using the matrix inverse code function available in the JNF library. The pseudoinverse of the Laplacian matrix is then obtained through intermediate matrix operations to finally establish the Kirchhoff index of the network in Isabelle/HOL as follows:

```
lemma KI_twobrdg_netw:
  assumes two_bridge_netw and connect1_ntw
  assumes inverse_mat (ℒ + (1/m) ·m (Jm m) = Minv
  shows Kirchh_index ℒ = 3723/110
```

5.2 Discussion

We successfully formalized the pseudoinverse of the Laplacian matrix, verified its core properties, and employed it to formally verify Kirchhoff index formula. Unlike the classical proofs of Equation (15) available in the literature, we provided a detailed, rigorous and mechanized verification of the compact form using Isabelle/HOL. During the formalization process, we encountered several challenges, particularly in reasoning about double summations. For instance, proving identities such as $\sum_{i=0}^{m}\sum_{j=0}^{m} f(i,i)+f(j,j)-2*f(i,j) = \sum_{i=0}^{m}\sum_{j=0,j\neq i}^{m} f(i,i)+f(j,j)-2*f(i,j)$, which are intuitively straightforward, often required significant decomposition into smaller subgoals to be tractable for automation. In addition to the theoretical formalization, we also verified the formal model of an horizontally embedded two-bridge circuit network by establishing its Kirchhoff index. For cross-validation of our formally verified result, we computed the Laplacian, pseudoinverse and Kirchhoff index of the same network using MATLAB[5] and obtained the exactly same result apart from some rounding effects experienced in MATLAB.

6 Conclusion

In this paper, we used Isabelle/HOL to formalize the pseudoinverse of the Laplacian matrix for symmetric weighted graphs, a concept with significant applicability in engineering and complex networked systems. We began by formalizing the pseudoinverse of matrices in a generic manner, encompassing both square and non-square, whether singular or non-singular. We then formally verified fundamental properties, such as uniqueness. Next, we focused on the Laplacian matrix of a graph, formalized its pseudoinverse, and verified several classical properties, including row/column linear dependence and commutativity with the original Laplacian matrix. These properties were verified under general conditions, where the number of nodes and edges is arbitrary, using the assumptions encoded in the `sym_wdg_sys` locale and the connectedness of the graph. To demonstrate the practical effectiveness of our formalization, we applied it to define and verify the Kirchhoff index for connected graphs, an important graph-theoretic invariant with applications in network science and electrical engineering. We also verified the Kirchhoff index of a two-horizontal bridge circuit network in Isabelle/HOL and cross-validated the result using MATLAB. In the future, we intend to extend our formal library to support deeper analysis of complex networked systems, incorporating key aspects such as stability and performance [19].

[5] https://www.mathworks.com/products/matlab.html.

References

1. Molitierno, J.J.: Applications of combinatorial matrix theory to Laplacian matrices of graphs. CRC Press (2012)
2. Myers, R.L.: The Basics of Physics. Bloomsbury Publishing USA (2005)
3. Monier, C.J.: Electric Circuit Analysis. Pearson (2001)
4. Aida, M., Takano, C., Murata, M.: Oscillation Model for network dynamics caused by asymmetric node interaction based on the symmetric scaled Laplacian matrix. In: Foundations of Computer Science, pp. 38–44. CSREA (2016)
5. Chiumento, A., Marchetti, N., Macaluso, I.: Energy efficient WSN: a cross-layer graph signal processing solution to information redundancy. In: International Symposium on Wireless Communication Systems, pp. 645–650. IEEE (2019)
6. Barata, J.C.A., Hussein, M.S.: The Moore-Penrose pseudoinverse: a tutorial review of the theory. Braz. J. Phys. **42**, 146–165 (2012)
7. Gutman, I., Mohar, B.: The Quasi-Wiener and the Kirchhoff Indices Coincide. J. Chem. Inf. Comput. Sci. **36**(5), 982–985. ACS Publications (1996)
8. Thulasiraman, K., Yadav, M., Naik, K.: Network science meets circuit theory: resistance distance, Kirchhoff index, and foster's theorems with generalizations and unification. IEEE Trans. Circuits Syst. I Regul. Pap. **66**(3), 1090–1103 (2018)
9. Saurabh, N., Varbanescu, A.L., Ranjan, G.: Computing the pseudo-inverse of a graph's laplacian using GPUs. In: IEEE International Parallel and Distributed Processing Symposium Workshop, pp. 265–274. IEEE (2015)
10. Harrison, J.: Handbook of Practical Logic and Automated Reasoning. Cambridge University Press (2009)
11. Heras, J., Poza, M., Dénès, M., Rideau, L.: Incidence simplicial matrices formalized in Coq/SSReflect. In: Davenport, J.H., Farmer, W.M., Urban, J., Rabe, F. (eds.) CICM 2011. LNCS (LNAI), vol. 6824, pp. 30–44. Springer, Heidelberg (2011). https://doi.org/10.1007/978-3-642-22673-1_3
12. Edmonds, C., Paulson, L.C.: Formalising Fisher's Inequality: formal linear algebraic proof techniques in combinatorics. In: Interactive Theorem Proving, LIPIcs. vol. 237, pp. 11:1–11:19 (2022)
13. Aksoy, K., Rashid, A., Hasan, O., Tahar, S.: Formal analysis of electrical circuit network topologies using theorem proving. In: 2025 International Systems Conference, pp. 1–8. IEEE (2025)
14. Nipkow, T., Wenzel, M., Paulson, L.C.: Isabelle/HOL: A Proof Assistant for Higher-Order Logic. Springer (2002)
15. Blanchette, J.C., Kaliszyk, C., Paulson, L.C., Urban, J.: Hammering towards QED. J. Formal. Reasoning **9**(1), 101–148 (2016)
16. Böhme, S., Weber, T.: Fast LCF-style proof reconstruction for Z3. In: Kaufmann, M., Paulson, L.C. (eds.) ITP 2010. LNCS, vol. 6172, pp. 179–194. Springer, Heidelberg (2010). https://doi.org/10.1007/978-3-642-14052-5_14
17. Barrett, C., et al.: CVC4. In: Computer Aided Verification, LNCS. vol. 6806, pp. 171–177. Springer (2011)
18. Blanchette, J.C.: Nitpick: a counterexample generator for Isabelle/HOL based on the relational model finder kodkod. EPiC Series Comput. **13**, 20–25 (2013)
19. Bullo, F., Cortés, J., Dörfler, F., Martínez, S.: Lectures on Network Systems. CreateSpace (2018)
20. Aksoy, K.: Proof Script: on the formalization of pseudoinverse of the Laplacian matrix in HOL (2025). https://hvg.ece.concordia.ca/code/Isabelle-hol/pilmat.zip

21. Gentle, J.E.: Matrix Algebra: Theory, Computations, and Applications in Statistics. Springer (2007)
22. Aksoy, K., Rashid, A., Tahar, S.: Formal Kinematic analysis of epicyclic bevel gear trains. In: Formal Engineering Methods, LNCS. vol. 15394, pp. 162–180. Springer (2024)
23. Gutman, I., Xiao, W.: Generalized inverse of the laplacian matrix and some applications. Bulletin (Académie serbe des sciences et des arts. Classe des sciences mathématiques et naturelles. Sciences mathématiques) 15–23 (2004)
24. Mohar, B.: Graph Laplacians. Top. Algebraic Graph Theory **102**, 113–136 (2004)
25. Klein, D.J., Randić, M.: Resistance distance. J. Math. Chem. **12**(1), 81–95 (1993)

A Generic Event-B Theory for the Formalisation of the International System of Units

Idir Ait-Sadoune(✉)

Paris-Saclay University, CentraleSupelec, LMF Laboratory, Plateau de Saclay, Gif-Sur-Yvette, France
idir.aitsadoune@centralesuplec.fr

Abstract. Formal verification of cyber-physical systems (CPS) requires a model that accurately represents physical measurements from the real world. Incorporating explicit units into these measurements enhances rigour by enabling the verification of unit compatibility and correction in computations. While formal methods such as Event-B support static type checking, they lack the capability to annotate variables with physical measurement units. This paper proposes extending the Event-B type-checking system by defining a generic theory that offers the possibility to annotate Event-B variables with measurement units. This approach allows the specification of physical quantities, units, and measurements using the Theory plug-in.

Keywords: Cyber-physical systems · International system of units · Event-B method · Type-checking

1 Introduction

Since its introduction, the Event-B formal method [1] has seen growing adoption and has been applied across a wide range of applications and domains [7]. Event-B is particularly well-suited for the analysis of discrete systems, with a type system that effectively supports the modelling of discrete behaviours. However, as the need to model and analyse hybrid systems-including complex and cyber-physical systems (CPS)-continues to grow, extending the Event-B type-checking system becomes increasingly important. In particular, enabling the specification and analysis of physical quantities and measurements in Event-B requires the integration of measurement unit definitions into the formalism.

The Rodin platform [2] is the most widely used development environment in the Event-B ecosystem. As it is based on Eclipse, it supports extensibility through plugins. Among the various plugins developed for Rodin, the Theory plugin [8] is primarily used to enhance the modelling capabilities of Event-B by

This work was supported by a grant from the French national research agency ANR ANR-19-CE25-0010 (EBRP Project https://www.irit.fr/EBRP/).

B. Ben Hedia et al. (Eds.): VECoS 2025, LNCS 16263, pp. 114–128, 2026.
https://doi.org/10.1007/978-3-032-20440-0_8

allowing the definition of custom theories. This plugin facilitates the creation of both mathematical and prover extensions. Mathematical extensions include new operator definitions, datatype definitions, and axiomatic specifications.

In this article, we propose the development of a measurement units theory using the Theory plugin. Our goal is to extend the Event-B type-checking system to support reasoning about measurement units. Specifically, we introduce a formal approach for annotating Event-B variables with associated units of measurement.

This paper is organized as follows. Section 2 introduces the main concepts of the Event-B method. Section 3 reviews related work on the formalization of measurement units using the Event-B method. Section 4 describes the proposed approach in detail, while Sect. 5 demonstrates its application through a simple example. Finally, Sect. 6 concludes the paper with a summary and perspectives for future work.

2 The Event-B Method

The Event-B method [1] is based on the notions of pre-conditions and post-conditions [14], weakest pre-condition, and the calculus of substitution [10]. It is a formal method based on first-order logic and set theory.

2.1 The Event-B Model

An Event-B model is made of two kinds of components: machines and contexts. The machines contain the dynamic parts, whereas the contexts contain the static parts. A machine can see one or several contexts. Moreover, a machine can be refined by another machine, and a context can be extended by another (cf. Listings 1.1 and 1.2).

Listing 1.1. The Event-B context

```
CONTEXT ctx_1 EXTENDS ctx_2
  SETS s
  CONSTANTS c
  AXIOMS A(s, c)
  THEOREMS T(s, c)
END
```

Listing 1.2. The Event-B machine

```
MACHINE mch_1 REFINES mch_2
  SEES ctx_i
  VARIABLES v
  INVARIANTS I(s, c, v)
  THEOREMS T(s, c, v)
  EVENTS
    < events_list >
END
```

A context is defined by a set of clauses as follows:

- `SETS` describes a set of abstract and enumerated types.
- `CONSTANTS` describes the constants used by a model.
- `AXIOMS` describes the properties of the constants.
- `THEOREMS` are properties that can be deduced from the axioms.

An Event-B machine is defined by variables that evolve thanks to events. It encodes a state transition system where the variables represent the state, and the events represent the transitions from one state to another. Similarly to contexts, a machine is defined by a set of clauses. Briefly, the clauses mean.

- `VARIABLES` represents the state variables of the specification model.
- `INVARIANTS` describes the properties of the model.
- `THEOREMS` are properties that can be deduced from the invariants.
- `EVENTS` defines all the events that occur in a given model. Each event is characterized by its guard and the actions performed when the guard is true.

The refinement operation offered by Event-B encodes model decomposition. A transition system is decomposed into another transition system with more and more design decisions while moving from an abstract level to a less abstract one. A refined machine is defined by adding new events, new state variables and a glueing invariant. Each event of the abstract model is refined in the concrete model by expressing how the new set of variables and events evolves.

Proof obligations (PO) are associated with any Event-B model. They define the formal semantics associated with each Event-B component. These PO need to be proved to ensure the correctness of the Event-B models. PO are automatically generated by *the PO generator plugin* and can be proved automatically or interactively by *the prover plugin* in the Rodin platform [2]. The rules for generating PO are listed in [1].

2.2 The Theory Plugin

To extend the Event-B modelling possibilities with new mathematical objects, the theory plugin [8] extends the Rodin platform by providing a new syntax to define mathematical and prover extensions with the theory component. A theory can contain new datatype definitions, polymorphic operator definitions, axiomatic definitions, theorems and associated rewrite and inference rules. The installation for the theory plugin is available under the main Rodin Update site[1] under the category "Modelling Extensions". More information about the Theory plugin is available on the user manual at this link[2].

2.3 Event-B Type Checking System

Formal methods like Event-B support static type checking with tool feedback if you use the Rodin platform or AtelierB. What makes the type-checking system even more interesting in these tools is the generation of proof obligations associated with correctly using arithmetic operators (called WD - Well Defined PO). These proof obligation rules ensure that a potentially ill-defined axiom, theorem, invariant, guard, action, variant, or witness is well-defined. For example, if we use the expression $E \div F$, we must ensure that $F \neq 0$.

[1] http://rodin-b-sharp.sourceforge.net/updates.

[2] https://wiki.event-b.org/images/Theory_Plugin.pdf.

In the context of modelling CPS systems, we need to use numerical variables that refer to physical measurements, and annotating such variables with physical units of measurement in Event-B is impossible. Formal verification of CPS systems requires a physical measurement model like The International System of Units (SI, abbreviated from the French "Système international d'unités") [6]. We cannot ignore that using explicit units in such model can allow a higher degree of rigour since we can ensure the compatibility of using quantities.

Our aim in this article is to propose a formal approach to annotating numerical variables with measurement units and to get an automatic checking of the correct use of measures when we write arithmetic expressions using measurable quantities or physics laws (by defining WD PO). For example, if we use the expression $b = v/2a_{max,brake}$ (the braking distance b depending on the speed v and the maximum braking deceleration $a_{max,brake}$), we must ensure that the unit of b is compatible with the unit of the expression $v/2a_{max,brake}$.

3 Related Works

Integrating reasoning about physical quantities, units and measurements in formal specifications is not a new challenge [9,11,13]. In this section we focus about different known tentatives to integrate measurement units in Classical B or Event-B methods. Krings and Leuschel [15] developed a plugin to extend ProB animator by the ability to perform unit analysis for formal models developed in B or Event-B by using annotations to infer the units of all variables and check the consistency of a machine. The proposed approach provides source-level error feedback to the user. Gibson and Mery proposed another approach [12] which consisted of explicitly formalising the units of measurement in the context of an Event-B model. Java implementations demonstrate the approach's feasibility, and Java unit tests were derived from the Event-B specifications. Finally, in the context of the Ait-Ameur et al. [3] work on the integration of knowledge modelled by ontologies in Event-B contexts, they proposed an approach similar to that of Gibson and Mery where all definitions and properties related to the units of measurement are axiomatised in Event-B contexts.

The problem with approaches that formalise units of measurement in Event-B contexts is that we have to adapt all arithmetic operators to each unit of measurement added to the model, which increases the complexity of the developed models. Another problem from a verification point of view is that these approaches do not offer any proof mechanism to verify the consistency of formulas manipulating units of measurement. In this article, we propose an approach that defines a generic theory that responds essentially to these two problems.

4 SI Units Formalisation

In the following sections, we will present different theories implementing our approach following the path defined in the Fig. 1. The central theory *thy_si_units* depends on the *thy_floating_point_numbers* (numerical representation) and *thy_si_dimensions* (dimensional reasoning) theories. It defines generic datatypes and operators. The *thy_si_base_units* theory uses the central theory and defines the seven base units (meter, kilogram, second, etc.), the *thy_length_units* theory defines the multiples and submultiples unites of a meter unit (millimetre, kilometre, etc.), the *thy_si_named_derived_units* theory defines named derived units like *Newton*, *Pascal*, etc., and finally, the *thy_si_other_derived_units* theory defines unnamed derived units (e.g., rad/s^2).

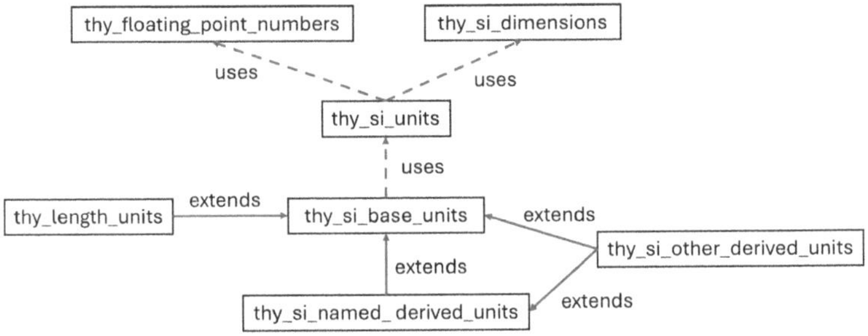

Fig. 1. The relation between different developed theories.

4.1 Floating-Point Numbers [4]

Formalising and analysing physical quantities sometimes requires manipulating small values (< 1) and converting from the smallest point of view to the most significant ones (from Milli to Kilo, for example). Representing such values is impossible in the Event-B mathematical language. To deal with this lack, we have proposed in a previous work [4] a theory to extend the Event-B type-checking system with the possibility of handling floating-point numbers.

The proposed approach represents floating-point numbers using an integer called the **significand**, scaled by an integer **exponent** of a fixed **base**. We have chosen that the base always equals ten in our models (see the following example).

$$\pi = 3.14159265359 = \underbrace{314159265359}_{\text{significand}} \times \underbrace{10}_{\text{base}}{}^{\overbrace{-11}^{\text{exponent}}}$$

To allow the Event-B language to embed this representation, we have developed a theory that formalises floating-point numbers by specifying the corresponding data type (`FLOAT_Type`), the supported arithmetic operators, and some axioms and theorems characterising the proposed modelling (cf. Listing 1.3). By using this theory, it is possible to create constants like 0 and

1 ($F0 = 0 \times 10^0$ or $F1 = 1 \times 10^0$) (cf. Listing 1.3). The proposed theory also redefines all essential numeric operators (comparison {`eq, gt, lt, ...`} and calculation operators {`plus, sub, mult, div, ...`}) (cf. article [4]). The *thy_floating_point_numbers* theory is also used to define a set of constants (the prefix part of a unit) like `MILLI`, `CENTI`, `DECI`, `DECA`, etc. (cf. Listing 1.3). The Event-B project containing this theory can be downloaded from this link[3].

Listing 1.3. The theory defining the floating-point numbers (extract)

```
THEORY thy_floating_point_numbers
DATATYPES
  FLOAT_Type ≙ NEW_FLOAT(s ∈ ℤ, e ∈ ℤ) // x = s(x) x 10^e(x)
OPERATORS
  F0 ≙ NEW_FLOAT(0,0)
  F1 ≙ NEW_FLOAT(1,0)
  ...
  MILLI ≙ NEW_FLOAT(1,-3) // 10^-3
  CENTI ≙ NEW_FLOAT(1,-2) // 10^-2
  DECI ≙ NEW_FLOAT(1,-1) // 10^-1
  DECA ≙ NEW_FLOAT(1,1) // 10^1
  HECTO ≙ NEW_FLOAT(1,2) // 10^2
  KILO ≙ NEW_FLOAT(1,3) // 10^3
  ...
END
```

4.2 Dimensions Formalisation

The International System of Units [6] comprises a coherent system of units of measurement starting with seven quantities, which are time (T), length (L), mass (M), electric current (I), thermodynamic temperature (Θ), amount of substance (N), and luminous intensity (J). All these quantities correspond to seven base dimensions. Thus, the SI was defined through seven base units from which the derived units were constructed as products of the powers of the base units. Physical quantities are organized in a system of dimensions, and each of the seven base quantities used in the SI has its dimension. In general the dimension of any quantity Q is written in the form of a dimensional product,

$$dim\ Q = T^{\alpha} L^{\beta} M^{\gamma} I^{\delta} \Theta^{\varepsilon} N^{\zeta} J^{\eta}$$

where the exponents $\alpha, \beta, \gamma, \delta, \varepsilon, \zeta$ and η, which can be positive, negative, or zero, are called the dimensional exponents. The Event-B theory described in listing 1.4 formalises this dimension concept by defining a new datatype called `SI_DIMENSION_Type` and its constructor `SI_DIMENSION`.

In the most used case, a quantity can have only one dimension different from zero. For this purpose, we have defined seven operators for creating dimensions associated with the seven quantities: length (`L_DIM`), mass (`M_DIM`), time (`T_DIM`), etc. In some cases, the dimension of a quantity can be deduced after multiplying or dividing two other quantities; this can be the case of a speed

[3] https://www.idiraitsadoune.com/recherche/modeles/eventb.theories.zip.

calculated from a distance and a time. For this need, we have provided two operators allowing a multiplication or a division of two dimensions (DIM_MULT and DIM_DIV). In other cases, we are brought to add or subtract (or compare) two quantities. These are possible for quantities with the same dimensions. Thus, we have provided an operator to compare exponents of two dimensions (HAVE_SAME_EXP_DIMENSIONS).

Listing 1.4. The Dimensions Theory (extract)

```
THEORY thy_si_dimensions
DATATYPES
  SI_DIMENSION_Type ≙ SI_DIMENSION(
    exp_d1 ∈ ℤ, // length dimension
    exp_d2 ∈ ℤ, // mass dimension
    exp_d3 ∈ ℤ, // time dimension
    exp_d4 ∈ ℤ, // electric current dimension
    exp_d5 ∈ ℤ, // thermodynamic temperature dimension
    exp_d6 ∈ ℤ, // amount of substance dimension
    exp_d7 ∈ ℤ) // luminous intensity dimension
OPERATORS
  // length quantity
  L_DIM (exp_d ∈ ℤ) ≙ SI_DIMENSION(exp_d,0,0,0,0,0,0)
  // mass quantity
  M_DIM (exp_d ∈ ℤ) ≙ SI_DIMENSION(0,exp_d,0,0,0,0,0)
  // time quantity
  T_DIM (exp_d ∈ ℤ) ≙ SI_DIMENSION(0,0,exp_d,0,0,0,0)
  ...
  DIM_MULT(dim1 ∈ SI_DIMENSION_Type, dim2 ∈ SI_DIMENSION_Type) ≙
    SI_DIMENSION(..., exp_di(dim1)+exp_di(dim2)), ...)

  DIM_DIV(dim1 ∈ SI_DIMENSION_Type, dim2 ∈ SI_DIMENSION_Type) ≙
    SI_DIMENSION(..., exp_di(dim1)−exp_di(dim2)), ...)

  HAVE_SAME_EXP_DIMENSIONS(
      dim1 ∈ SI_DIMENSION_Type, dim2 ∈ SI_DIMENSION_Type) ≙
    dim1=dim2
  ...
END
```

4.3 Unit of a Quantity

The proposed approach represents a unit using a product of a **multiplier** with **dimension** shifted by an **offset**:

$$unit = multiplier \times dimension + offset$$

The **multiplier** part is used to formalise the prefix of a base unit like MILLI, CENTI, DECI, DECA, KILO, etc., and the **offset** is helpful to define a shift from a base unit in case of some units like the *degree Celsius* that is offset by 273.15 units compared to *degree Kelvin* unit.

The Event-B theory presented in the listing 1.5 formalises this unit definition by the SI_UNIT_Type datatype and its constructor SI_UNIT. This theory fragment provides also functions that allow the composition of units (e.g., $Newton = kg.m/s^2$) through operations like multiplication and division.

UNIT_MULT and UNIT_DIV functions define the multiplication and division operators for SI units : the new multiplier is the product/quotient of the two input multipliers, the new dimension is computed using DIM_MULT/DIM_DIV, a function that multiplies/divides dimensions (the resulting offset is fixed to F0 since offsets do not make sense in unit multiplication/division).

Listing 1.5. The SI theory (extract)

```
THEORY thy_si_units
DATATYPES
  SI_UNIT_Type ≙ SI_UNIT(
    multiplier ∈ FLOAT_Type,
    dimension ∈ SI_DIMENSION_Type,
    offset ∈ FLOAT_Type)
  ...
OPERATORS
  UNIT_MULT(u1 ∈ SI_UNIT_Type, u2 ∈ SI_UNIT_Type) ≙
    SI_UNIT(
      multiplier(u1) mult multiplier(u2),
      DIM_MULT(dimension(u1), dimension(u2)), F0)

  UNIT_DIV(u1 ∈ SI_UNIT_Type, u2 ∈ SI_UNIT_Type) ≙
    SI_UNIT(
      multiplier(u1) div multiplier(u2),
      DIM_DIV(dimension(u1), dimension(u2)), F0)
  ...
END
```

The value of a physical measure is generally expressed as the product of the quantity (float value) and its unit. The proposed theory formalises the physical measure by a new datatype called MEASURE_Type and its constructor MEASURE taking as input a value and its unit. The proposed theory also provides a new operator called SI_MEASURE_Type (behaving like a constructor) to allow the creation of a new measurement datatype with a specific unit t (cf. Listing 1.6).

The defined theory also provides a set of operators comparing two measurements: SI_EQ defines an equality operation for measurements $m1$ and $m2$, and others that are not detailed in this paper. As a remark, the two measurements to be compared must have the same unit. For this purpose, we have defined an operator called HAVE_THE_SAME_UNIT that checks whether two measurements have the same unit (cf. Listing 1.6). The proposed theory also redefines all essential calculation operators: SI_PLUS defines an addition operation for two measurements $m1$ and $m2$ (they must have the same unit, and the result is a new measurement with the sum of the values and the same unit), SI_MULT defines a multiplication operation for two measurements $m1$ and $m2$ (their values are multiplied and their units are combined by using the UNIT_MULT operator). The same reasoning is used to define the subtraction and the division operators.

The last generic operation defined in this theory is SI_CONVERT (cf. Listing 1.6). It establishes a conversion operation, allowing a measurement m with a specific unit to be converted into another unit u. The conversion is only valid if the source and target units have the same dimensions. The conversion itself involves a formula that transforms the value $v1$ in the source unit into $v2$ in the target unit using the formula:

$$v2 = (v1 - o1) \times \frac{(m1 \times d1)}{(m2 \times d2)} + o2$$

where $o1$ and $o2$ are offsets, and $m1$, $m2$, $d1$, and $d2$ are multipliers and dimensions involved in the conversion.

Listing 1.6. The SI theory (extract)

```
THEORY thy_si_units
DATATYPES
  ...
  MEASURE_Type ≙
    MEASURE(value ∈ FLOAT_Type, unit ∈ SI_UNIT_Type)
OPERATORS
  SI_MEASURE_Type(t ∈ SI_UNIT_Type) ≙
    {x · x ∈ MEASURE_Type ∧ unit(x) = t | x}

  HAVE_THE_SAME_UNIT(m1 ∈ MEASURE_Type, m2 ∈ MEASURE_Type) ≙
    unit(m1) = unit(m2)

  SI_EQ(m1 ∈ MEASURE_Type, m2 ∈ MEASURE_Type) ≙
    wd : HAVE_THE_SAME_UNIT(m1,m2)
    def : value(m1) eq value(m2)
  ...
  SI_PLUS(m1 ∈ MEASURE_Type, m2 ∈ MEASURE_Type) ≙
    wd : HAVE_THE_SAME_UNIT(m1,m2)
    def : MEASURE(value(m1) plus value(m2), unit(m1))
  ...
  SI_MULT(m1 ∈ MEASURE_Type, m2 ∈ MEASURE_Type) ≙
    MEASURE(value(m1) mult value(m2), UNIT_MULT(unit(m1), unit(m2)))
  ...
  SI_CONVERT(u ∈ SI_UNIT_Type, m ∈ MEASURE_Type) ≙
    wd : HAVE_SAME_EXP_DIMENSIONS(dimension(unit(m)),dimension(u))
    def : // v2 = (v1 − o1) × (m1 × d1)/(m2 × d2) + o2
END
```

As a reminder, our main goal in this article is to propose a formal approach to annotating numerical variables with measurement units and to get an automatic check of the correct use of measures when writing arithmetic expressions. The proposed theory defines and formalises Well-Definedness (WD) conditions in all proposed operations (for example, to compare two measures, they must have the same unit), and these WD expressions allow the Rodin platform to automatically generate proof obligations to check if they are correctly defined/used.

After defining the generic part of the proposed theory, we give the parts formalising the SI base units, the derived and coherent derived units, and some non-SI units in the following subsections.

4.4 SI Base Units Formalisation

Listing 1.7. The SI base unit theory

```
THEORY thy_si_base_units
OPERATORS
  METRE_UNIT ≙ SI_UNIT(F1, L_DIM(1), F0) // m
  KILO_GRAM_UNIT ≙ SI_UNIT(KILO, M_DIM(1), F0) // kg
  SECOND_UNIT ≙ SI_UNIT(F1, T_DIM(1), F0) // s
  AMPERE_UNIT ≙ SI_UNIT(F1, I_DIM(1), F0) // A
  KELVIN_UNIT ≙ SI_UNIT(F1, O_DIM(1), F0) // K
  MOLE_UNIT ≙ SI_UNIT(F1, N_DIM(1), F0) // mol
  CANDELA_UNIT ≙ SI_UNIT(F1, J_DIM(1), F0) // cd
END
```

The *thy_si_base_units* theory essentially defines the seven base SI units used to measure physical quantities in the International System of Units (SI [6]) (METRE_UNIT, KILO_GRAM_UNIT, SECOND_UNIT, etc.). Each unit is associated with a physical dimension (such as length L_DIM(1), mass M_DIM(1), time T_DIM(1), etc.) and is defined using the SI_UNIT constructor with one as a scaling factor (except *kg* unit that uses KILO as a scaling factor) and a base dimension with a power equals to one (cf. Listing 1.7).

Listing 1.8. The length unit theory (extract)

```
THEORY thy_length_units
OPERATORS
  MILLI_METRE_UNIT ≙ SI_UNIT(MILLI, L_DIM(1), F0) // mm
  CENTI_METRE_UNIT ≙ SI_UNIT(CENTI, L_DIM(1), F0) //cm
  DECI_METRE_UNIT ≙ SI_UNIT(DECI, L_DIM(1), F0) //dm
  DECA_METRE_UNIT ≙ SI_UNIT(DECA, L_DIM(1), F0) //dam
  HECTO_METRE_UNIT ≙ SI_UNIT(HECTO, L_DIM(1), F0) //hm
  KILO_METRE_UNIT ≙ SI_UNIT(KILO, L_DIM(1), F0) //km
  ...
END
```

Each SI base unit can be used to define a formal model expressing different units of a physical quantity. For example, the *thy_si_base_units* theory can be extended to define length units within the SI system. Thus, the *thy_length_units* theory defines various units related to the length dimension (cf. Listing 1.8). For example, this theory contains definitions of multiples and submultiples of the METRE_UNIT. For example, the MILLI_METRE_UNIT represents the millimetre (mm). It uses the MILLI coefficient (which represents 10^{-3}), indicating that 1 millimetre is 10^{-3} of a meter. The other multiples and submultiples are defined by following the same template.

4.5 SI Derived Units Formalisation

Derived units are defined as products of powers of the base units (dimensions). When the numerical factor of this product is one, the derived units are called coherent derived units. The word *coherent* here means that equations between the numerical values of quantities take the same form as the equations between the quantities themselves. Some coherent derived units in the SI are given special names (twenty-two units like *radian*, *hertz*, *coulomb*, *degreeCelsius*, etc.). Together with the seven base units, they form the core of the SI units [6].

Listing 1.9. The SI named derived unit theory (extract)

```
THEORY thy_si_named_derived_units
OPERATORS
  HERTZ_UNIT ≙ UNIT_INV(SECOND_UNIT) // 1/s
  COULOMB_UNIT ≙ UNIT_MULT(SECOND_UNIT, AMPERE_UNIT) // s A
  NEWTON_UNIT ≙ // kg m / s^2
    UNIT_MULT(KILO_GRAM_UNIT,
      UNIT_DIV(METRE_UNIT, UNIT_MULT(SECOND_UNIT,SECOND_UNIT)))
  ...
END
```

The *thy_si_named_derived_units* theory defined in the listing 1.9 formalises the twenty-two named units by combining the seven base units. For example, the HERTZ_UNIT is the inverse of the SECOND_UNIT, the COULOMB_UNIT is obtained by multiplying the SECOND_UNIT and the AMPERE_UNIT units, while the NEWTON_UNIT is obtained by multiplying the KILO_GRAM_UNIT with the METRE_UNIT divided by the square of the SECOND_UNIT.

Listing 1.10. The SI other derived unit theory (extract)

```
THEORY thy_si_other_derived_units
OPERATORS
  SQUARE_METRE_UNIT ≙ //area m^2
    UNIT_MULT(METRE_UNIT, METRE_UNIT)
  CUBIC_METRE_UNIT ≙ // volume m^3
    UNIT_MULT(SQUARE_METRE_UNIT, METRE_UNIT)
  METRE_PER_SECOND_UNIT ≙ // speed, velocity m/s
    UNIT_DIV(METRE_UNIT, SECOND_UNIT)
  METRE_PER_SECOND_SQUARED_UNIT ≙ // acceleration m/s^2
    UNIT_DIV(METRE_UNIT, UNIT_MULT(SECOND_UNIT, SECOND_UNIT))
  ...
  COULOMB_PER_CUBIC_METRE_UNIT ≙ // electric charge density
    UNIT_DIV(COULOMB_UNIT, CUBIC_METRE_UNIT) // coulomb/m^3 = s.A/m^3
  ...
END
```

The seven base units and twenty-two units with special names may be combined to express the units of other derived physical quantities. The *thy_si_other_ derived_units* theory defined in the listing 1.10 contains some derived units definitions expressed in terms of base units like SQUARE_METRE_UNIT (area quantity) or METRE_PER_SECOND_UNIT (velocity quantity), and other derived units defined in terms of base and derived named units like COULOMB_PER_ CUBIC_METRE_UNIT to express electric charge density.

As you can see, due to the space limitations, all presented listings contain only extracts of the developed theories. The Event-B project, containing all developed theories, can be downloaded from this link[4].

---

[4] https://www.idiraitsadoune.com/recherche/modeles/eventb.theories.si-units.zip.

4.6 Non-SI Units Formalisation

As consequence of haw the SI_UNIT_Type is formalised, and the form of most used Non-SI units that accepted for use with the SI Units and that we can find in the official SI Brochure [6], it becomes possible to formalise the Non-SI unit as a SI_UNIT_Type datatype with a specific constructor called NONSI_UNIT (cf. the *thy_non_si_units* theory in the listing 1.11).

Listing 1.11. The non SI unit theory

```
THEORY thy_non_si_units
OPERATORS
  NONSI_UNIT(v ∈ FLOAT_Type, u ∈ SI_UNITE_Type) ≙
      SI_UNIT(v mult multiplier(u), dimension(u), offset(u))
  ...
  MINUTE_UNIT ≙ NONSI_UNIT(FLOAT(60), SECOND_UNIT)
  HOUR_UNIT ≙ NONSI_UNIT(FLOAT(3600), SECOND_UNIT)
  HECTARE_UNIT ≙ NONSI_UNIT(FLOAT(10000), SQUARE_METRE_UNIT)
  LITRE_UNIT ≙ NONSI_UNIT(NEW_FLOAT(1,-3), CUBIC_METRE_UNIT)
  ...
END
```

The NONSI_UNIT constructor defines the value of a non-SI unit (parameter v) in the SI base unit of the same dimension (parameter u). For example, we have defined the MINUTE_UNIT and the HOUR_UNIT in the *time* dimension, the HECTARE_UNIT in the *area* dimension, the LITRE_UNIT in the *volume* dimension, etc.

5 The Case Study

To illustrate our approach for extending the Event-B core with the floating-point numbers and SI units datatypes, we propose to model a system that continuously calculates a moving object's speed. The main objective of this example is to show some modelling and validation problems that we can face when we analyse physical phenomena. The studied system contains two functional properties: **P 1 -** the speed of the moving object is equal to the *travelled_distance* divided by the *measured_time* ($v = d/t$), and **P 2 -** the object moves when its speed is different from zero.

To formalise this system, we have used the Event-B refinement to deal separately with the problem of using small values and the problem of correctly using measurement units. The first machine m_1 (cf. Listing 1.12) formalises the **P 1** and **P 2** properties by the invariants *@inv7* and *@inv8*. Moreover, the main event called *get_speed* captures the new position of the moving object and calculates the new values of the *measured_time*, *travelled_distance*, and *speed* variables. These new values depend on the initial position stored in the *starting_time* and *starting_position* variables captured by another event that doesn't interest us in this study. This Event-B machine correctly specifies our requirements and deal with the limitations of the basic Event-B language that do not allow us to validate continuous behaviours requirements (cf. our previous work in [4]).

Listing 1.12. The Event-B model calculating the speed of a moving object

```
MACHINE m1
...
INVARIANTS
  @inv1: travelled_distance ∈ PFLOAT_Type
  @inv2: measured_time ∈ PFLOAT_Type ∧ s(measured_time) ≠ 0
  @inv3: speed ∈ PFLOAT_Type
  @inv4: starting_position ∈ PFLOAT_Type
  @inv5: starting_time ∈ PFLOAT_Type
  @inv6: div_WD(travelled_distance, measured_time)
  @inv7: speed eq travelled_distance div measured_time
  @inv8: travelled_distance gt F0 ⇒ speed gt F0
EVENTS
...
get_speed ≙
  any p t where
    @grd1: p ∈ PFLOAT_Type ∧ p gt starting_position
    @grd2: t ∈ PFLOAT_Type ∧ t gt starting_time
    @grd3: div_WD(v minus starting_position, t minus starting_time)
  then
    @act1: travelled_distance := p minus starting_position
    @act2: measured_time := t minus starting_time
    @act3: speed := (p minus starting_position) div (t minus starting_time)
  end
END
```

The second step of our modelling process is to integrate measurement units in the Event-B model by refinement. The machine m_2 refines the previous machine m_1 by annotating all its variables with a SI measure unit (cf. listing 1.13). This refinement introduces a more concrete representation of physical quantities—distance, time, and speed—using the `SI_MEASURE_Type` constructor. The invariants associate specific variables (*si_td*, *si_mt*, *si_s*, etc.) with their respective SI unit types (*meters*, *seconds*, *meters/second*), ensuring consistency of physical measurements throughout the system. For each concrete variable (*si_td*, *si_mt*, *si_s*, etc.), a glueing invariant guarantees that its value is the same as its abstract one used in the first machine m_1.

Additionally, the `get_speed` event encapsulates the logic to compute speed as the quotient of traveled distance and measured time, while carefully handling unit operations using typed expressions like `SI_MINUS` and `SI_DIV`. This Event-B machine generates PO to be checked, guaranteeing that the two operands of the `SI_MINUS` operator have the same unit and the unit of the speed (`METRE_PER_SECOND_UNIT`) is coherent with the unit obtained after dividing the traveled distance (`METRE_UNIT`) by the measured time (`SECOND_UNIT`). Regarding the complexity of the proof, the integration of the units of measurement theory did not increase the complexity of the proof process since all generated PO uses comparison operators to assure the correct use of the units declared in the model, unlike the floating point numbers theory that generates more complex PO (cf. [4]).

Listing 1.13. The Event-B refinement calculating the speed of a moving object

```
MACHINE m2 REFINES m1
...
INVARIANTS
  @inv1: si_td ∈ SI_MEASURE_Type(METRE_UNIT) ∧
           value(si_td) = travelled_distance
  @inv2: si_mt ∈ SI_MEASURE_Type(SECOND_UNIT) ∧
           value(si_mt) = measured_time
  @inv3: si_s ∈ SI_MEASURE_Type(METRE_PER_SECOND_UNIT) ∧
           value(si_s) = speed
  @inv4: si_sp ∈ SI_MEASURE_Type(METRE_UNIT) ∧
           value(si_sp) = starting_position
  @inv5: si_st ∈ SI_MEASURE_Type(SECOND_UNIT) ∧
           value(si_st) = starting_time
EVENTS
...
get_speed ≙
  any si_p si_t where
    @grd1: si_p ∈ SI_MEASURE_Type(METRE_UNIT) ∧ ...
    @grd2: si_t ∈ SI_MEASURE_Type(SECOND_UNIT) ∧ ...
    ...
  then
    @act1: si_td := si_p SI_MINUS si_sp
    @act2: si_mt := si_t SI_MINUS si_st
    @act3: si_s := (si_p SI_MINUS si_sp) SI_DIV (si_t SI_MINUS si_st)
  end
END
```

6 Conclusion and Future Work

In this article, we have proposed an approach using the Theory plugin to extend the Event-B type-checking system with the possibility of standard units of measurement defined by the International System of Units (SI). We have defined a generic theory to offer the possibility to define all measurement units (the seven base units, the named or not derived units, etc.) and to provide an adapted set of all arithmetic operators to have the possibility to check expressions typed with measurement units.

Providing a floating-point number and SI measurement units theories will be helpful in modelling cyber-physical systems, and these works will be integrated into our framework [5] for generating the Event-B model from ontologies that can define concepts in the context of hybrid systems.

References

1. Abrial, J.R.: Modeling in event-B: system and software engineering. Cambridge Uni. Press (2010). https://doi.org/10.1017/CBO9781139195881
2. Abrial, J., Butler, M.J., Hallerstede, S., Hoang, T.S., Mehta, F., Voisin, L.: Rodin: an open toolset for modelling and reasoning in Event-B. Int. J. Softw. Tools Technol. Transf. **12**(6) (2010). https://doi.org/10.1007/s10009-010-0145-y
3. Aït-Ameur, Y., Laleau, R., Méry, D., Singh, N.K.: Towards leveraging domain knowledge in state-based formal methods. In: Logic, Computation and Rigorous Methods. LNCS, vol. 12750 (2021). https://doi.org/10.1007/978-3-030-76020-5_1

4. Aït-Sadoune, I.: A floating-point numbers theory for Event-B. In: Model and Data Engineering - 12th International Conference, MEDI 2023. LNCS, vol. 14396. https://doi.org/10.1007/978-3-031-49333-1_3
5. Aït-Sadoune, I., Mohand-Oussaïd, L.: Building formal semantic domain model: an Event-B based approach. In: Model and Data Engineering - 9th International Conference, MEDI 2019. LNCS, vol. 11815. https://doi.org/10.1007/978-3-030-32065-2_10
6. The international bureau of weights and measures (BIPM): The international system of units (SI). 9th edition. https://www.bipm.org/en/publications/si-brochure. Paris, France (2024)
7. Butler, M., et al.: The first twenty-five years of industrial use of the B-method. In: ter Beek, M.H., Ničković, D. (eds.) FMICS 2020. LNCS, vol. 12327, pp. 189–209. Springer, Cham (2020). https://doi.org/10.1007/978-3-030-58298-2_8
8. Butler, M., Maamria, I.: Practical theory extension in event-B. In: Liu, Z., Woodcock, J., Zhu, H. (eds.) Theories of Programming and Formal Methods. LNCS, vol. 8051, pp. 67–81. Springer, Heidelberg (2013). https://doi.org/10.1007/978-3-642-39698-4_5
9. Cooper, J., McKeever, S.: A model-driven approach to automatic conversion of physical units. Softw. Pract. Exp. **38**(4) (2008). https://doi.org/10.1002/SPE.828
10. Dijkstra, E.W.: A Discipline of Programming. Prentice-Hall (1976)
11. Foster, S., Wolff, B.: Automated reasoning for physical quantities, units, and measurements in Isabelle/HOL. In: 27th International Conference on Engineering of Complex Computer Systems, ICECCS (2023). https://doi.org/10.1109/ICECCS59891.2023.00025
12. Gibson, J.P., Méry, D.: Explicit modelling of physical measures: from Event-B to Java. In: Joint Workshop IMPEX/FM&MDD 2017. EPTCS, vol. 271. https://doi.org/10.4204/EPTCS.271.5
13. Hayes, I.J., Mahony, B.P.: Using units of measurement in formal specifications. Formal Aspects Comput. **7**(3), 329–347 (1995). https://doi.org/10.1007/BF01211077
14. Hoare, C.A.R.: An axiomatic basis for computer programming. Commun. ACM **12**(10) (1969). https://doi.org/10.1145/363235.363259
15. Krings, S., Leuschel, M.: Inferring physical units in B models. In: Software Engineering and Formal Methods - 11th International Conference, SEFM 2013. LNCS. https://doi.org/10.1007/978-3-642-40561-7_10

Reversibility-Aware Step Graphs for State Space Reduction and Reversibility Checking in Concurrent Systems

Hao Dou[1], Mengchu Zhou[1](✉), Shouguang Wang[2](✉), Dan You[2], and Wenli Duo[3]

[1] Macao Institute of Systems Engineering and Collaborative Laboratory for Intelligent Science and Systems, Macau University of Science and Technology, Macao 999078, China
haodou1@foxmail.com, zhou@njit.edu

[2] School of Information and Electronic Engineering, Zhejiang Gongshang University, Hangzhou 310018, China
{wangshouguang,youdan}@zjgsu.edu.cn

[3] School of Statistics and Mathematics, Zhejiang Gongshang University, Hangzhou 310018, China
duowenli@foxmail.com

http://www.springer.com/gp/computer-science/lncs

Abstract. Reversibility is a critical property of concurrent systems, reflecting their ability to return to the initial state without external intervention. Petri nets (PN) are widely used to model such systems, as they effectively capture complex interleavings and asynchronous behaviors. Traditional approaches to reversibility checking typically rely on constructing the reachability graph (RG) of a PN, which often encounters state-space explosion. Although partial order methods have been proposed to mitigate this issue by eliminating redundant interleavings, few are tailored to reversibility analysis. In this work, we propose a novel approach based on the notion of sound steps and introduce a definition called reversibility-aware score. Each transition is annotated with a reversibility-aware score indicating the likelihood of returning to the initial marking after its firing. At a given marking, transitions with the highest scores in a maximal sound step are grouped and fired simultaneously, resulting in a new marking. This procedure is conducted iteratively until no new markings are generated, producing a reversibility-aware step graph (RASG). We formally prove that RASG preserves the presence of deadlocks and enables efficient reversibility checking.

Keywords: Concurrent systems · Petri nets · Reachability graphs · Partial order methods · Reversibility

B. Ben Hedia et al. (Eds.): VECoS 2025, LNCS 16263, pp. 129–142, 2026.
https://doi.org/10.1007/978-3-032-20440-0_9

1 Introduction

Concurrent systems [1,2] are composed of multiple components operating independently yet interacting through shared resources or synchronization events. Such systems are common in engineering domains [3], including automated manufacturing systems and network protocols [4,5]. The inherent complexity of such systems, arising from nondeterminism, concurrency, and synchronization, requires rigorous analysis to ensure their desired behavioral properties [6]. Among these, reversibility, the ability of a system to return to its initial configuration without external intervention, is crucial for enhancing fault recovery, reducing energy consumption, and improving system robustness [7–10]. Hence, a reversible system is required in most engineering applications.

Petri nets (PN) [11] are widely used for modeling concurrent systems due to their ability to capture asynchronous and nondeterministic behaviors. Reversibility checking in PN typically involves constructing their reachability graphs (RG). However, the number of markings in RG grows exponentially with the size of PN and its initial marking, a phenomenon known as the state-space explosion, which greatly limiting the applicability of this approach to large systems.

To address this challenge, researchers have developed state-space reduction techniques such as abstraction [12], symbolic representation [13], and partial order methods [14–19]. Among them, partial order techniques are particularly effective in reducing redundant interleavings while preserving key behavioral properties. For instance, methods like covering step graphs (CSG) [19] and maximal good step graphs (MGSG) [20–22] have been proposed to preserve the liveness and the presence of deadlocks of a PN. Other methods, like hybrid persistent step graphs (PSG) [23] and weak-persistent step graphs (WPSG) [24], are proven to preserve the presence of deadlocks. However, these approaches are not specifically designed to preserve reversibility.

Reversibility plays a crucial role in manufacturing systems and healthcare workflows, where it is essential to determine whether a system can return to a safe or initial configuration after a sequence of actions. However, existing partial order methods have not addressed the question of reversibility preservation during state-space reduction. This leads to a critical research gap: Can we reduce the state space of a PN while preserving its reversibility?

To answer this important question, we propose a novel approach called reversibility-aware step graphs (RASG). Our method introduces a mechanism for selecting steps based on their contribution to reversibility. Specifically, we adopt the definition of sound steps and propose a new concept of reversibility-aware score. Each transition is annotated with a reversibility-aware score, representing the likelihood that firing this transition will eventually lead the system back to the initial marking. At each marking, transitions in a maximal sound step with the highest scores are grouped and fired together. This process continues iteratively to build a compact and reversibility-aware graph. The main contribution of this paper are as follows:

1) We introduce the concept of reversibility-aware transitions and propose a formal criterion for selecting transitions to be fired together, forming a step that is aware of reversibility. An algorithm is developed for the step construction, and its computational complexity is analyzed; and
2) We design a procedure to generate RASG of a PN. Besides, we formally prove that RASG preserves the presence of deadlocks and enables efficient reversibility checking for PN.

2 Preliminaries

Let A be an alphabet. The sets of strings over A are denoted by A^* and A^+, where $A^* = A^+ \cup \{\epsilon\}$ and ϵ represents the empty string. In addition, $\mathbb{N}$ and $\mathbb{N}^+$ represent the sets of non-negative and positive integers, separately. These notations are used throughout the paper.

A labeled directed graph is a triple $G = (V, E, L)$, where V is a finite set of nodes, $E \subseteq V \times V$ is a set of directed edges (arcs), and $L : E \to A$ is a labeling function that assigns a symbol from an alphabet A to each arc. A general PN is a 4-tuple $N = (P, T, F, W)$, which can be considered as a labeled directed graph. P and T represent the set of nodes, where P is a place set and T denotes a transition set. $F \subseteq (P \times T) \cup (T \times P)$ is the set of arcs connecting places to transitions and transitions to places. Additionally, $W : (P \times T) \cup (T \times P) \to \mathbb{N}$ is a weight function that assigns a non-negative integer to an arc. If $W(t, p) = W(p, t) = 1$ holds for all arcs, PN is called an ordinary one and we denote it as $N = (P, T, F)$. For a transition $t \in T$, its preset and postset are denoted as ${}^\bullet t = \{p \in P | (p, t) \in F\}$ and $t^\bullet = \{p \in P | (t, p) \in F\}$, respectively. For a place $p \in P$, the preset and postset are similarly defined as ${}^\bullet p = \{t \in T | (t, p) \in F\}$ and $p^\bullet = \{t \in T | (p, t) \in F\}$, separatively.

A marking $M : P \to \mathbb{N}$ assigns a number of non-negative number of tokens to each place. The number of tokens in a place $p \in P$ is denoted by $M(p)$. Besides, we always use $\sum_{p \in P} M(p)p$ to denote the vector M. A PN with an initial marking M_0 is called a marked net or a net system, which is denoted by (N, M_0). The set of reachable markings from M_0 is denoted as $R(N, M_0)$. A transition $t \in T$ is enabled at a marking M, denoted by $M[t\rangle$, if $\forall p \in {}^\bullet t$, $M(p) > W(p, t)$. The set of enabled transitions at M is denoted as $E(M) = \{\forall t \in T | M[t\rangle\}$. The firing of an enabled transition t yields a new marking M', denoted by $M[t\rangle M'$, if $\forall p \in P$, $M'(p) = M(p) - W(p, t) + W(t, p)$.

Let $\sigma = t_1 t_2 \ldots t_n$ be a sequence of transitions, where $n \in \mathbb{N}^+$. A marking M'' is reachable from M by the firing of σ, denoted by $M[\sigma\rangle M''$, if $\exists M_1, M_2, \ldots, M_n \in R(N, M_0)$ such that $M[t_0\rangle M_1 \wedge M_1[t_1\rangle M_2 \wedge \cdots \wedge M_n[t_n\rangle M''$. The Parikh vector of a sequence σ is a function $\overrightarrow{\sigma} : T \to \mathbb{N}$, where $\overrightarrow{\sigma}(t)$ denotes the number of occurrences of t in σ. Two sequences $\sigma_1, \sigma_2 \in T^*$ are equivalent, denoted as $\sigma_1 \equiv \sigma_2$, if their Parikh vectors are the same, i.e., $\overrightarrow{\sigma_1} = \overrightarrow{\sigma_2}$. Two transitions $t, t' \in T$ are independent under a marking M, denoted by $t \wr t'$, if they are both enabled at M, and the firing order does not affect the resulting marking. Formally, $\forall M', M'' \in R(N, M)$, $M[t\rangle M'$, $M[t'\rangle M'' \Rightarrow \exists M''' \in R(N, M)$,

$M'[t'\rangle M''' \wedge M''[t\rangle M'''$. A set of transitions $\tau \subseteq T$ is called an enabled step at M if: 1) $\forall p \in \bigcup_{t\in\tau} {}^{\bullet}t$, $M(p) \geq \Sigma_{\forall t\in\tau} W(p,t)$, and 2) $\forall t, t' \in \tau$, $t \wr t'$. The set of transitions included in a sequence σ is denoted by $||\sigma||$.

Given a PN (N, M_0), it is bounded if there exists a constant $k \in \{1, 2, \dots, n\}$ such that $\forall M \in R(N, M_0)$, $\forall p \in P$, $M(p) \leq k$ holds. A transition $t \in T$ is live if $\forall M \in R(N, M_0)$, $\exists M' \in R(N, M)$, $M'[t\rangle$. A PN (N, M_0) is live if each transition $t \in T$ is live. It is dead if $\forall t \in T$, $\exists M \in R(N, M_0)$, $\neg M[t\rangle$. A marking $M \in R(N, M_0)$ is called a home marking if $\forall M' \in R(N, M)$, we have $M \in R(N, M')$. If M_0 is a home marking, the net system (N, M_0) is reversible.

In this paper, we focus on bounded and ordinary PN. For more information of PN, kindly consult the reference [25].

3 Generation of Reversibility-Aware Step Graphs

Given a PN (N, M_0), its RG is constructed by iteratively firing all enabled transitions at each reachable marking. Each firing leads to a new marking, and the process continues until no new marking is produced. The resulting RG can be viewed as a labeled directed graph $\Omega_R = (\mathbb{M}_R, \mathbb{E}_R, \mathbb{L}_R, M_0)$, where $\mathbb{M}_R = R(N, M_0)$ denotes the set of nodes corresponding to reachable markings, $\mathbb{E}_R \subseteq \mathbb{M}_R \times \mathbb{M}_R$ represents the set of arcs connecting pairs of markings, and $\mathbb{L}_R : \mathbb{E}_R \to T$ assigns a transition to each arc.

Since the size of RG may grow exponentially with the size of the net and the initial marking, this leads to the well-known state-space explosion problem. To alleviate this issue, various partial order techniques have been proposed, including CSG, PSG, WPSG, and MGSG. Among them, MGSG has demonstrated the most effective state-space reduction [20–22]. However, MGSG cannot be applied to verify the reversibility of a PN. To overcome this limitation, we introduce a new partial order technique designed to preserve reversibility while reducing the state space as much as possible.

The remainder of this section is organized as follows. We first recall the definition of sound steps, and then introduce a new concept called reversibility-aware scores, which are used in conjunction with sound steps to determine which transitions should be fired at a given marking to maintain reversibility. Based on this idea, Algorithm 1 is developed to compute reversibility-aware steps. We then further present Algorithm 2 to construct RASG of a PN. Theoretical results in Theorems 1–3 show that RASG preserves the presence of deadlocks and supports reversibility checking. A simple example is provided to illustrate the applicability of the proposed method.

Definition 1 *[20] Given a PN (N, M_0), let M be a reachable marking and τ an enabled step at M. A transition $t \in \tau$ is* **sound** *at M w.r.t. τ if for any other transition $t' \in \tau \backslash \{t\}$, the following conditions hold:*

1) $\forall \sigma \in (T\backslash\{t\})^+$, $M[t'\sigma\rangle \wedge \neg M[t'\sigma t\rangle \Rightarrow$

1.1) $\exists \sigma' \in (T\backslash\{t\})^+, M[\sigma'\rangle \wedge M[t'\sigma\sigma' t\rangle$, *or*

1.2) $\exists t_1 \in E(M)\backslash\tau$, $\exists \sigma_1 \in (T\backslash\{t\})^*, (t_1\sigma_1 \equiv \sigma) \wedge M[t_1 t'\sigma_1\rangle$;

2) $\forall \sigma \in (T\backslash\{t\})^+, M[t'\sigma t\rangle \Rightarrow \exists \delta \in (T\backslash\{t\})^+, (\delta \equiv \sigma) \wedge M[tt'\delta\rangle$.

The step τ is sound at M if all transitions in it are sound at M w.r.t. τ.

Roughly speaking, a transition is sound if, no matter how it interacts with the other transitions in τ, it will not be permanently disabled. Specifically, Condition 1 implies that if firing t' followed by a sequence σ disables t at M, then at least one of the following must hold:

1) Condition 1.1: There exists a sequence σ' enabled at M such that firing σ' after $t'\sigma$ at M can re-enable t.
2) Condition 1.2: To avoid the situation where t is disabled by $t'\sigma$, we can omit the sequence $t'\sigma$ and instead consider its equivalent sequence that starts with another enabled transition t_1 outside of τ. In this case, the information contained in $t'\sigma$ can be preserved and extended through its equivalent sequence $t_1t'\sigma_1$, where $t_1 \in E(M)\backslash\tau$.

Condition 2 enforces that if firing $t'\sigma$ does not disable t, then the firing of t must also not disable $t'\delta$ where $\delta \equiv \sigma$. Note that a sound step τ is said to be maximal at a marking M if there exists no other sound step τ' such that τ is a subset of τ' and τ' is also sound at M.

While firing the maximal sound step at each marking can significantly reduce the state space, this strategy may compromise the reversibilty of a PN. Specifically, a transition that individually enables a path back to the initial marking may lose this ability when executed together with other transitions as a step. In such cases, the system's ability to return to the initial state can no longer be guaranteed. To address this issue, we propose a mechanism called reversibility-aware score, which quantifies the contribution of each transition to the system's reversibility. This concept is used to guide the construction of steps at each marking, ensuring that reversibility is preserved during state-space reduction.

Definition 2 *Given a PN (N, M_0), let M be a reachable marking and t an enabled transition at M. Firing t at M yields a marking $M' \in R(N, M_0)$, i.e., $M[t\rangle M'$. We define the* ***reversibility-aware score*** *of a transition t, denoted by $\rho(t) \in [0, 1]$, to quantify the similarity between the generated marking M' and the initial marking M_0. The score $\rho(t)$ indicates the extent to which firing t at M contributes to reaching M_0:*

$$\rho(t) = \frac{\sum_{p \in ({}^\bullet t \cup t^\bullet)} \Big(1 - \Delta\big(M'(p), M_0(p)\big)\Big)}{|{}^\bullet t \cup t^\bullet|},$$

where the indicator function $\Delta(\cdot, \cdot)$ is given by

$$\Delta\big(M'(p), M_0(p)\big) = \begin{cases} 0, & \text{if } M'(p) = M_0(p), \\ 1, & \text{if } M'(p) \neq M_0(p). \end{cases}$$

Intuitively, the value of $\rho(t)$ lies between 0 and 1 (inclusive). We refer to a transition t with its reversibility-aware score $\rho(t)$ as a **reversbility-aware transition**, denoted by $t^{(\rho(t))}$. In Definition 2, the indicator function

$\Delta(M'(p), M_0(p)) \in \{0,1\}$ returns a binary outcome. If $M'(p) = M_0(p)$, then $\Delta = 0$, indicating that the token count of p is consistent with the initial marking. Otherwise, $\Delta = 1$, meaning that the token count of p deviates from the initial marking. Hence, the term $1 - \Delta\big(M'(p), M_0(p)\big)$ evaluates to 1 if p remains unchanged compared to M_0, and 0 otherwise. $|{}^\bullet t \cup t^\bullet|$ represents the number of places directly connected to transition t. Overall, $\rho(t)$ measures the fraction of those places whose token counts remain consistent with the initial marking after firing t.

For instance, consider a PN (N_2, M_0) shown in Fig. 1(a) with $M_0 = p_1 + p_2 + p_3$. Its RG is shown in Fig. 1(b). At a marking $M_4 = p_1 + p_3 + p_4$, two transitions t_1 and t_4 are enabled. Firing t_1 yields $M_5 = p_2 + p_3 + p_4$. We can compute $\rho(t_1)$ as

$$\rho(t_1) = \frac{(1-\Delta(M_5(p_1),M_0(p_1)))+(1-\Delta(M_5(p_2),M_0(p_2)))}{|\{p_1,p_2\}|} = \frac{(1-1)+(1-0)}{2} = 0.5.$$

Therefore, the reversibility-aware score of t_1 at M_4 is 0.5. t_1 is denoted as $t_1^{(0.5)}$, called a reversbility-aware transition. Firing t_4 at M_4 can lead directly to M_0 since both p_2 and p_4 return to their initial token counts. We compute $\rho(t_4)$ as

$$\rho(t_4) = \frac{(1-(M_5(p_4),M_0(p_4)))+(1-(M_5(p_2),M_0(p_2)))}{|\{p_2,p_4\}|} = \frac{(1-0)+(1-0)}{2} = 1.$$

Hence, t_4 is denoted as $t_4^{(1)}$, indicating a maximal contribution to reaching the initial marking.

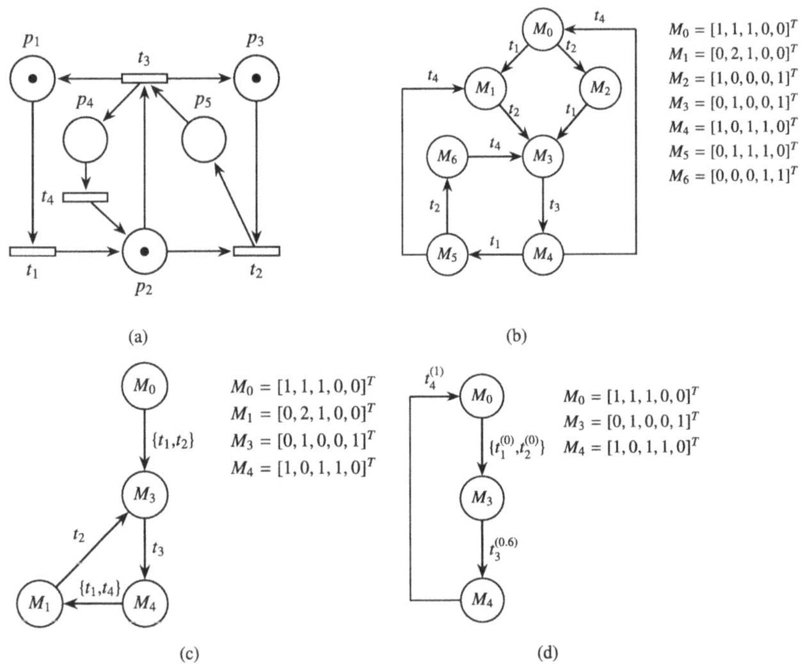

Fig. 1. (a) A PN (N_1, M_0), its (b) RG, (c) MGSG, and (d) RASG.

We use $\rho(t)$ to evaluate, at the current marking M, how advantageous firing t is for returning to the initial marking M_0. A higher value of $\rho(t)$ signifies greater progress toward moving back to M_0 from M. The reversibility-aware score is applied together with sound steps to maintain the reversibility of a PN. Given a maximal sound step τ at M, we compare the reversibility-aware scores of all transitions in τ, and those with the highest scores are fired simultaneously as a reversibility-aware step. Note that firing only the highest-scoring transition at each marking, without enforcing the soundness constraint, could permanently disable some enabled transitions that are necessary for the sequence leading back to M_0. By combining with sound steps, as defined in Definition 1, we guarantee that transitions in τ do not permanently disable each other (Condition 2). In addition, if a sequence starting with one transition in τ appears to disable another, such a sequence can be restored either by reordering or by using its equivalent sequence (Condition 1). Consequently, selecting the subset of transitions with the highest scores within τ does not eliminate any sequences returning to M_0 that were already preserved by τ.

Algorithm 1: Computing Reversibility-Aware Steps.

Input: A PN (N, M_0), marking M, and a maximal sound step τ at M.
Output: A reversibility-aware step at M.

1 Let $\pi = \emptyset$;
2 **for** $\forall t \in \tau$ **do**
3   Compute ${}^\bullet t$ and $t^\bullet$;
4   Compute the reachable marking M' with $M[t\rangle M'$;
5   Compute $\rho(t)$ by Definition 2;
6   Denote t as $t^{(\rho(t))}$;
7     $\pi = \pi \cup \{t^{(\rho(t))}\}$;
8 $\rho_{max} = max_{t \in \tau}\rho(t)$;/*Compute the maximal value among transitions in τ*/
9 **if** $\forall t \in \tau, \rho(t) = \rho_{max}$ **then**
10   π is fired at M;
11 **else**
12     $\pi = \{t \in \pi | \rho(t) = \rho_{max}\}$;
13   π is fired at M;
14 **Return** π;

The procedure for generating a reversibility-aware step at the current marking is detailed in Algorithm 1. Given a PN (N, M_0) and a marking M, it is assumed that a maximal sound step τ at M has already been computed. For each transition t in τ, its reversibility-aware score is calculated according to Definition 2 (Steps 2–7). Once the scores for all transitions in τ are computed, the highest score is identified (Step 8). If all transitions in τ have identical scores, the entire step is fired (Steps 9–10). Otherwise, transitions with the highest score are fired simultaneously as a step (Steps 11–13). The primary computational effort lies in the loop over all transitions inτ, where each transition's preset and postset must be accessed. Let $|\tau|$ represent the number of transitions in a max-

Algorithm 2: RASG Generation of a PN (N, M_0)

```
Input: A PN (N, M_0)
Output: An RASG Ω = (𝕄, 𝔼, 𝕃, M_0)
Obtain an initial marking M_0 and draw a root node v_0 corresponding to M_0;
Ψ ← (v_0); /*Nodes are stored in Ψ.*/
Θ ← {M_0}; /*Nodes correspond to markings in Θ.*/
Γ ← ∅; /*Arcs of RASG are stored in Γ.*/
Π ← ∅; /*Steps that label arcs are stored in Π.*/
while Ψ ≠ () do
    v ← pop(Ψ); /*Choose the last node v from Ψ.*/
    M_v is a marking corresponding to the node v;
    if E(M_v) ≠ ∅ then
        Compute the set MSS(M_v) of maximal sound steps under M_v /*Refer
          to [20].*/;
        if MSS(M_v) ≠ ∅ then
            for ∀τ ∈ MSS(M_v) do
                Compute the reversibility-aware step π ⊆ τ by Algorithm 1;
                Π = Π ∪ {π};
        else
            for ∀t ∈ E(M) do
                Compute ρ(t) by Definition 1 and denote t as t^(ρ(t));
                Π = Π ∪ {t^(ρ(t))};
        for each π ∈ Π do
            Compute the marking M_w reached from M_v, where M_v[ξ⟩M_w;
            if M_w ∉ Θ then
                Create a node w;
                Γ ← Γ ∪ {(v, w)};
                Label (v, w) by π;
                M_w is a marking corresponding to the node w;
                Θ ← Θ ∪ {M_w};
                Ψ ← push(Ψ, w); /*Add w into Ψ as the last node.*/
            else
                Obtain the node w of M_w;
                Γ ← Γ ∪ {(v, w)};
                Label (v, w) by π;
𝔼 ← Γ;
𝕃 ← Π;
Output: Ω = (𝕄, 𝔼, 𝕃, M_0).
```

imal sound step τ and $|{}^{\bullet}t \cup t^{\bullet}|$ denote the number of places connected to each transition t in τ, the overall complexity of this algorithm is $O(|\tau| \cdot |{}^{\bullet}t \cup t^{\bullet}|)$. Based on this procedure, Algorithm 2 is introduced to construct a reversibility-aware step graph (RASG) for a PN. In summary, Algorithm 1 is used to compute a reversibility-aware step at each marking, and by iteratively applying this process to all yielded markings, RASG of a PN is generated.

By Algorithm 2, only the initial marking M_0 of a PN is known at first, which serves as the starting node of RASG (Step 8). We begin by computing the set of enabled transitions at M_0, then proceed to identify all maximal sound steps at this marking. If there are maximal sound steps at M_0, for each one, we compute the reversibility-aware transition for every transition it contains. Transitions with the highest scores are grouped together and fired as a reversibility-aware step from M_0 (Steps 9–14). If no maximal sound step exists at M_0, the reversibility-aware scores are computed for each enabled transition separately, and all are fired from M_0 (Steps 15–18). For each resulting step, we evaluate the marking it leads to (Steps 19–20). If the resulting marking has already been encountered, we add an arc labeled with the corresponding step from the current marking to the existing one (Steps 2831). If the resulting marking is new, then a new node is created, and a labeled arc is added from the current node to this new one. The newly generated marking is then added to the set of markings to be explored (Steps 2127). This process repeats iteratively until no new marking is generated. The complexity of this algorithm mainly depends on the number of markings in RASG. In the worst case, if no sound step exists at any marking, all enabled transitions must be explored individually at each marking. Thus, the number of markings in RASG matches that in RG, making the complexity of computing RASG is exponential in the worst case.

Example 1 For a PN (N_1, M_0) illustrated in Fig. 1(a), its MGSG and RASG are shown in Figs. 1(c) and (d), respectively. At the initial marking M_0, transitions t_1 and t_2 can be fired together as a sound step. According to Definition 2, the reversibility-aware scores are $\rho(t_1) = \rho(t_2) = 0$. By Algorithm 1, since all transitions in the sound step share the same value, the step $\{t_1^{(0)}, t_2^{(0)}\}$ is fired from M_0. At $M_4 = p_1 + p_3 + p_4$, transitions t_1 and t_4 form a sound step $\{t_1, t_4\}$. According to Definition 2, their reversibility-aware scores are $\rho(t_1) = 0.5$ and $\rho(t_4) = 1$, respectively. Applying Algorithm 1, transition t_4 has the highest score and is therefore selected and fired individually. As a result, only $t_4^{(1)}$ is executed from M_4 in RASG. According to Algorithm 2, RASG of a PN (N, M_0) is constructed as shown in Fig. 1(d). ■

Theorem 1 *[21] Firing maximal sound steps at each marking preserves the presence of deadlocks in a PN (N, M_0).*

Theorem 2 *RASG computed by Algorithm 2 preserves the presence of deadlocks in a PN (N, M_0)*

Proof According to Theorem 1, firing maximal sound steps at each marking preserves the presence of deadlocks in a PN. To construct the RASG of (N, M_0) using Algorithm 2, there are two cases to consider at each marking:

Case 1: No maximal sound step exists. According to Steps 15–18 of Algorithm 2, each enabled transition is annotated with its reversibility-aware score and fired at the current marking. It can be considered as constructing RG of (N, M_0). Thus, all markings including deadlock ones are preserved. Deadlock preservation is guaranteed in this case.

Case 2: Maximal sound steps exist. According to Steps 10–14 of Algorithm 2, transitions with the highest reversibility-aware scores are selected and fired as a step. Let τ denote a maximal sound step and $\pi \subseteq \tau$ be the subset of transitions with the highest probabilities. Two subcases arise:

(a) All transitions in τ have equal scores. In this case, the maximal sound step τ is fired at the marking. According to Theorem 1, firing maximal sound steps at each marking preserves the presence of deadlocks.
(b) Only a subset π of τ has the highest score. In this case, only π is fired at the marking. By the definition of sound steps (Definition 1), each $t \in \pi$ is sound for every $t' \in (\tau \setminus \pi)$. Suppose there exists a deadlock marking M_D reachable from the current marking M by firing the sequence $\tau\sigma$, i.e., $M[\tau\sigma\rangle M_D$. Assume, for contradiction, that M_D is not reachable from M after firing any sequence starting with π. However, since $\pi \subseteq \tau$ and all transitions in $(\tau \setminus \pi)$ are sound with respect to π, it follows that there exists an interleaving $\pi(\tau \setminus \pi)\sigma$ such that $M[\pi(\tau \setminus \pi)\sigma\rangle M_D$, contradicting the assumption.

In both cases, the presence of deadlocks is preserved. Hence, RASG constructed by Algorithm 2 preserves the deadlocks of a PN if existing. ■

Theorem 3 *Reversibility of a PN (N, M_0) can be verified by its RASG constructed by Algorithm 2.*

Proof Suppose that a PN (N, M_0) is reversible, meaning that for every reachable marking $M \in R(N, M_0)$, the initial marking M_0 is also reachable from M. We aim to show that PN's reversibility property can be verified by using its RASG generated by Algorithm 2. There are two cases:

Case 1: No maximal sound step exists at any marking. In this case, the RASG construction defaults to firing all enabled transitions annotated with their reversibility-aware scores at each marking (Steps 15–18 of Algorithm 2). Consequently, the resulting RASG is identical to RG of (N, M_0). Since RG can always be used to verify reversibility, the equivalent RASG also maintains reversibility.

Case 2: Maximal sound steps exist at some markings. In this case, the reversibility-aware score for each transition in a maximal sound step is calculated and annotated with the corresponding transition (Steps 2–7 of Algorithm 1), and the transitions with the highest scores are fired together as a step. If (N, M_0) is reversible, then $\exists \sigma, \delta \in T^*$, $\exists M, M' \in R(N, M_0)$, $\exists t \in E(M)$, such that $M_0[\sigma\rangle M \wedge M[\delta\rangle M' \wedge M'[t\rangle M_0$, where $\rho(t) = 1$ by Definition 2. Since there must exist a maximal sound step at a reachable marking according to the precondition, let M be a reachable marking under which a maximal sound step τ is fired. Suppose that RASG cannot preserve the reversibility of (N, M_0), which means that $M[\delta\rangle M' \wedge M'[t\rangle M_0$ does not hold for RASG. It is obvious that we have $M[\delta t\sigma\rangle M$, and τ is a maximal sound step at M. According to Algorithm 1, transitions with the highest scores can be fired together as a reversibility-aware step at M, denoted by π. Since reversibility-aware step is just the subset of a maximal sound step, the step π still satisfies the constraints on sound steps defined in Definition 1, i.e., $\exists \omega \in T^*$, s.t. $M[\pi\omega\rangle M$ with $\pi\omega \equiv \delta t\sigma$. Then, there are several cases shown as follows:

1) $\pi \subseteq ||\delta||$. In this case, $\exists \omega_1 \in T^*$ such that $\pi\omega_1 \equiv \delta$. Since the firing of π does not forbid the firing of the sequence $\delta t\sigma$, we have $\pi\omega_1 t\sigma \equiv \delta t\sigma \equiv \pi\omega$. Therefore, $M[\pi\omega_1\rangle M' \wedge M'[t\rangle M_0$ hold for RASG, which contradicts our assumption. Reversibility of (N, M_0) can be verified by its RASG in this case.
2) $\pi = ||\delta t||$. In this case, M_0 is obviously reached from M.
3) $||\delta t|| \subsetneq \pi \subseteq ||\delta t\sigma||$. We can divide π into π_1 and π_2 with $\pi = \pi_1 \cup \pi_2$, where $\pi_1 = ||\delta||$. Besides, $\exists \sigma_1, \sigma_2 \in T^*$ s.t. $\sigma_1\sigma_2 \equiv \sigma$, $\pi_2 = ||t\sigma_1||$, and $\pi_2\sigma_2 \equiv t\sigma_1\sigma_2 \equiv t\sigma$. Thus, we have $\pi\omega \equiv \pi_1\pi_2\sigma_2$ and $M[\pi_1\rangle M' \wedge M'[\pi_2\sigma_2\rangle M$. Since $t \in \pi_2$ and $M'[t\rangle M_0$, we can obtain $\rho(t) = 1$ at M' according to Definition 2 and $\forall t' \in \pi_2$, $\rho(t') = 1$ at M' by Algorithm 1. Then, we have $M'[\pi_2\rangle M_0$.

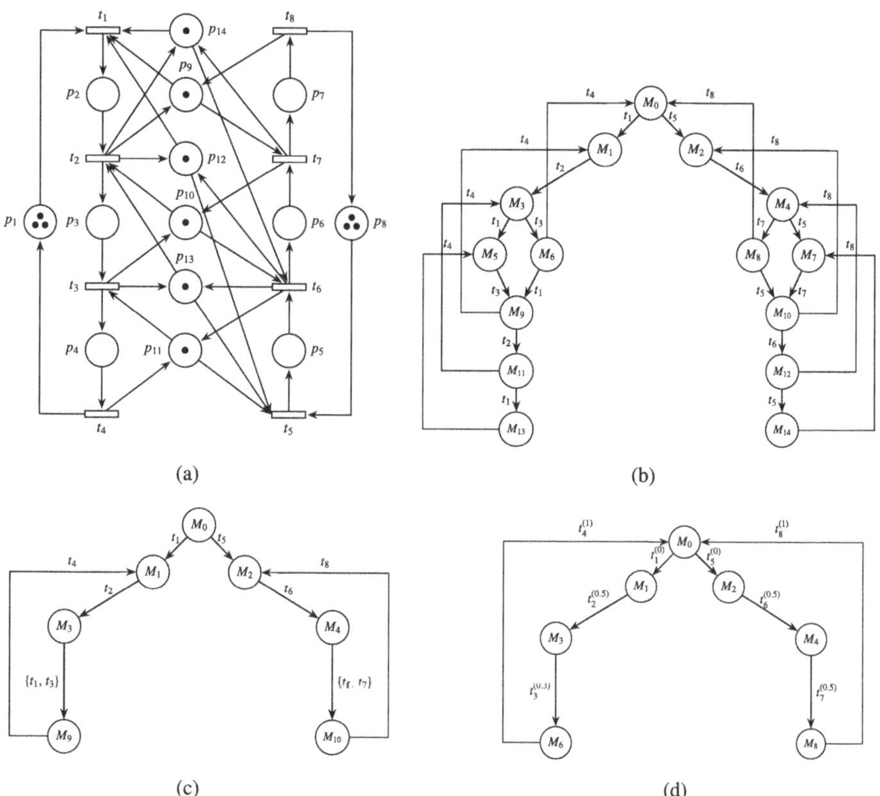

Fig. 2. (a) A PN (N_2, M_0), its (b) RG, (c) MGSG, and (d) RASG.

Thus, it is obvious that $M[\pi_1\rangle M' \wedge M'[\pi_2\rangle M_0 \Rightarrow M[\pi\rangle M_0$, which contradicts our assumption.

Overall, the initial marking of (N, M_0) can be reached in RASG, indicating that it can be used to verify the reversibility of a PN (N, M_0). ■

Example 2 The PN model (N_2, M_0) is shown in Fig. 2(a), with its corresponding RG, MGSG, and RASG depicted in Figs. 2(b)–(d), respectively. In its RG, all reachable markings can reach the initial marking M_0. However, in its MGSG, all markings M_1–M_4, M_9, and M_{10} fail to reach the initial marking, thereby preventing the verification PN reversibility based on MGSG alone.

In contrast, the proposed RASG enables reversibility checking. At markings M_3 and M_4, transitions t_3 and t_7 exhibit higher reversibility-aware scores (0.5) compared to t_1 and t_5 (0). As a result, only t_3 and t_7 are selected and fired at the corresponding markings, yielding M_6 and M_8, respectively. These markings subsequently lead back to M_0. This demonstrates that RASG successfully preserves and verifies the reversibility of (N_2, M_0).

Notably, both RASG and MGSG comprise 7 markings, significantly fewer than 15 markings in RG, highlighting the efficiency of the proposed approach in mitigating state-space explosion. ■

4 Conclusion and Future Work

This paper presents a novel reversibility-checking approach called reversibility-aware step graphs (RASG), which not only verify the reversibility of Petri nets (PN) but also address the state-space explosion problems encountered in reachability graph (RG) analysis. We first review the definition of sound steps and propose a new concept called reversibility-aware scores, which quantifies the likelihood that a transition contributes to reaching the initial marking. By integrating reversibility-aware scores with transitions in sound steps, we develop an algorithm that determines which transitions within a sound step should be fired simultaneously to preserve reversibility. Based on this mechanism, we further design an algorithm for constructing RASG of a PN. The resulting graph has been theoretically shown to preserve deadlocks and support reversibility checking.

Despite its advantages, the proposed method primarily targets reversibility preservation, which may come at the cost of state-space compression. In particular, compared to existing partial order approaches such as MGSG, RASG may include more markings since certain transitions that can be fired together in MGSG are selectively excluded in RASG to ensure reversibility. This trade-off may limit its effectiveness in scenarios where aggressive state-space reduction is critical. Furthermore, the current approach is limited to ordinary PN. In future work, we aim to extend the proposed framework to more expressive PN classes and explore the integration with other reduction techniques to enhance both of its scalability and generality.

Acknowledgment. This work was supported in part by the National Natural Science Foundation of China under Grant 62302448, and in part by the FDCT (Fundo para o Desenvolvimento das Ciencias e da Tecnologia) under Grant No. 0147/2024/AFJ.

References

1. Ben-Ari, M.: Principles of Concurrent and Distributed Programming, 2nd edn. Addison-Wesley, Boston (2006)
2. Groote, J.F., Mousavi, M.R.: Modeling and Analysis of Communicating Systems. MIT Press, Cambridge (2014)
3. Xiang, Z.Y., Chen, Y.F., Wu, N.Q., Li, Z.W.: On the existence of nonblocking bounded supervisors for discrete-event systems. IEEE Trans. Autom. Control **69**(11), 8003–8010 (2024)
4. Xiang, Z.Y., Chen, Y.F., Wu, N.Q., Li, Z.W.: Over-approximation state estimation for networked timed DES with communication delays and losses. IEEE Trans. Syst. Man Cybern. Syst. **55**(2), 1215–1229 (2025a)
5. Xiang, Z., Chen, Y., Wu, N., Li, Z.: Supervisory control of networked timed discrete event systems with bandwidth constraints. IEEE Trans. Autom. Control **70**(7), 4849–4856 (2025b)
6. Murata, T.: Petri nets: properties, analysis and applications. Proc. IEEE **77**(4), 541–580 (1989)
7. Huang, B., Zhou, M.C.: Supervisory Control and Scheduling of Resource Allocation Systems: Reachability Graph Perspective. IEEE Press/Wiley, Hoboken, NJ (2020)
8. Jiang, Z., Li, Z., Wu, N.Q., Zhou, M.C.: A petri net approach to fault diagnosis and restoration for power transmission systems to avoid the output interruption of substations. IEEE Syst. J. **12**(3), 2566–2576 (2018)
9. Zhou, M.C., Venkatesh, K.: Modeling, Simulation and Control of Flexible Manufacturing Systems: A Petri Net Approach. World Scientific, Singapore (1999)
10. Zhou, M.C., DiCesare, F.: Petri Net Synthesis for Discrete Event Control of Manufacturing Systems. Springer, New York, NY (1993)
11. Cassandras, C.G., Lafortune, S.: Introduction to Discrete Event Systems. Springer, Boston, MA, USA (2008)
12. Mover, S.: Abstraction techniques for symbolic model checking of infinite-state discrete and continuous systems. Ph.D. dissertation, Institut Polytechnique de Paris, Paris, France (2024)
13. He, L.F., Liu, G.J., Zhou, M.C.: Petri-net-based model checking for privacy-critical multiagent systems. IEEE Trans. Comput. Soc. Syst. **10**(2), 563–576 (2022)
14. Godefroid, P.: Using partial orders to improve automatic verification methods. In: Clarke, E.M., Kurshan, R.P. (eds) Computer-Aided Verification. CAV 1990. Lecture Notes in Computer Science, vol 531, pp. 176–185. Springer, Berlin, Heidelberg (1991). https://doi.org/10.1007/BFb0023731
15. Godefroid, P., Peled, D., Staskauskas, M.: Using partial-order methods in the formal validation of industrial concurrent programs. IEEE Trans. Software Eng. **22**(7), 496–507 (1996)
16. Peled, D., Wilke, T.: Stutter-invariant temporal properties are expressible without the next-time operator. Inf. Process. Lett. **63**(5), 243–246 (1997)
17. Valmari, A., Hansen, H.: Can stubborn sets be optimal? Fund. Inform. **113**(3–4), 377–397 (2011)

18. Godefroid, P., Leeuwen, J., Hartmanis, J., Goos, G., Wolper, P.: Partial-order methods for the verification of concurrent systems: an approach to the state-explosion problem. In: Lect. Notes Comput. Sci., vol. 1032. Springer, Heidelberg (1996)
19. Vernadat, F., Azema, P., Michel, F.: Covering step graph. In: Billington, J., Reisig, W. (eds.) Application and Theory of Petri Nets. ICATPN 1996. Lecture Notes in Computer Science, vol 1091, pp. 516–535. Springer, Heidelberg (1996). https://doi.org/10.1007/3-540-61363-3_28
20. Dou, H., Barkaoui, K., Boucheneb, H., Jiang, X.N., Wang, S.G.: Maximal good step graph methods for reducing the generation of the state space. IEEE Access **7**, 155805–155817 (2019)
21. Dou, H., Zhou, M.C., Wang, S.G., Albeshri, A.: An efficient liveness analysis method for petri nets via maximally-good-step graphs. IEEE Trans. Syst. Man Cybern. Syst. **54**(7), 3908–3919 (2024)
22. Dou, H., You, D., Wang, S.G., Zhou, M.C.: Designing liveness-enforcing supervisors for manufacturing systems by using maximally good step graphs of petri nets. IEEE Trans. on Autom. Sci. Eng. **22**, 7312–7323 (2024)
23. Ribet, P.O., Vernadat, F., Berthomieu, B.: On combining the persistent sets method with the covering steps graph method. In: Peled, D.A., Vardi, M.Y. (eds.) Formal Techniques for Networked and Distributed Sytems, FORTE 2002. Lecture Notes in Computer Science, vol 2529, pp. 344–359. Springer, Berlin, Heidelberg (2002). https://doi.org/10.1007/3-540-36135-9_22
24. Barkaoui, K., Boucheneb, H., Li, Z.W.: Exploiting local persistency for reduced state-space generation. Innovations Syst. Software Eng. **16**(2), 181–197 (2020)
25. Li, Z.W., Zhou, M.C.: Deadlock Resolution in Automated Manufacturing Systems: A Novel Petri Net Approach. Springer Science & Business Media, Cham (2009)

Tuning NB-IoT Power Battery Lifetime Using SPN Modeling

Mohammed Djahafi(✉) and Nabila Salmi

MOVEP Laboratory, USTHB University, Bab-Ezzouar, 16111 Algiers, Algeria
{mdjahafi,nsalmi}@usthb.dz, mohameddjahafi20@gmail.com

Abstract. Nowadays, with the rapid expansion of Internet of Things (IoT) networks, extending device battery lifetime has emerged as a paramount challenge. The 3GPP Narrowband IoT (NB-IoT) standard introduces advanced power-saving mechanisms, notably Power Saving Mode (PSM) and extended Discontinuous Reception (eDRX), designed to enhance device energy efficiency. However, achieving optimal energy savings necessitates a comprehensive evaluation of energy consumption under varying traffic conditions and configuration parameters. This paper proposes a stochastic Petri net (SPN) model to rigorously analyze the energy dynamics of NB-IoT devices, providing system designers with a robust analytical tool for performance evaluation and energy optimization. The model accurately reflects real-world device behavior by integrating Radio Resource Control (RRC) states, stochastic uplink and downlink traffic patterns, and critical 3GPP timer settings to simulate battery drain scenarios. Performance analyses conducted across diverse traffic loads and configurations of PSM intervals and eDRX cycles enable the quantification of energy consumption and the identification of optimal parameter settings to maximize battery lifetime. Validation results confirm the model's effectiveness, particularly in characterizing mean sojourn times across operational states. Ultimately, this approach empowers NB-IoT system designers to tailor configurations that balance power efficiency with performance requirements, thereby facilitating the deployment of more sustainable IoT networks. While the model provides valuable insights for device-level parameter tuning under idealized conditions, future extensions should address dynamic traffic patterns, network-level effects, and broader empirical validation to enhance real-world applicability.

Keywords: Narrow-band IoT (NB-IoT) · Power Saving Mode (PSM) · Extended Discontinuous Reception (eDRX) · Stochastic Petri Nets (SPN)

1 Introduction

The Internet of Things (IoT) [1] is transforming human life and industries by enabling billions of interconnected devices to communicate efficiently. Large and diverse sectors are targeted, ranging from precision agriculture and smart cities to healthcare, industrial automation, and environmental monitoring.

B. Ben Hedia et al. (Eds.): VECoS 2025, LNCS 16263, pp. 143–157, 2026.
https://doi.org/10.1007/978-3-032-20440-0_10

A critical requirement for most IoT devices is long-term energy autonomy, demanding uninterrupted operation over several years without manual battery replacement. This is particularly vital for devices deployed in remote or hard-to-access areas, where frequent maintenance is impractical.

Traditional cellular communication technologies, optimized for high data throughput and low latency, are inherently unsuited to the typical IoT traffic profile, which is characterized by small, infrequent data transmissions and relaxed latency constraints. To address this mismatch, the 3rd Generation Partnership Project (3GPP) [2] introduced Narrowband Internet of Things (NB-IoT) in Release 13 [3–5], as a dedicated Low Power Wide Area (LPWA) technology [6].

NB-IoT leverages existing LTE (Long Term Evolution) [7] infrastructure while incorporating innovations aimed at reducing device complexity, enhancing signal coverage, and minimizing energy consumption.

At the heart of NB-IoT's energy efficiency are two advanced power-saving mechanisms: Power Saving Mode (PSM) and Extended Discontinuous Reception (eDRX) [8]. These mechanisms allow devices to enter deep sleep states or reduce radio activity while maintaining network registration, thus significantly extending battery life. PSM enables devices to sleep for long durations and waking up only when necessary to transmit or receive data, while eDRX intelligently controls the intervals at which devices check for incoming messages, striking a trade-off between energy use and communication responsiveness.

Although these power-saving features offer substantial energy gains, configuring them optimally is non-trivial. Prolonged sleep cycles can lead to missed communications or increased latency, while frequent wake-ups may quickly deplete battery resources. Therefore, achieving an optimal balance between energy efficiency and performance is essential for effective NB-IoT deployment.

To address this need, we propose using SPN modeling and analysis to assess performance and energy consumption, enabling detection of configurations that preserve energy while maintaining adequate performance. Our SPN model captures the dynamic energy behavior and state transitions of NB-IoT devices. SPN modeling is particularly suitable due to its ability to model concurrency, synchronization, and stochastic timing, critical elements for realistically modeling NB-IoT device operation under various network conditions.

The proposed method is applicable to single NB-IoT devices operating under typical IoT scenarios with periodic or event-driven data transmission patterns, focusing on battery lifetime optimization through PSM and eDRX parameter tuning.

Using the GreatSPN tool [9], we analyze our model and assess energy consumption during different operational states through various experimental studies. The impact of configured parameters (PSM and eDRX timers) is quantified, providing invaluable insights for engineering IoT systems that meet both energy constraints and application-specific requirements.

This work focuses on device-level energy optimization under controlled traffic assumptions, we acknowledge that real-world NB-IoT deployments involve additional complexities including dynamic traffic patterns, network congestion effects, and interference conditions. The proposed model serves as a foundational analytical framework that can be extended to incorporate these network-level phenomena and validated against diverse empirical scenarios in future research.

The remaining sections of this paper are structured as follows: Sect. 2 reviews existing research on NB-IoT energy modeling. Section 3 provides foundational information on the NB-IoT standard and its associated power-saving mechanisms. Section 4 introduces the Stochastic Petri Net (SPN) formalism. Section 5 presents the proposed SPN model for NB-IoT power-saving mechanisms. Section 6 discusses the energy consumption analysis, and experimental results are presented in Sect. 7. Finally, Sect. 8 concludes the paper and outlines avenues for future research.

2 Related Work

Several studies have analyzed NB-IoT device energy consumption to evaluate battery lifetime.

García-Martín et al. [10] developed an analytical model for estimating NB-IoT UE energy consumption across various configurations. Similarly, Sultania et al. [11] presented an analytical MATLAB model for NB-IoT devices, particularly emphasizing the use of PSM and eDRX mechanisms. Notably, their model assumed Poisson-distributed uplink and downlink packet arrivals. Furthermore, Andres-Maldonado et al. [12] provided an overview and performance analysis of new small data transmission optimizations introduced in 3GPP Release 13 for NB-IoT. They based their proposal on an analytical model that extends previous work to include specific NB-IoT features.

Also, Syed et al. [13] proposed a mathematical model analyzing energy requirements of user equipment when receiving DL packets, considering various parameters like repetitions, sub-frames. Other researchers [14] explored uplink scheduling optimization in NB-IoT systems to enhance energy efficiency while ensuring reliability, delay, and resource allocation constraints.

A recent study by Tsoukaneri et al. [15] provides a comprehensive analysis of energy consumption characteristics of commercial NB-IoT devices through detailed experimental measurements. Sørensen et al. [16] proposed a power consumption model for NB-IoT and LTE-M, integrating PHY-level measurements, to improve battery lifetime estimation. Their model, validated through empirical experiments, achieves an estimation error below 5%.

Another key contribution, Jano et al. [17], introduced a Markov chain energy model tailored for 5G RedCap [18] IoT devices. Their model extends traditional NB-IoT analysis by considering 5G-specific RRC states and DRX configurations, demonstrating significant energy savings under short inter-arrival times (IAT).

Following a similar approach, Andres-Maldonado et al. [19] proposed an analytical Markov chain model to predict NB-IoT power consumption. Their model was validated through experimental measurements on commercial devices. It demonstrated a maximum estimation error of 21% in battery lifetime prediction.

Expanding on this research, Oh et al. [20] analyzed battery consumption of an NB-IoT device, specifically focusing on the impact of downlink data reception and RRC connected state duration. They developed a mathematical model to evaluate the battery consumption rate, emphasizing the time a device spends in the RRC connected state.

Furthermore, Radfar et al. [21] introduced and validated an analytical model for NB-IoT energy consumption and delay, utilizing a 6-state Markov chain to estimate the average energy consumption and latency of user equipment sending periodic uplink reports via control plane optimization. Much existing work has also focused on Discontinuous Reception (DRX) optimization for LTE systems [22–25].

Despite these studies, a significant gap remains: no stochastic model of both PSM and eDRX has been proposed, except Markov chain models, but Markov chains are known as state models, not addressing concurrency and parallelism aspects. Our paper addresses this gap by introducing a stochastic Petri net model designed to accurately optimize NB-IoT energy usage while capturing concurrent system behaviors.

3 Overview of NB-IoT Power-Saving Mechanism

Narrowband IoT is a cellular-based Low Power Wide Area Network (LPWAN) technology, standardized by the 3GPP, to enable low-cost, low-power, and long-range communication for massive IoT deployments. As part of Release 13 (2016), NB-IoT was introduced to address IoT devices unique requirements, such as extended battery life, improved coverage, and high connection density, which were not adequately supported by traditional cellular networks.

3.1 NB-IoT Power Management Overview

3GPP defines several energy-saving techniques to provide prolonged battery life in NB-IoT devices. Figure 1 illustrates the state transition diagram of NB-IoT power-saving modes.

Power Saving Mode (PSM). Power Saving Mode represents the most aggressive energy-saving technique developed by 3GPP specifically for NB-IoT devices. This technique allows devices to enter deep sleep states for configurable periods up to 310 h via the T3412 extended timer, while preserving critical network parameters, including registration [26]. During PSM, devices effectively switch off most radio and processing components, becoming temporarily unreachable by the network for downlink communications. The network buffers (cache) any downlink data packets received during these deep sleep periods, ensuring delivery upon the device's exit from the PSM cycle. Devices in PSM can waking up independently to transmit uplink (UL) data. Upon generating a UL packet, the device goes through the Paging state to request an UL grant, then to the Connected state for transmission (see Fig. 1).

Extended Discontinuous Reception (eDRX). It is also introduced in 3GPP Release 13. It enhances the traditional LTE DRX mechanism [27] by enabling significantly longer sleep cycles, particularly in the RRC Idle state, thereby optimizing the trade-off between device energy conservation and network accessibility. An eDRX cycle is structured into an *On Duration*, during which the device monitors the Narrowband Physical Downlink Control Channel (NPDCCH) for paging messages, and an *eDRX period*, where the device conserves energy by disabling channel monitoring. The T3324 timer defines device residence time in RRC Idle state before transitioning to PSM in the absence of uplink or downlink activity, with the eDRX timer dictating the frequency of paging opportunities during this phase. While applicable in both RRC Connected and Idle states, eDRX's primary benefits emerge in the RRC Idle state, where cycles can extend up to 10,485.76 s, in contrast to a maximum of 10.24 s in RRC Connected.

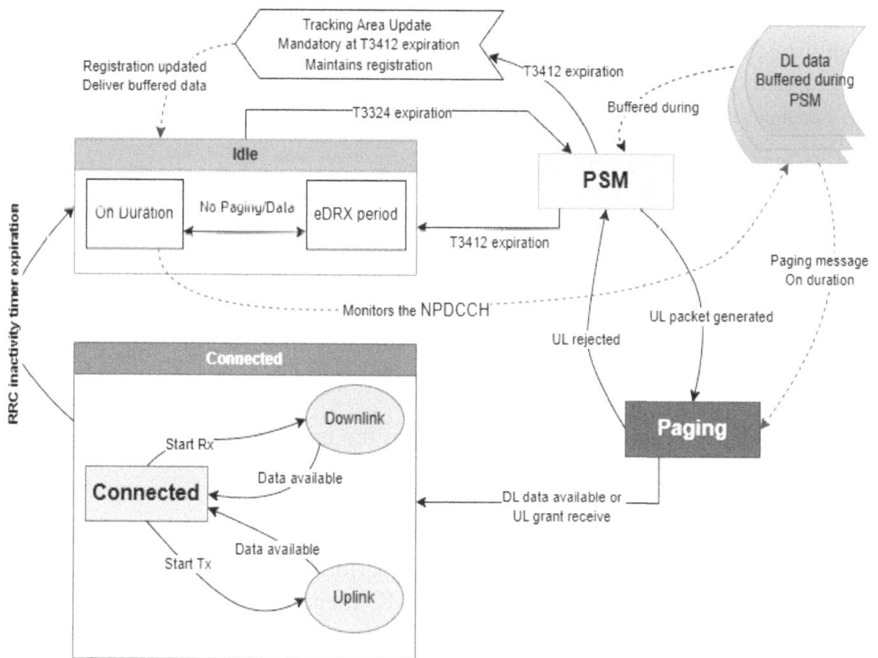

Fig. 1. State Transition Diagram of NB-IoT Power Saving Modes.

Radio Resource Control (RRC) States. In NB-IoT networks, device operation is structured around distinct RRC states, each strategically designed to manage the trade-off between energy efficiency and network responsiveness. The RRC Connected state represents the most power-intensive mode, where the device actively maintains an RRC connection with the eNodeB, continuously monitoring the NPDCCH for downlink data and uplink grants while sustaining dedicated bearers for data exchange. Upon connection release, the device moves to the RRC Idle state, periodically waking to check for paging messages with considerably reduced power consumption, as no active connection is preserved. For further energy optimization, the device may enter PSM mode, a deep sleep state where it remains registered to the network but becomes temporarily unreachable for downlink communication, minimizing power usage to the lowest possible level. State transitions management, and timing are governed by critical timers such as T3324 and T3412.

State Transitions. Efficient state transitions are crucial for optimizing NB-IoT devices functioning. Devices switch between states based on network activity and predefined timers. (See Fig. 1).

4 Stochastic Petri Net Formalism

4.1 Definition

A Stochastic Petri Net (SPN) [28] is a mathematical modeling formalism designed to represent and analyze the dynamic, concurrent, and stochastic behavior of complex systems. Extending the classical Petri net [29], SPNs associate with each transition a probabilistic timing through a random firing delay, typically governed by exponential or other probability distributions.

A Stochastic Petri Net is a tuple $N = (P, T, Pre, Post, \theta, M_0)$ defined as follows:

- ***P*** is a finite set of places.
- ***T*** is a set of timed transitions with a stochastic firing delay.
- ***Pre***: $P \times T \rightarrow \mathbb{N}$ is the input function, specifying for each arc from place p to transition t the number of tokens required to enable t.
- ***Post***: $T \times P \rightarrow \mathbb{N}$ is the output function, specifying for each arc from transition t to place p the number of tokens added to p when t fires.
- **θ**: $T \rightarrow \mathbb{R}^+$ associates a strictly positive firing rate to each transition. The firing delay of a transition t, once enabled, is a random variable following an exponential distribution with rate parameter $\theta(t)$.
- M_0: $P \rightarrow \mathbb{N}$ is the initial marking, indicating the initial number of tokens in each place.

4.2 Quantitative Performance Analysis of an SPN

Quantitative evaluation of an SPN models is performed through equivalence with continuous-time Markov chains (CTMC). CTMC numerical methods for computing performance metrics apply to SPN underlying stochastic states. SPN analysis requires:

1. First, verify essential SPN properties including liveness (no deadlocks) and boundedness (finite states). The cyclic nature of NB-IoT state transitions in our model ensures liveness, as timer-based transitions prevent permanent blocking. Deadlock detection would require model correction before steady-state analysis.
2. Generate the reachability graph of the SPN, by computing all possible markings (states).
3. Compute stationary probabilities represented by the (π) vector, by solving the following system of equations:

$$\begin{cases} \pi.\mathrm{Q} = 0 \\ \sum \pi_i = 1 \end{cases}$$

Using the stationary probability vector, several steady-state performance parameters can be computed.

5 Proposed SPN Model for NB-IoT Power Saving Mechanisms

This section presents our proposed SPN model for NB-IoT device energy management, illustrated in Fig. 2. The model maps operational characteristics of NB-IoT devices onto interconnected places and transitions, each serving specific roles in simulating realistic power-saving and data communication scenarios.

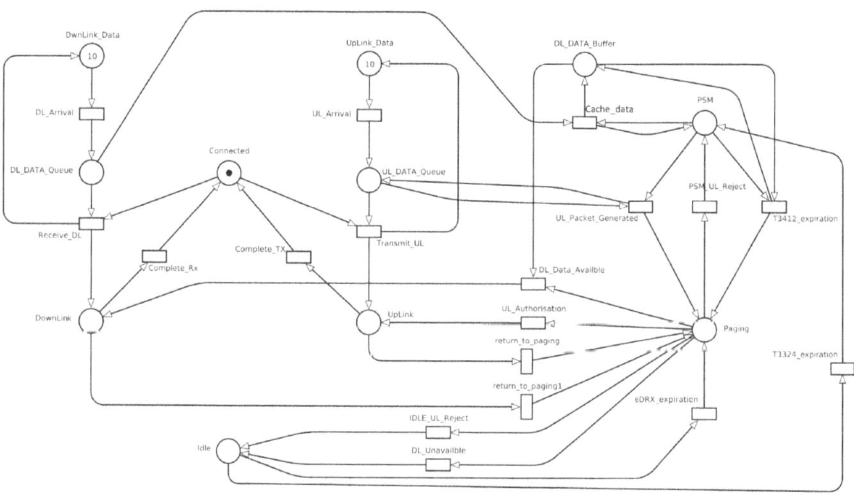

Fig. 2. Stochastic Petri Net Model for NB-IoT Power Saving Mechanisms.

Places in our model, detailed in Table 1, represent various RRC states and data buffering conditions of the NB-IoT device.

Transitions orchestrate dynamic NB-IoT device behavior, representing events enabling state transitions, data consumption/production, or network timer interactions. Each transition has specific firing rates, typically exponentially distributed, modeling event timing. Table 2 details these transitions and their functions.

The SPN model operation follows these key behavioral patterns:

- The SPN model begins with the first state of a device being in the *Connected* state, ready for active communication.
- Upon inactivity periods, detected by inactivity timers, the device moves to the Idle state to conserve energy.
- In the Idle state, the model captures eDRX cycles, where the device periodically wakes (*eDRX_expiration*) to check for paging messages. If no activity occurs within the T3324 timer's duration, the *T3324_expiration* transition fires, causing the device to enter into the deep sleep PSM state.
- When uplink packets are generated, either in PSM or Idle, the device enters the Paging state to request an uplink grant. If authorized, device moves to Connected for *Transmit_UL*; if rejected, it returns to respective power-saving mode via *PSM_UL*_Reject or *IDLE_UL_Reject*.
- Similarly, incoming downlink data (*DL_Arrival*, *DL_Data_Available*) can trigger transitions to Paging or Connected for *Receive_DL*.
- After data exchange or prolonged inactivity, the device typically returns to Idle or PSM via relevant timers to optimize battery life.

Table 1. Places in the NB-IoT SPN Model

Place Name	Description
PSM	Represents the Power Saving Mode state, where the device is in a deep sleep to conserve energy
Idle	Represents the RRC Idle state, where the device periodically wakes to monitor paging occasions, consuming less power than the active Connected state
Connected	Represents the RRC connection with the eNodeB, enabling data transmission and reception
Paging	Represents a state where the device is actively monitoring for network messages or requesting an uplink grant
UL_DATA_Queue	Represents a buffer for uplink data packets awaiting transmission
DL_DATA_Queue	Models a buffer for downlink data packets awaiting delivery to the device
DL_DATA_Buffer	Models a buffer holding downlink data packets on the network side, specifically when the device is in PSM and is temporarily unreachable
UpLink_Data Down-Link_Data	Models data ready for transmission or reception
UpLink DownLink	Represent available channels for respective data flows

It is important to note that the exponential modeling of 3GPP timers (T3324_expiration, T3412_expiration, eDRX_expiration) represents the stochastic nature of system events triggering these timers rather than the deterministic timer values themselves. In practice, these transitions fire based on network conditions, traffic arrivals, and system state changes that can be approximated as exponentially distributed events for analytical tractability.

Table 2. Transitions and Their Rates in the NB-IoT SPN Model.

Transition Name	Description
T3324_expiration	Models the maximum duration a device remains in the RRC Idle state before transiting to PSM
Transmit_UL	Represents the transmission of uplink data by the device
DL_Arrival	Models the downlink data arrival for the device
Receive_DL	Models receiving downlink data
UL_Arrival	Models the uplink data generation or arrival within the device
T3412_expiration	Represents the T3412 extended timer expiration, which governs the duration of PSM sleep cycles
PSM_UL_Reject	Represents uplink grant request rejection, while the device is in PSM, leading to a return to PSM
IDLE_UL_Reject	Represents uplink grant request rejection while the device is in RRC Idle
DL_Unavailable	Represents a scenario where downlink data becomes unavailable or is unable to be delivered to the device
Idle_Timer_Expiration	Moves the device from the Connected state to the Idle state upon prolonged inactivity
eDRX_expiration	Models the expiration of cyclic sleep periods within the Idle state, regulating when the device wakes to check for paging messages
UL_Packet_Generated	Represents the internal event within the device where an uplink packet is generated and made ready for transmission
UL_Authorization	Represents the network granting authorization for uplink transmission
DL_Data_Available	Represents available downlink data for the device
Cache_data	Caching or buffering data
return_to_paging return_to_paging_1	Represents the action of returning to a paging-listening state following various events

6 Energy Consumption Analysis

This section outlines the experimental methodology for quantitatively evaluating effects of different NB-IoT timer configurations on device energy consumption.

Energy consumption quantification is fundamentally linked to the device time spent in various power states. Assuming given average power consumption rates when being in a specific state, we define the amount of energy consumed by a device while residing in a given state (represented by place p) as:

$$Energy = T^*(p) \times E(p) \tag{1}$$

where:

- $T^*(p)$: Represents the mean sojourn time a token resides in place p, it is derived using Little's Law, computed as $T^*(p) = \frac{M^*(p)}{Post(p,\cdot)*\theta^*}$
- $E(p)$: Denotes the average power consumption rate specific to the operational state represented by place p. The assumed power consumption rates for these operational states are summarized in Table 3. These power consumption values are representative averages based on literature, and may vary across different NB-IoT chipsets and implementations.
- $M^*(p)$: Represents the mean number of tokens in place p.
- $Post(p, *)$: Refers to the row vector of the post-incidence matrix, indicating tokens produced when firing transitions from place p.

This analysis assumes ideal network conditions without considering congestion or interference effects that may impact real deployments.

Table 3. Average Power Consumption Rates for NB-IoT Operational States.

State	Power Consumption
PSM	15 μW
Idle	3 mW
Connected	160 mW

7 Experimental Results

To investigate the influence of specific timers used in the NB-IoT approach, we perform a systematic parametric analysis by varying the firing rates of key transitions that represent timers in our SPN model. This process is orchestrated by customized Perl scripts. For each configuration, the GreatSPN tool is utilized to perform steady-state analysis, leading to the stationary probability distribution of the SPN. The steady-state probabilities are used to compute sojourn times, from which we can estimate energy consumption.

Influence of T3324 timer (T3324_expiration). This timer defines the maximum duration an NB-IoT device can reside in the RRC Idle state before transitioning to PSM mode. Figure 3 shows energy consumption versus T3324_expiration rate.

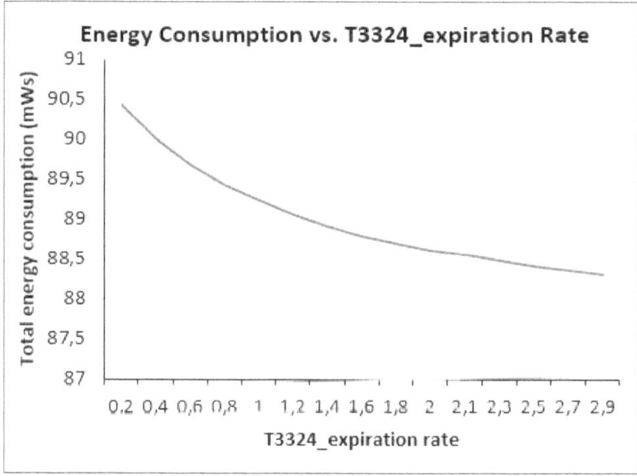

Fig. 3. Energy consumption vs. T3324_expiration rate

Analysis of varying T3324_expiration rate (inverse of T3324 timer duration) reveals its impact on the NB-IoT device energy consumption. As depicted in Fig. 3, the total energy consumption shows decreasing trend as T3324_expiration rate increases, indicating shorter T3324 timer durations (higher rates) lead to lower overall energy consumption.

These results highlight that accelerating the T3324 expiration (i.e., setting a shorter T3324 timer) is an effective strategy for reducing overall energy consumption. This is possible by minimizing the time the device spends in the Idle state before moving to the ultra-low power PSM state. While the Connected state remains the largest energy drain, reducing idle time by configuring a shorter T3324 timer is a direct means to enhance energy efficiency. This optimization involves trade-offs: very short T3324 timers might reduce device readiness for immediate downlink communications due to frequent deep sleep entry.

Influence of Idle_Timer_Expiration. Figure 4 depicts *Idle_Timer_Expiration* rate impact on NB-IoT device energy consumption. This parameter dictates device transition rate from *Connected* to *Idle* state following inactivity period of. Higher *Idle_Timer_Expiration* rate means shorter inactivity duration required in the *Connected* state before this transition occurs.

As observed in Fig. 4, increasing *Idle_Timer_Expiration* rate leads to a substantial decrease in total energy consumption. For example, at an *Idle_Timer_Expiration rate* of 0.2, the total energy consumed is approximately 171.23 mWs. This value significantly drops to about 40.48 mWs when the rate increases to 3.2. This clear trend indicates that configuring shorter inactivity timers enables NB-IoT devices to spend less time in high-power states, resulting in considerable energy savings.

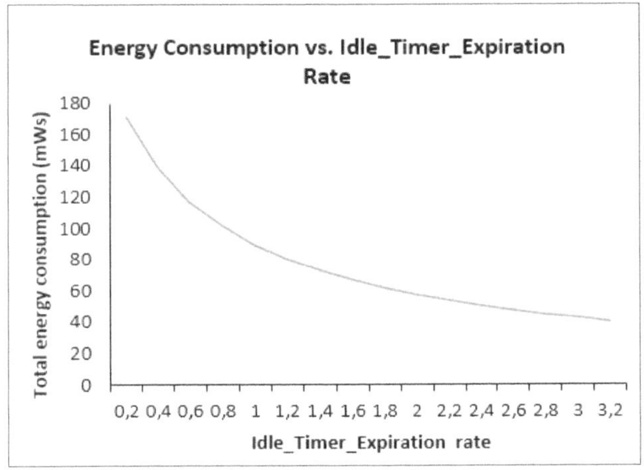

Fig. 4. Energy Consumption vs. Idle_Timer_Expiration Rate.

Influence of eDRX cycle timer (eDRX_expiration). This timer enables devices to remain reachable for extended periods while significantly conserving power by defining intervals at which they wake up to monitor paging messages. *eDRX_expiration* parameter directly influences sleep cycles lengths, with higher value indicating longer eDRX cycle. Figure 5 illustrates varying *eDRX_expiration* impact. As *eDRX_expiration* values increase (longer eDRX cycles), Connected state energy exhibits slight increases. For example, Connected state energy rises from 87.27 mWs at *eDRX_expiration* of 1 to 88.58 mWs at *eDRX_expiration* of 10.

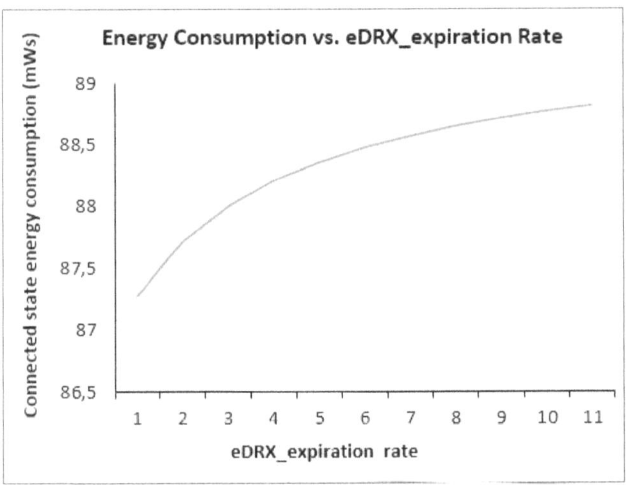

Fig. 5. Energy consumption by connected place vs. eDRX_expiration rate.

Energy consumption increases because frequent wake-up events and associated overhead during these periods demand more device power. Even when utilizing power-saving mechanisms like eDRX, configurations lead to short sleep cycles or increased wake-up frequency for paging message monitoring and connection management require more power than deep sleep. This includes radio activation energy, network synchronization, and potential buffered data handling or connection re-establishment—all more power-intensive than deep sleep states.

While this analysis focuses on energy optimization, real NB-IoT deployments must balance energy savings with latency and reliability requirements. Aggressive power saving (shorter T3324, longer eDRX cycles) may increase message delivery latency and reduce device reachability. The current validation is limited to analytical results and requires empirical validation using commercial devices across diverse network conditions and chipset variants.

8 Conclusion

This paper proposes a novel Stochastic Petri Net model for analyzing energy consumption in NB-IoT devices. Our approach addresses limitations of existing analytical models by capturing concurrent and stochastic behavior inherent in NB-IoT power management systems.

The SPN model integrates critical operational aspects including RRC state transitions, 3GPP timer configurations (T3324, T3412), and realistic traffic patterns to provide comprehensive energy consumption assessments. Using GreatSPN tool, we demonstrated model effectiveness in quantifying device energy usage and identifying optimal parameter configurations balancing power efficiency with performance requirements.

Experimental results reveal significant insights into key timer parameters impacts on battery lifetime, enabling system designers to make adequate decisions regarding NB-IoT deployment configurations.

Future research directions include extending the model to incorporate more sophisticated traffic patterns beyond exponential distributions, integrating network-level effects such as congestion and interference, and conducting broader empirical validation using commercial NB-IoT devices under diverse real-world conditions. Additionally, developing automated optimization algorithms for dynamic parameter adjustment will enhance the model's practical applicability.

References

1. Rose, K., Eldridge, S., Chapin, L.: The internet of things: an overview. Internet Soc. (ISOC) **80**, 1–53 (2015)
2. 3GPP – The Mobile Broadband Standard. 3GPP. https://www.3gpp.org. Accessed 16 June 2025
3. Standardization of NB-IoT completed. https://www.3gpp.org/news-events/3gpp-news/nb-iot-complete. Accessed 07 July 2025
4. Chen, M., Miao, Y., Hao, Y., Hwang, K.: Narrow band internet of things. IEEE Access **5**, 20557–20577 (2017)
5. Ratasuk, R., Mangalvedhe, N., Zhang, Y., Robert, M., Koskinen, J.-P.: Overview of narrowband IoT in LTE Rel-13. In: 2016 IEEE Conference on Standards for Communications and Networking (CSCN), pp. 1–7. IEEE (2016)

6. Raza, U., Kulkarni, P., Sooriyabandara, M.: Low power wide area networks: an overview. IEEE Commun. Surv. Tutor. **19**(2), 855–873 (2017)
7. Dahlman, E., Parkvall, S., Skold, J.: 4G: LTE/LTE-Advanced for Mobile Broadband. Academic Press (2013)
8. Schlienz, J., Raddino, D.: Narrowband Internet of Things Whitepaper. White Paper, Rohde&Schwarz, pp. 1–42 (2016)
9. Baarir, S., Beccuti, M., Cerotti, D., De Pierro, M., Donatelli, S., Franceschinis, G.: The GreatSPN tool: recent enhancements. SIGMETRICS Perform. Eval. Rev. **36**, 4–9 (2009). https://doi.org/10.1145/1530873.1530876
10. García-Martín, J.P., Torralba, A.: Energy consumption analytical modeling of NB-IoT devices for diverse IoT applications. Comput. Netw. 109855 (2023)
11. Sultania, A.K., Zand, P., Blondia, C., Famaey, J.: Energy modeling and evaluation of NB-IoT with PSM and eDRX. In: 2018 IEEE Globecom Workshops (GC Wkshps), pp. 1–7. IEEE (2018)
12. Andres-Maldonado, P., Ameigeiras, P., Prados-Garzon, J., Navarro-Ortiz, J., Lopez-Soler, J.M.: Narrowband IoT data transmission procedures for massive machine-type communications. IEEE Network **31**, 8–15 (2017)
13. Syed Ariz, M., Verma, S., Sindhu Hak, G.: Analysis and optimization of downlink energy in NB-IoT. Sustain. Comput. Inform. Syst. **35**, 100757 (2022)
14. Yassine, F., El Helou, M., Lahoud, S., Bazzi, O.: Energy-efficient uplink scheduling in narrowband IoT. Sensors **22**(20), 7744 (2022)
15. Tsoukaneri, G., Garcia, F., Marina, M.K.: Narrowband IoT device energy consumption characterization and optimizations. In: EWSN, pp. 1–12 (2020)
16. Sørensen, A., et al.: Modeling and Experimental Validation for Battery Lifetime Estimation in NB-IoT and LTE-M. arXiv preprint arXiv:2106.13286v3 (2022)
17. Jano, A., Alejandre Garana, P., Mehmeti, F., Mas-Machuca, C., Kellerer, W.: Modeling of IoT devices energy consumption in 5G networks. IEEE (2023)
18. Giorgi, G., Narduzzi, C.: How 5G can support worker well-being: the RedCap solution. In: 2024 IEEE International Symposium on Measurements & Networking (M&N), pp. 1–6. IEEE (2024)
19. Andres-Maldonado, P., Lauridsen, M., Ameigeiras, P., Lopez-Soler, J.M.: Analytical modeling and experimental validation of NB-IoT device energy consumption. IEEE Internet Things J. **6**(3), 5691–5701 (2019)
20. Oh, S.M., Jung, K.R., Bae, M., Shin, J.: Performance analysis for the battery consumption of the 3GPP NB-IoT device. In: International Conference on Information and Communication Technology Convergence, pp. 981–983 (2017)
21. Radfar, M., Nakhlestani, A., Le Viet, H., Desai, A.: Battery management technique to reduce standby energy consumption in ultra-low power IoT and sensory applications. IEEE Trans. Circuits Syst. I Regul. Pap. **67**, 336–345 (2019)
22. Wang, X., Sheng, M.J., Lou, Y.Y., Shih, Y.Y., Chiang, M.: Internet of things session management over LTE balancing signal load, power, and delay. IEEE Internet Things J. **3**(3), 339–353 (2016)
23. Tseng, C.C., Wang, H.C., Kuo, F.C., Ting, K.C., Chen, H.H., Chen, G.Y.: Delay and power consumption in LTE/LTE-a DRX mechanism with mixed short and long cycles. IEEE Trans. Veh. Technol. **65**(3), 1721–1734 (2016)
24. Zhou, L., Xu, H., Tian, H., Gao, Y., Du, L., Chen, L.: Performance analysis of power saving mechanism with adjustable DRX cycles in 3GPP LTE. In: IEEE Vehicular Technology Conference, pp. 1–5 (2008)

25. Koc, A.T., Jha, S., Vannithamby, R., Torlak, M.: Optimizing DRX configuration to improve battery power saving and latency of active mobile applications over LTE-a network. In: Wireless Communications and Networking Conference (WCNC) IEEE, pp. 568–573. Shanghai, China (2013)
26. Liu, K., Cui, G., Li, Q., Zhang, S., Wang, W., Li, X.: An optimal PSM duration calculation algorithm for NB-IoT. In: 2019 IEEE 5th International Conference on Computer and Communications (ICCC), pp. 447–452. IEEE (2019)
27. Bontu, C.S., Illidge, E.: DRX mechanism for power saving in LTE. IEEE Commun. Mag. **47**(6), 48–55 (2009)
28. Molloy, M.K.: Performance analysis using stochastic petri nets. IEEE Trans. Comput. C **31**(9), 913–917 (1982)
29. Murata, T.: Petri nets: properties, analysis and applications. Proc. IEEE **77**(4), 541–580 (2002)

Correct-by-Construction Code Generation from Event-B to Python

Neeraj Kumar Singh(✉)

INPT-ENSEEIHT/IRIT, University of Toulouse, Toulouse, France
neeraj.singh@toulouse-inp.fr

Abstract. There is an increasing demand for automation in system engineering, particularly for the development of complex systems, to speed up the development process and minimise the risk of coding errors. In current setting, Python has increasingly become a preferred choice for developers and industries for prototype development, particularly due to its robust ecosystem of open-source libraries and frameworks. However, it lacks safe coding features for critical systems. Formal methods are important for designing safe systems by verifying essential safety properties. Event-B and B methods are already in the core industrial practices for the verification and validation of system requirements. These verified models can be further used for code generation. However, manual code generation can be prone to errors and is often time-consuming, which may result in serious system failures. To produce safe Python code from formal models, we advocate for automating the code generation process. This paper introduces a code generation methodology, along with tool support, for generating Python code from Event-B models. Additionally, we have implemented and tested a plugin, called EB2Py, on several Event-B examples to demonstrate scalability and reliability of our approach.

Keywords: Formal methods · Refinement and Proofs · Correct-by-construction · Event-B · Code generation · EB2Py

1 Introduction

Our daily lives are increasingly reliant on both simple and complex systems, ranging from everyday applications to advanced technologies designed to enhance our activities. These systems are evolving rapidly, driven through advancements in software and hardware. To effectively handle the complexities of designing and implementing such systems, it is essential to adopt various approaches that ensure correct functionalities while keeping pace with the rapid technological changes.

To effectively design reliable and safe systems, formal methods play a key role for specifying complex systems. Notably, formal techniques like Event-B [2] and B methods [1] have been widely adopted across various industries [4,9], such as RATP, Siemens, Alstom and others, for the rigorous development of complex systems and for identifying flaws in system requirements. These methods allow software engineer to create an abstract model that can be progressively refined into concrete specifications

B. Ben Hedia et al. (Eds.): VECoS 2025, LNCS 16263, pp. 158–173, 2026.
https://doi.org/10.1007/978-3-032-20440-0_11

closely aligned with the source code. However, transforming these concrete models into source code manually can be error prone. Thus, there is a growing demand for tools that can automate the source code generation process. Meanwhile, Python has emerged as a preferred language for developers and industries engaged in prototype development, largely due to its robust ecosystem of open-source libraries and frameworks. However, it lacks safe coding features for critical systems. Despite the advantages of these methodologies and tools, a significant gap remains: to our knowledge, there are currently no tools available that enable the automatic generation of Python code from Event-B models. This represents both a challenge and an opportunity for further advancement, particularly in promoting a correct-by-construction methodology for designing complex systems and implementing them in Python for rapid prototyping.

To tackle the challenges associated with translating Event-B models into executable code, this paper presents a robust mechanism designed to generate Python code from Event-B models. Event-B models utilise set-theoretical notations that often resist direct translation into conventional programming languages. To bridge this gap, our translator rewrites these complex formal notations into a format that is readily translatable into Python. This ensures that the resulting code can be executed using standard interpreter tools, facilitating easier transition from formal models to low level implementations.

In support of this transformation mechanism, we have developed a new code generation tool, EB2Py, as part of the EB2ALL [11,14,15]. EB2ALL is a versatile code generation framework that automates the code generation across multiple programming languages, including C, C++, Java, C#, and Solidity. The EB2Py tool specifically enables users to generate Python code from Event-B models, developed using the correct-by-construction approach, while preserving the required properties. Furthermore, this tool has been developed as a plug-in using Eclipse, functioning within the Rodin framework to ensure seamless integration into existing workflows.

To validate the efficacy of our code generation mechanism, we applied EB2Py to several complex case studies and standard examples. The results not only demonstrated the reliability and scalability of the tool, but also highlighted its potential to enhance the modelling, verification, and implementation processes in the rapid development of complex system prototypes using Python. This makes EB2Py an invaluable asset for software engineers and academics engaged in the design and implementation of advanced formal methods for complex systems.

This paper is structured as follows: In Sect. 2, we present an overview of the key elements of both the Event-B modelling language and the Python programming language. Section 3 details the transformation mechanisms from Event-B to Python, focusing on the implementation of the Rodin plugin known as EB2Py. In Sect. 4, we present a case study that exemplifies our approach. Related work is presented in Sect. 5, and we conclude the paper in Sect. 6 and outline some future perspectives.

2 Background

This section describes the Event-B modelling language and its refinements for modelling and designing complex reactive systems. It also includes background information on Python programming language that is used as a target language for code generation.

2.1 Event-B Modelling Language

Event-B is a state-based modelling language that employs set theory and first-order logic (FOL) to model and design complex systems using the correct-by-construction methodology. This language has two main components: *context* and *machine*, which define the system's static and dynamic behaviours, including safety properties. A *context* describes the static features of a system using *carrier sets* (s), *constants* (c), *axioms* ($A(s, c)$), and *theorems* ($T_c(s, c)$). In contrast, a *machine* focuses on the dynamic components by incorporating *variables* (v) to represent states, *invariants* ($I(s, c, v)$) that characterise states in predicate form for defining typing and safety properties, *theorems* ($T_m(s, c, v)$) that express advanced and auxiliary system properties, *variants* ($V(s, c, v)$) that highlight convergence properties, and guarded *events* ($E(s, c, v, x)$) that detail the evolution of states through before-after predicates (BAP). The overall structure of an Event-B model is illustrated in Fig. 1.

CONTEXT	MACHINE
ctxt_id_2	*machine_id_2*
EXTENDS	**REFINES**
ctxt_id_1	*machine_id_1*
SETS	**SEES**
s	*ctxt_id_2*
CONSTANTS	**VARIABLES**
c	v
AXIOMS	**INVARIANTS**
$A(s, c)$	$I(s, c, v)$
THEOREMS	**THEOREMS**
$T_c(s, c)$	$T_m(s, c, v)$
END	**VARIANT**
	$V(s, c, v)$
	EVENTS
	Event evt
	any x
	where $G(s, c, v, x)$
	then
	$v :\|BAP(s, c, v, x, v')$
	end
	END

Fig. 1. Event-B model structure

Theorems	$A(s, c) \Rightarrow T_c(s, c)$ $A(s, c) \wedge I(s, c, v)$ $\Rightarrow T_m(s, c, v)$
Invariant preservation	$A(s, c) \wedge I(s, c, v)$ $\wedge G(s, c, v, x)$ $\wedge BAP(s, c, v, x, v')$ $\Rightarrow I(s, c, v')$
Event feasibility	$A(s, c) \wedge I(s, c, v)$ $\wedge G(s, c, v, x)$ $\Rightarrow \exists v'.BAP(s, c, v, x, v')$
Variant progress	$A(s, c) \wedge I(s, c, v)$ $\wedge G(s, c, v, x)$ $\wedge BAP(s, c, v, x, v')$ $\Rightarrow V(s, c, v') < V(s, c, v)$

Fig. 2. Proof obligations

Event-B modelling language supports various proof obligations (POs), including invariant preservation, the feasibility of non-deterministic actions, guard strengthening in refinements, simulation, variant, and well-definedness, among others. Figure 2 highlights some key proof obligations. There are two types of theorems: $T_c(s, c)$ and $T_m(s, c, v)$. The proof obligation associated with the context theorem $T_c(s, c)$ verifies that it can be derived from the defined axioms. In contrast, the proof obligation associated with the machine theorem $T_m(s, c, v)$ ensures that it can be derived from previously established invariants as well as the specified axioms $A(s, c)$. Invariant preservation guarantees that every invariant is maintained by the initialization event $Init(x)$ as well as other model events $BAP(e)(s, c, v, x, v')$. The subsequent proof obligation is related to feasibility, ensuring that the non-deterministic action is feasible when event e is enabled. The last proof obligation is related to variant V, which maps a state v to a natural number, guarantees that each convergent event strictly decreases V. Additionally, other proof obligations, such as guard strengthening in refinements, ensure that the concrete guards in a refining event are more robust than the abstract ones, while simulation verifies that each action in a concrete event effectively simulates the corresponding abstract action.

The Event-B modelling language enables a *correct by construction* approach that refines a model (a transition system) into a more detailed transition system, including additional design choices, resulting in a transition from a higher to a lower level of abstraction. This refinement process allows for the incremental modelling of a system, with safety properties introduced at each refined stage. The refined model reduces the degree of non-determinism by strengthening the guards and/or predicates. During each refinement, new variables and events may be introduced, increasing the specificity of the system's behaviour. These refinements define the relationship between the abstract model and the refined concrete model. The introduction of *gluing invariants* establishes the relationship between defined abstract and concrete state variables. The correctness of refinement operations is ensured by establishing new proof obligations.

The Rodin Platform [3] offers a comprehensive suite of tools for developing models in the Event-B modelling language. Its features include project management, model development, proof generation, model checking, animation, and automatic code generation. Once an Event-B model is modelled and syntactically checked within the Rodin Platform, the system automatically generates a series of proof obligations using its built-in tools. The integrated Rodin prover then processes these proof obligations. In [2], the author provides more information on proof obligations.

2.2 Python

G. Rossum developed Python, an interpreted, object-oriented, high-level programming language with dynamic semantics, which was released in 1991 [18]. It is simple to learn and has been used in various domains, including web development, data analysis, scientific computing, automation, and many more. This is one of the open source programming languages that includes a large library to cover all aspects of a system, as well as modularity and code reusability, making it suitable for rapid prototype development. This subsection describes the major Python constructs that are relevant to our work for transforming Event-B model to Python code. More information about Python programming language can be found in [18].

Python's core syntax is heavily influenced by other programming languages, such as ABC, C and Java. Python uses indentation to separate code blocks like loops, conditionals, and functions, unlike other languages that use braces '{ ... }' or specific keywords for this purpose. Furthermore, it provides a variety of control structures such as `for`, `while`, `do-while`, and `if-else`. Additionally, it supports a variety of operators, including arithmetic, comparison, logical, assignment, bitwise, identity, and membership operators. These diverse operators enable complex functionalities for handling different data types, playing a important role in performing calculations, making comparisons, and controlling the flow of Python programs.

Python is a dynamically typed scripting programming language, which means we can define variables without specifying their type, such as integer, string, or float. In fact, the runtime type of a variable is determined by the value assigned to it. In Python, there are numerous elementary types that can be combined to create more complex types (see Table 1). Furthermore, it also supports wide range of complex data types such as sequences, arrays, dictionaries, and frozensets. It should be noted that the Python language lacks "variables" in the sense of C or Java. In Python, a variable is simply a tag that can be applied to any object, as opposed to a name that references a specific memory location. In Python, a variable is not defined until it is assigned a value.

Table 1. Python Value and Composite Types

Value and Composite Types	Keyword	Description
Boolean Type	$bool$	possible values $true$ and $false$
Integer Types	int	signed integers
String Types	str	strings are immutable sequences of Unicode code points.
List Types	$list = [\ldots]$	a list of mutable sequences to store homogeneous items
Dictionaries Types	$dict = \{\ldots\}$	dictionaries are used to store data values in `key:value` pairs.
Tuple Types	$tuple = (\ldots)$	a tuple is a collection of immutable items similar to list
Enumerated Type	$enum$	a set of symbolic names bound to unique values

In Python, a namespace organises identifiers and their corresponding objects to prevent naming conflicts. There are four major namespaces: `built-in`, `global`, `local`, and `enclosing`. To access the global namespace, use the predefined function `globals()`; for the local namespace, use `locals()`. The `nonlocal` keyword is used to modify variables within an enclosing scope. Errors are handled in Python using the `try`, `except`, `finally`, and `else` blocks. Such mechanisms allow developers to handle errors that occur during line by line execution. Python has a number of built-in functions that can be called directly from the program, but it also allows us to define new functions with input arguments that can be invoked within the program.

3 Code Generation: Event-B to Python

Figure 3 illustrates the core architecture, emphasising the essential processes involved in the code generation workflow, as well as their integration into tool development. The following sections describe each step of the code generation process in detail.

3.1 Translation of Event-B to Python

The primary objective of our work is to transform an Event-B model into Python. To achieve this, we have developed a translator that relies on a set of transformation rules designed to facilitate the mapping between Event-B and Python. Table 2 provides a comprehensive list of transformation functions designed to generate Python code from Event-B components.

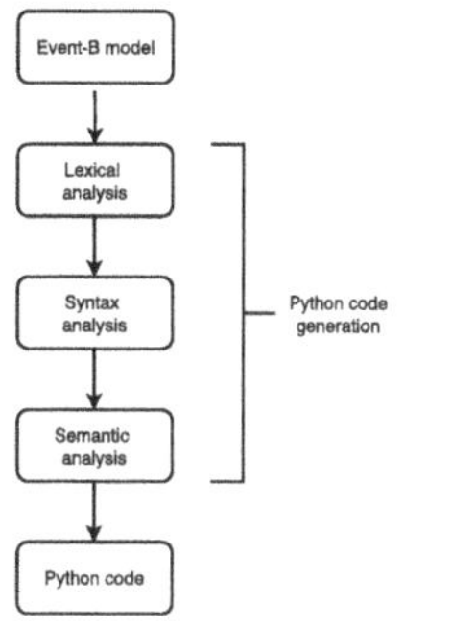

Fig. 3. Code generation workflows: Event-B to Python

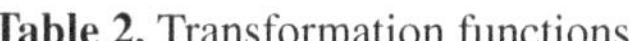

Table 2. Transformation functions

T_{decl}	:	Datatype and Constant declaration translation function
T_{st}	:	State variables translation function
T_{axm}	:	Axioms translation function
T_{pred}	:	Predicate translation function
T_{evt}	:	Events translation function
T_{prm}	:	Event parameters translation function
T_{grd}	:	Event's guards translation function
T_{act}	:	Event's actions translation function
T_{exp}	:	Expressions translation function

Table 3 presents a comprehensive collection of symbols supported by the code generation mechanism and the implemented EB2Py tool. This table illustrates a subset of Event-B syntax alongside its corresponding representation in Python code. In this development, we adhere to the formal notations of Event-B [2] and utilize an Abstract Syntax Tree (AST) to encapsulate the Event-B grammar. Our code generation tool is equipped to process various expressions, including conditional, arithmetic, and logical expressions, derived from formal models. Note that the Event-B models that contain both machines and contexts are translated into Python code seamlessly. Below, we summarise the essential steps involved in the code generation process, specifically for handling both Event-B context and machine models.

– **Context models.** The context of an Event-B model includes *sets*, *enumerated sets*, *constants*, and *functions*, each associated with its respective type. To facilitate the translation process, the transformation rules are derived to accommodate all types of context components. The generated Python code has all the semantic attributes of Event-B specification to ensure correct transformation. Table 4 presents a mapping between Event-B types and various Python types. The constants, sets, and enumerated sets from the Event-B model are translated into Python constants, type declarations, and enumerated types using the defined transformation functions (see Table 2).

The direct mapping between Event-B enumerated sets and Python enumerated types simplifies the translation process. The connection between Event-B and Python concerning integer values is important for ensuring both the efficiency of the generated code and the accuracy of the translation.

While a preprocessing step is recommended for other EB2ALL code generation plugins to produce correct and safe code, this is not necessary for our code generation mechanism and the implemented tool EB2Py. Unlike many programming languages, Python does not require explicit type declarations. In Python, variables are used to store data that can be referenced and manipulated throughout the program's execution.

In programming, a constant is a name that represents a value which remains unchanged throughout the execution of a program. However, Python does not provide specific syntax for defining constants. Instead, Python constants are essentially

Table 3. Event-B to Python

Event-B	Pyhton	Comment
const_x $\in \mathbb{N} \wedge$ cons_x=120	const_x : Final[int] = 120	Constant declaration
x $\in \mathbb{Z}$	x : int = random.randint(-32768, 32767)	Integer variable declaration
x $\in \mathbb{N}$	x : int = random.randint(0, 32767)	Unsigned integer variable declaration
b $\in$ BOOL	b : bool = False	Boolean variable declaration
x $\in 1..m \rightarrow \mathbb{Z}$	x = [0] $*$ m	Array declaration with default value 0
x = y	if(x == y): ...	Conditional statement
x $\neq$ y	if(x != y): ...	Conditional statement
x $<$ y	if(x<y): ...	Conditional statement
x $\leq$ y	if(x<=y): ...	Conditional statement
x $>$ y	if(x>y): ...	Conditional statement
x $\geq$ y	if(x>=y): ...	Conditional statement
(x>y) $\wedge$ (x$\geq$z)	if ((x>y) and (x>=z)): ...	Conditional statement
(x>y) $\vee$ (x$\geq$z)	if ((x>y) or (x>=z)): ...	Conditional statement
$\neg$x<y	if(not (x<y)): ...	Logical not
X$\Rightarrow$Y	if(not X or Y): ...	Logical Implication
X$\Leftrightarrow$Y	if((not X or Y) and (not Y or X)): ...	Logical Equivalence
x := y + z	x = y + z	Arithmetic assignment
x := y - z	x = y - z	Arithmetic assignment
x := y * z	x = y * z	Arithmetic assignment
x := y $\div$ z	x = y / z	Arithmetic assignment
x := a(y)	x = a[y]	Array assignment
x := y	x = y	Scalar action

$\forall i.i \in 1..100 \Rightarrow fun(i) < 50$	for i in range(1,100):
	if(fun(i)<50):
	return False
		$\forall$ Quantifier

$\exists i.i \in 1..100 \wedge fun(i) < 20$	exist_tf = False
	i = 1
	while(i < 100) and not exist_tf:
	i = i+ 1
	if((fun(i)<20) and not exist_tf):
	exist_tf = True
	elif ((i == 100) and not exist_tf):
	return False
		$\exists$ Quantifier

a := a $\Leftarrow$ {x$\mapsto$y}	a[x] = y	Array action
a := a $\Leftarrow$ {x$\mapsto$y} $\Leftarrow$ {i$\mapsto$j}	a[x]=y a[i]=j	Array action
fun $\in \mathbb{N} \times \mathbb{N} \rightarrow \mathbb{N}$	def fun($arg1$, $arg2$): ... returns res	Function definition

Table 4. Event-B and Python mapping

Event-B types	Python language
Enumerated sets	Enumerated types
Basic integer sets	Basic Integer type
Event-B array types	Python arrays
Function	Python function structure

variables that are intended to remain immutable. To create a constant that aligns with Event-B semantics, we can use the `typing.Final` qualifier to indicate that certain variables cannot be reassigned ensuring compliance with Event-B standards. The *mypy* command can be utilised to check for any unauthorised reassignment of these constants, preventing further modifications to final names within type-checked code. Event-B constants can be directly translated into Python due to the straightforward correspondence between Event-B and Python integer types.

The translation between the Event-B array type and the Python array type is not straightforward. In Event-B, an array is defined as a total function, whereas in Python, arrays correspond to a contiguous block of memory characterised by their starting address and size. Nonetheless, the semantic relationship between an array element *arr(i)* in Event-B and the value at the position *arr[i]* in Python can be easily established.

Translating the Event-B function into a Python function is a straightforward process. The developed prototype tool supports only the total function from Event-B. Input and output arguments for the Python function can be easily identified by examining the left and right sides of the total function symbol ($\rightarrow$) in the Event-B function specification. This formal definition can be effectively mapped to the structure of a Python function.

In the generated code, the context model components are declared in global scope, allowing them to be accessed throughout the program. The type information for these context elements is extracted from the context axioms that serve as their type definitions.

– **Machine models.** An Event-B machine model consists of *variables*, *invariants*, and *guarded events*. The variables defined in the Event-B machine can be transformed into Python variables. However, they cannot be declared in advance because Python is entirely object-oriented and not *statically typed*. Additionally, the Event-B machine may include function and array declarations, which can be transformed according to the established rules for functions and arrays within the context model. The required typing information for such declarations can be extracted from the Event-B invariants.

In the Event-B specification, variables are categorised into two main classes: *global variables* and *local variables*. Global variables are directly derived from variable declarations and have a global scope, allowing them to be accessed throughout the entire model. In contrast, local variables are created within the context of specific event clauses and are restricted to those events. When a function structure is generated, all declarations of local variables are included as a list of input arguments.

The transformation mechanism employs a recursive approach to generate Python code for each event in the Event-B specification. During this process, it continuously monitors for the presence of a *'null'* event, which signifies a guard with a false condition. When such an event is encountered, the mechanism refrains from generating source code and inserts a relevant comment to maintain traceability. For instance, if an event is associated with a single guard that evaluates to $false$, the resulting Python code will completely omit that event. This automatic exclusion is designed to prevent the generation of unreachable runtime code, thereby enhancing the efficiency and clarity of the final output.

The initialisation event of the Event-B machine is represented by an initial Python function. Within this function, all variables are assigned their default values, which are directly derived from the action predicates of the Event-B initialisation event. This method guarantees that the default initial values in the Python program are in harmony with the specifications of the Event-B model, ensuring a precise alignment with the evolution of all variables as outlined in the Event-B model traces.

The handling of guards in Event-B can be quite ambiguous due to the multiple interpretations associated with them. These ambiguities stem from various factors, including the definition of local variable types, the assignment of values to these variables, and the construction of condition statements that involve logical operators such as negation ($\neg$), conjunction ($\wedge$), disjunction ($\vee$), implication ($\Rightarrow$), and equivalence ($\Leftrightarrow$). To tackle this complexity, we propose a recursive technique aimed at parsing and identifying the distinct components of Event-B guards for more effective transformation. For instance, when our transformation mechanism encounters implication ($\Rightarrow$) and equivalence ($\Leftrightarrow$) operators, it automatically reformulates the predicates into equivalent expressions that only use conjunction ($\wedge$), disjunction ($\vee$), and negation ($\neg$) operators.

Additionally, the quantifiers *exists* ($\exists$) and *forall* ($\forall$) have been carefully implemented. To incorporate both quantifiers, we utilize `for` loops to determine a fixed number of steps when checking the specified Event-B predicates. The equivalent Python code generated from the quantified Event-B predicates is presented in Table 3.

Another notable aspect to consider is the functional-image relation, which effectively illustrates a data array or an external function. Once the event guards are classified, we use these guards that convey local variable type information to generate variable declarations within the function. The remaining guards are leveraged to create local assignment and conditional statements. Furthermore, we derive local variable type information in a manner similar to how we infer global variables from the guard.

Event-B events are transformed into Python functions, where the parameters of each event are passed as arguments to their respective functions. To guarantee that these functions are invoked correctly, we generate additional conditions derived from the guard predicates of the Event-B events. In Event-B, actions are executed concurrently, and modifications to the state made during an action take effect only after the event's guards are fully satisfied. Therefore, it is important to perform dependency checks to ensure that no state variable, designated as an action assignee, is updated before it is used. To facilitate this process, we introduce a set of temporary variables that capture the values of the state variables prior to executing the before-after predicates. This approach allows us to maintain the semantics of atomic actions by ensuring that all changes appear to occur simultaneously. Next, we rewrite the event actions as assignment statements within the function body, utilising these pre-defined temporary variables. This transformation ensures that the integrity of the state is preserved during execution. Additionally, our transformation mechanism is versatile: it supports assignments to scalar variables, allows for overriding statements on array-type variables, and accommodates complex arithmetic expressions. Finally, after executing the action statements, we update all relevant state variables with the values stored in the temporary variables, completing the transition while maintaining consistency within the system.

3.2 EB2Py Plugin: Implementation and Installation

This section describes the implementation of our code generation mechanism, designed to transform Event-B models into Python code. We present our newly developed plugin tool, EB2Py[1], which facilitates the seamless generation of Python code from Event-B models within the Rodin platform. The EB2Py plugin builds upon the existing EB2ALL framework [11, 14], which has established itself as a robust toolset for developing code generation methodologies that convert Event-B models into various target programming languages. Our plugin, EB2Py, leverages the core architecture of EB2ALL by parsing Rodin projects and employing a set of transformation rules for code generation, ensuring that the resulting Python code accurately corresponds to the Event-B models.

EB2Py is primarily implemented in Java and uses the Rodin core libraries. Leveraging the existing interface and class structure of Rodin, we automate the transformation mechanisms outlined in several transformation rules (see Table 2). This process involves parsing the models and conducting both syntactical and semantic analyses of the context and machine models and it enables the generation of Python code that is derived from various modelling components of an Event B model, including axioms, enumerated sets, variables, invariants, events, guards, actions, and other predicates. We have previously discussed some transformation principles, which are implemented into this plugin to produce reliable code corresponding to different elements of Event-B models.

After successfully installing the plug-in, users will find a new Translator/EB2Py menu and a corresponding tool button conveniently integrated within the Rodin environment. Figure 4 illustrates a screen capture of EB2Py seamlessly integrated within the Rodin environment, allowing users to effortlessly generate Python code while leveraging Eclipse's intuitive interface. To generate Python code for a formal model, users can choose between the EB2Py menu or the tool button. This action will open a dialog box shows a list of active projects, enabling users to select the desired project for code generation. After selecting a Rodin project, the tool automatically generates the corresponding Python code and saves it in a designated file within the project folder. EB2Py also offers a significant advantage by maintaining a detailed log of the code generation process. This log provides valuable information for troubleshooting potential issues. Users will receive immediate feedback through a dialog box confirming the successful generation of code or highlighting any errors that require attention. Additionally, a log file documenting the code generation process will be created and stored in the Rodin project folder, facilitating further analysis of the code generation process.

4 Case Study

To evaluate the efficiency and reliability of our proposed code generation mechanism, as well as the performance of our implemented tool, EB2Py, we use several small and large examples. Among these, we formalised the specifications for several complex systems, including a cardiac pacemaker, an insulin infusion pump, a cardiac resynchronization therapy (CRT) device, and an automatic rover protection system. Note that, we have chosen the CRT case study as a particularly interesting and complex example. In this section, we will outline the formal development of the CRT case study and discuss how we use our tool, EB2Py, to generate Python code.

[1] Download: https://sites.google.com/site/singhnne/eb2py.

Fig. 4. Screenshot of the EB2Py plugin in Rodin.

4.1 Informal Description

A *Cardiac Resynchronization Therapy* (CRT) [16, 17], or multi-site pacing device, is an advanced type of pacemaker designed to address a specific type of heart failure characterised by poor synchronisation between the two lower chambers of the heart. Here, we focus on biventricular sensing and pacing (BiSP) mode of CRT, which enables pacing and sensing in three heart chambers. Biventricular pacing coordinates contractions of the left and right ventricles (LV and RV), aligning them with the natural sinus rhythm detected in the right atrium (RA). The process involves monitoring intrinsic events in the LV and RV to adjust pacing intervals, taking into account variations in the atrioventricular interval (AVI). Timing is crucial for electrode activity across all chambers, as delays in pacing between the RV and LV can complicate biventricular pacing. These parameters define the atrioventricular (AV) and ventriculoatrial (VA) escape intervals, which are essential for dual-chamber pacing.

4.2 Formal Development in Event-B

This section summarises the formal development of CRT using the *correct-by-construction* approach.

– **Abstract model: Introducing actuators and sensors.** The abstract model of CRT describes the pacing and sensing functions of electrodes located within three heart chambers: the right atrium (RA), right ventricle (RV), and left ventricle (LV). To capture the static characteristics of CRT, we develop a context model that includes an enumerated set, *Status*, to represent `ON` and `OFF` states of electrods. For modelling dynamic behaviour, we define several state variables that represent the actuators and sensors for each chamber. This abstract model focuses on pacing and sensing activities, without addressing timing constraints. We introduce 12 events, each accompanied by guards based on the actuators and sensors' states, along with BAP that modify the defined states.

– **First refinement: Introducing time for managing pacing and sensing activities.** This refinement refines the abstract model and introduces a logical clock to formalise the timing properties related to pacing and sensing activities. It defines four new constants: AVI, VAI, LVI, and RVI, each defined with specific value ranges. Additionally, some constraints are defined as axioms for various intervals. In the machine model, a variable called now is defined as a clock counter that increments with each tick, while another variable, $RecPS$, is introduced to monitor pacing and sensing activities, which facilitates the determination of future actions for any chamber. Several new safety properties are introduced to ensure the necessary functionalities in the BiSP mode of CRT. This refinement consists of 18 events that enhance the abstract events by specifying how actuators and sensors should function under the new timing constraints. A key event, $Clock\_tic$, is introduced to model the clock's ticking behavior, incrementing the now counter. Initially, this event has no guard; however, future refinements will include guards to ensure the proper evolution of pacing and sensing activities.
– **Second refinement: Detecting intrinsic heart activities by introducing thresholds.** In this refinement, we focus on the detection of intrinsic heart activities using electrode sensors in CRT. By continuously monitoring heart activity and comparing it against predefined standard thresholds for each heart chamber, the CRT can deliver appropriate stimulation when necessary. We define a set of constants in the context model for each chamber: *STA_THR_A* for the atrial chamber, *STA_THR_LV* for the left ventricle, and *STA_THR_RV* for the right ventricle. To ensure the accurate detection of intrinsic activities, CRT sensors are designed to monitor heart function at specific intervals and are programmed to respond when sensed signals exceed these standard thresholds. If intrinsic activity is not detected, an electrical pulse is triggered to stimulate the relevant chamber. To guarantee the proper operation of each electrode, we defined a set of safety invariants. We also introduce new event actions aimed at resetting counters, further refining the CRT functionalities.
– **Third refinement: Introducing blanking and refractory periods.** The last refinement introduces refractory and blanking periods for the atrial and ventricular chambers, enhancing signal detection and minimising over-sensing issues. Several new constants are defined to represent these refractory and blanking periods. Furthermore, six safety properties are established to ensure the proper functioning of the sensors and actuators during varying refractory and blanking periods. To improve system responsiveness, a new guard is added to the $Clock\_tic$ event, enabling time advancement that accurately reflects the system's activities in pacing and sensing, as described in the BiSP mode.

4.3 Model Validation and Analysis

This section presents the proof statistics for the generated POs and uses the ProB model checker [10] to validate the CRT model. The POs include consistency checks, invariants satisfaction, refinement steps and others. In total, 184 POs are generated, in which 181 (98.37%) POs are automatically proved and the remaining 3 (1.63%) POs require interactive proofs. Furthermore, model analysis and animation are performed using ProB to find potential deadlocks and hidden properties that may not be addressed during the CRT modelling. The ProB animation facilitates an exploration of the expected behaviour of the CRT across various scenarios, confirming the integrity of the formal models developed and ensuring that no errors or counterexamples exist.

4.4 Code Generation for CRT in Python

The EB2Py tool[1] has been successfully applied to several complex case studies, demonstrating its effectiveness and scalability in generating Python code from Event-B models. For our selected CRT case study, we use the EB2Py tool to illustrate the generation of Python code from our verified CRT model. Before employing the tool, we refine our concrete model to eliminate any abstract operations and unsupported symbols. Prior to generating the Python code for the CRT model, it is necessary to discharge all newly generated proof obligations (POs) to guarantee correct code generation.

The EB2Py tool generates Python code from the refined CRT model, producing files that include constants, variables, functions, and related definitions derived from the original Event-B models. The formalised CRT model consequently generates a set of functions based on event analysis, which examines various components such as local parameters, guards, and actions. Each Event-B event is translated into a corresponding Python function, with event parameters serving as function arguments. The actions associated with these events are converted into Python assignment expressions. To execute the set of actions within any function, all specified guards must evaluate to TRUE; if not, the statements within the function body will be skipped. An excerpt of the generated code corresponding to the defined events is provided in Fig. 4. The final Python code generated for the CRT model is directly executable by the Python interpreter.

5 Related Work

In [5], the authors introduce a method for generating efficient code from B models to C specifically for smart card applications in the RNTL BOM project to cover important criteria, including correctness, memory management, runtime error-free operation, adaptability to the 8-bit AVR platform, and compliance with industrial standards. In [19], the author discusses the creation of a code generation plugin, B2C, designed to generate C code from Event-B models. However, this plugin supports only a limited subset of Event-B notations necessary for capturing the Instruction Set Architecture (ISA) properties of a virtual machine known as MIDAS. This tool is very limited and cannot be used for handling complex Event-B expressions and predicates. In [13], the authors present EventB2Java, a code generation tool designed to convert Event-B models into Java programs annotated with JML. One of the main advantages of this JML-annotated Java code is that it facilitates the verification of the generated code using JML tools. This tool also supports only subset of Event-B notations. In [12], the authors propose generation of VHDL code from Event-B models. This approach primarily revolves around linking the structure of the Event-B model with the syntax of hardware description languages. Finally, this approach is implemented as a plugin for the Rodin framework, enabling the automatic generation of VHDL code. In [8], the authors introduced a framework for translating Event-B models into Python code. They discussed a set of translation rules designed to map components of Event-B models into

Python classes. Note that no supporting tool has been provided to facilitate this translation process. In the work by Andreas et al. [7], the authors introduce a methodology to guarantee the correctness of program code generated from Event-B models. This is accomplished through the application of refinement and well-definedness restrictions, which help mitigate runtime errors stemming from semantic differences and variations in the interpretation of integer values. Additionally, the authors propose an intuitive scheduling language for defining sequences of event executions and associated assertion properties. Note that there is no tool has been implemented to support this approach. In [6], the authors describe an approach for deriving concurrent programs in Ada from Event-B by using tasking and shared machines.

In [11,14], the authors introduced a suite of plugins known as EB2ALL, which is designed to facilitate source code generation across multiple programming languages. The initial release of this tool included four main plugins: EB2C, EB2C++, EB2J, and EB2C#, enabling code generation in C, C++, Java, and C#, respectively, from the Event-B models. The underlying principle of source code generation closely aligns with the structure of Event-B events, where each event is represented as a function with specified arguments. These functions can be invoked from the main program either through scheduling or in the development of complex software systems. Since its initial release in 2011, EB2ALL has significantly evolved, receiving numerous enhancements that include new features, additional modelling constructs, and improved compatibility with the latest Java versions and associated repositories. For instance, it includes support for quantifiers and integrates the semantics of Event-B BAP assignment. This is one of the most current plugins for the latest Rodin IDE designed to facilitate code generation from Event-B models.

Python has emerged as one of the most popular programming languages today, known for its simple and user-friendly syntax, open-source nature, and extensive support for advanced libraries like Pandas, NumPy, and TensorFlow. Major tech companies such as Google and Meta have adopted Python, making it a preferred choice for designing rapid prototypes across various domains. To integrate formal methods into complex systems that utilise Python as the primary implementation language, we aim to generate Python code from Event-B models. To our knowledge, there is currently no existing plugin or tool that facilitates the automatic generation of Python code from Event-B models. Conversely, EB2Py supports a comprehensive subset of Event-B operators and continues to evolve by incorporating additional features, benefiting from ongoing development within the EB2ALL. Other code generation tools related to Event-B are outdated, poorly maintained, and no longer have active web links. This study presents a code generation mechanism, along with a tool implementation, specifically designed for generating Python code from Event-B models.

6 Conclusion

This paper presents a code generation process along with a supporting tool that effectively transforms Event-B models into Python code. We chose to focus on Python due to its extensive range of open-source libraries suitable for different applications and its ease of use in mainstream prototype development. Our main tool, EB2Py, is a prototype designed to automatically generate source code from verified Event-B models. Setting it up as a plugin for the Rodin platform, we detail the code generation mechanism that employs a set of transformation functions. The core of our approach relies on syntax-directed translation and a methodology that ensures correct transformation, enabling the generation of Python code from Event-B models. Although the current implementation focuses on a limited syntax, it effectively accommodates numerical applications and facilitates robust static analysis techniques. The initial version of EB2Py specifically targets a subset of the Event-B to generate the corresponding Python code efficiently.

To illustrate the practical application of our proposed approach, we developed a comprehensive case study on the CRT that successfully transitioned from abstract modelling to real-world implementation. This case study was fully developed and validated within the Rodin platform, leading to the generation of Python code using EB2Py. Additionally, to evaluate the effectiveness of our code generation mechanism, we conducted tests of EB2Py on various complex case studies. The results demonstrated not only the reliability and scalability of the tool but also its significant potential to enhance the modelling, verification, and implementation processes for complex systems. Consequently, EB2Py emerges as an invaluable tool for software engineers and researchers engaged in advanced formal methods for complex system design and implementation.

Currently, EB2Py supports only a subset of the Event-B modelling language. Given the richness of Event-B, we plan to extend this subset to provide greater flexibility in modelling and reasoning, enabling the generation of Python code from any level of refinement. Additionally, we intend to expand EB2Py to include more constructs from Event-B and its extension, including algebraic theories, to enable animation for validation purposes. Furthermore, we will focus on integrating advanced concepts of Python classes to enhance our tool capabilities. An important future task will involve validating the translation principles defined for EB2Py. To achieve this, we will develop a meta-model in higher-order logic to verify the correctness of our transformation rules. This initiative is proposed to ensure that the Python code generated from Event-B models will be certifiable and reliable.

Acknowledgements. The author acknowledges the ANR-19-CE25-0010 *EBRP:EventB-Rodin-Plus* project.

References

1. Abrial, J.: The B-Book - Assigning Programs to Meanings. Cambridge University Press, Cambridge (1996)
2. Abrial, J.: Modeling in Event-B - System and Software Engineering. Cambridge University Press, Cambridge (2010)
3. Abrial, J.R., Butler, M., Hallerstede, S., Hoang, T.S., Mehta, F., Voisin, L.: Rodin: an open toolset for modelling and reasoning in Event-B. Int. J. Softw. Tools Technol. Transf. **12**(6), 447–466 (2010)
4. Behm, P., Benoit, P., Faivre, A., Meynadier, J.-M.: Météor: a successful application of B in a large project. In: Wing, J.M., Woodcock, J., Davies, J. (eds.) FM 1999. LNCS, vol. 1708, pp. 369–387. Springer, Heidelberg (1999). https://doi.org/10.1007/3-540-48119-2_22

5. Bert, D., Boulmé, S., Potet, M.-L., Requet, A., Voisin, L.: Adaptable translator of B specifications to embedded C programs. In: Araki, K., Gnesi, S., Mandrioli, D. (eds.) FME 2003. LNCS, vol. 2805, pp. 94–113. Springer, Heidelberg (2003). https://doi.org/10.1007/978-3-540-45236-2_7
6. Edmunds, A., Rezazadeh, A., Butler, M.: Formal modelling for ADA implementations: tasking Event-B. In: Brorsson, M., Pinho, L.M. (eds.) Reliable Software Technologies - Ada-Europe 2012, pp. 119–132. Springer, Berlin (2012)
7. Fürst, A., Hoang, T.S., Basin, D., Desai, K., Sato, N., Miyazaki, K.: Code generation for Event-B. In: Albert, E., Sekerinski, E. (eds.) Integrated Formal Methods, pp. 323–338. Springer International Publishing, Cham (2014)
8. Karmakar, R.: A framework for component mapping between Event-B and Python. In: Hu, Y.C., Tiwari, S., Trivedi, M.C., Mishra, K.K. (eds.) Ambient Communications and Computer Systems, pp. 129–139. Springer Nature Singapore, Singapore (2022)
9. Lecomte, T., Deharbe, D., Prun, E., Mottin, E.: Applying a formal method in industry: a 25-year trajectory. In: Cavalheiro, S., Fiadeiro, J. (eds.) SBMF 2017. LNCS, vol. 10623, pp. 70–87. Springer, Cham (2017). https://doi.org/10.1007/978-3-319-70848-5_6
10. Leuschel, M., Butler, M.J.: ProB: an automated analysis toolset for the B method. Springer Int. J. STTT **10**(2), 185–203 (2008)
11. Méry, D., Singh, N.K.: Automatic code generation from Event-B models. In: Thang, H.Q., Tran, D.K. (eds.) Proceedings of the 2011 Symposium on Information and Communication Technology, SoICT 2011, Hanoi, Viet Nam, 13–14 October 2011, pp. 179–188. ACM (2011)
12. Ostroumov, S., Tsiopoulos, L.: VHDL code generation from formal Event-B models. In: 2011 14th Euromicro Conference on Digital System Design, pp. 127–134 (2011)
13. Rivera, V., Cataño, N., Wahls, T., Rueda, C.: Code generation for Event-B. Int. J. Softw. Tools Technol. Transfer **19**(1), 31–52 (2017)
14. Singh, N.K.: Using Event-B for critical device software systems. Springer (2013). https://doi.org/10.1007/978-1-4471-5260-6
15. Singh, N.K., Fajge, A.M., Halder, R., Alam, M.I.: Chapter 8 - formal verification and code generation for solidity smart contracts. In: Pandey, R., Goundar, S., Fatima, S. (eds.) Distributed Computing to Blockchain, pp. 125–144. Academic Press
16. Singh, N.K., Lawford, M., Maibaum, T.S.E., Wassyng, A.: Formalizing the cardiac pacemaker resynchronization therapy. In: Duffy, V.G. (ed.) DHM 2015. LNCS, vol. 9185, pp. 374–386. Springer, Cham (2015). https://doi.org/10.1007/978-3-319-21070-4_38
17. Singh, N.K., Lawford, M., Maibaum, T.S.E., Wassyng, A.: Chapter 9 verifying trustworthy cyber-physical systems using closed-loop modeling. In: Romanovsky, A., Ishikawa, F. (eds.) Trustworthy Cyber-Physical Systems Engineering, pp. 199–236. Taylor & Francis Group, 6000 Broken Sound Parkway NW, Suite 300, Boca Raton, FL, pp. 33487–2742. CRC Press (2016)
18. Van Rossum, G., Drake, F.L.: Python 3 Reference Manual. CreateSpace, Scotts Valley, CA (2009)
19. Wright, S.: Automatic generation of C from Event-B. In: Workshop on Integration of Model-based Formal Methods and Tools (2009)

FETMA: A Tool for Functional Block Diagram and Event Tree Based Safety Analysis

Mohamed Abdelghany, Adnan Rashid(✉), and Sofiène Tahar

Department of Electrical and Computer Engineering, Concordia University, Montreal, QC, Canada
{m_eldes,rashid,tahar}@ece.concordia.ca

Abstract. Functional Block Diagrams (FBDs) are widely used for safety analysis in complex industrial electronic systems, such as smart grids and autonomous platforms. They model stochastic behaviors and cascading dependencies of system components using hierarchical Functional Blocks (FBs). Event Tree (ET) modeling is typically integrated with FBDs to capture complete and partial failure scenarios. This paper introduces FETMA (Functional Block Diagram and Event Tree Modeling and Analysis), a software tool for automating FBD construction and safety evaluation. We use FETMA to analyze an automated smart grid substation comprising three levels: Station, Bay, and Process. The tool identifies all possible failure and reliability events across these levels. To evaluate FETMA's scalability, accuracy and execution time, we compare its results with MATLAB-based Monte Carlo simulations, the Isograph software and manual analysis.

Keywords: Functional Block Diagram · Event Tree · Safety Analysis · Python · Smart Grids · Smart Automated Substation

1 Introduction

Meeting rigorous safety standards has become essential in the design of modern industrial systems, such as smart grids and autonomous platforms. To address these challenges, engineers are increasingly relying on reliability modeling techniques aligned with standards, like IEC 61850 [11] and ISO 26262 [12]. Event Tree (ET) analysis [15] is a widely used method for probabilistic risk assessment, offering a structured way to represent all possible failure and success scenarios at the system level. For complex hierarchical systems, ETs can be integrated into Functional Block Diagrams (FBDs) [14], which provide a visual abstraction of system functionality and interconnections[1]. In an FBD, each Functional Block

[1] This notion of FBD is a graphical approach used to represent system components and their interconnections, focusing on failure behavior. It is different from the FBD used in IEC 61131-3 [16], which is a graphical programming language used to design control systems by focusing on data and control flow between functions.

B. Ben Hedia et al. (Eds.): VECoS 2025, LNCS 16263, pp. 174–189, 2026.
https://doi.org/10.1007/978-3-032-20440-0_12

(FB) models a subsystem's behavior by embedding its success and failure pathways using an ET structure. By combining subsystem-level ETs across all FBs, a comprehensive system-wide reliability model can be constructed. FBD-based analysis supports informed decision-making during system design by quantifying the likelihood of critical events and identifying improvement opportunities. For example, Papakonstantinou et al. [13] applied FBD analysis to classify safety levels in a Boiling Water Reactor (BWR) and its associated steam turbine generator within a nuclear power plant.

Traditionally, FBD analysis has relied on manual paper-based methods [14], which are prone to human error due to the complexity involved in constructing hierarchical ET models. While commercial tools such as Isograph[2] and ITEM[3] offer intuitive interfaces and advanced ET modeling features, they lack support for FBD modeling and cannot handle hierarchical ET structures at the subsystem level. These tools also suffer from notable limitations: (1) they require users to manually create a system-level ET diagram, which becomes impractical for large-scale systems; and (2) they do not offer functionality for selecting and analyzing specific sets of ET scenarios based on accident-triggering events, which is essential for accurate probability calculations. Although random-based techniques like, MATLAB Monte Carlo (MC) simulation [20] offer faster computation for ET analysis, they also lack support for hierarchical FBD modeling [10], limiting their utility for structured safety analysis in complex systems.

To address the limitations of existing methods and tools, we introduce a novel software: $\mathbb{FETMA}$ (*Functional Block Diagram and Event Tree Modeling and Analysis*), developed in Python. $\mathbb{FETMA}$ extends a previously developed preliminary tool, ($\mathcal{ETMA}$) [1], which was limited to system-level ET modeling and analysis, only. In contrast, $\mathbb{FETMA}$ supports the modeling and analysis of more hierarchical Event Tree structures, making it well-suited for complex industrial systems. $\mathbb{FETMA}$ offers the following key functionalities: (i) *FBD Construction*: builds a hierarchical FBD model from a list of FBs representing subsystems; (ii) *ET Generation*: automatically creates complete ET models for each FB; (iii) *ET Reduction*: prunes redundant nodes and branches from the generated ETs to reflect accurate subsystem behavior; (iv) *ET Composition*: links the ETs from individual FBs to construct a complete subsystem-level ET model; (v) *ET Partitioning*: selects specific ET scenarios associated with system-level accident events; and (vi) *Probabilistic Analysis*: computes the likelihood of various ET scenarios based on different failure and success conditions to classify safety outcomes. The software is implemented in Python programming language [18], chosen for its robust libraries supporting GUI development, numerical computation and data manipulation. A distinguishing feature of $\mathbb{FETMA}$ is its ability to handle large-scale systems with subsystems/components exhibiting multiple operational states, including complete failure, partial failure, partial success, and complete success. To demonstrate $\mathbb{FETMA}$'s effectiveness, we conduct an FBD-based safety analysis of an industrial automated substation within a smart grid.

---

[2] https://www.isograph.com.
[3] https://itemsoft.com/eventtree.html.

We identify all possible subsystem-level safety classes and compare 𝔽𝔼𝕋𝕄𝔸's results with those obtained through manual mathematical analysis, the Isograph tool, and MATLAB-based Monte Carlo simulation.

The rest of the paper is organized as follows: In Sect. 2, we briefly present the fundamentals of FBDs. The internal structure and the software process of 𝔽𝔼𝕋𝕄𝔸 is described in Sect. 3. Section 4 provides the step-wise safety analysis of a smart automated substation, including the redundancy analysis for the substation critical-components, as well as a comparison with other existing approaches. Lastly, Sect. 5 concludes the paper.

2 Functional Block Diagrams

An FBD is a probabilistic risk assessment method that is based on constructing hierarchical ET structures to perform the subsystem-level safety analysis of industrial systems. To provide a better understanding of the FBD-based safety analysis, we consider a steam turbine governor system of a thermal power plant, as shown in Fig. 1. This system controls the position of a Steam Inlet Valve (V), which in turn regulates the steam flow to the turbine and thus controls the output power. The valve operates with an Induction Motor (IM) that is energized by a Power Supply (PS). The main objective of the valve is to control the Steam Flow (SF) at point B given the flow situation at point A and a command signal C that dictates the required operation of the valve, i.e., opening or closing.

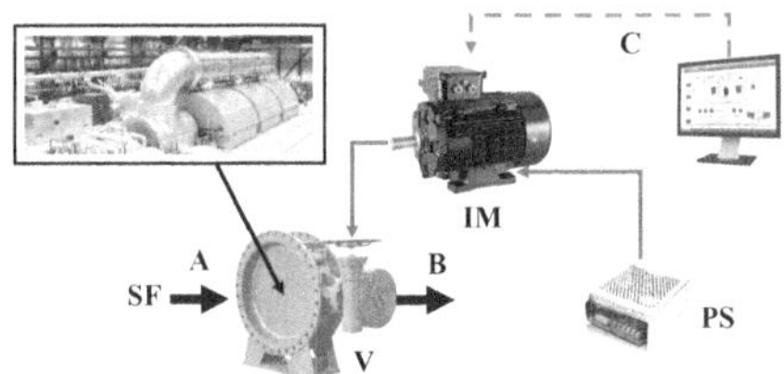

Fig. 1. Steam-Turbine Governor System.

The six step FBD analysis is as follows:

1. **FBD Construction**: Develop an FBD of the system using the engineering knowledge, which consists of FBs representing the subsystem-level behavior, as depicted in Fig. 2.
2. **ET Generation**: Construct a complete ET model corresponding to each subsystem FB. Assuming each subsystem component is represented by two operating states only, i.e., Success (S) or Fail (F). Figure 3 depicts all subsystems' complete ETs of the steam-turbine governor, i.e., $ET_{1(Complete)}$, $ET_{2(Complete)}$ and $ET_{3(Complete)}$ corresponding to FB_1, FB_2 and FB_3, respectively.
3. **ET Reduction**: Reduce the ETs by removing some nodes/branches according to the subsystems' functionality. For instance, in the steam turbine governor $FB_2(ET_{2(Complete)})$, if the critical component power supply FB_1 fails, then the whole IM fails regardless of the status of its other elements, as shown in Fig. 3.

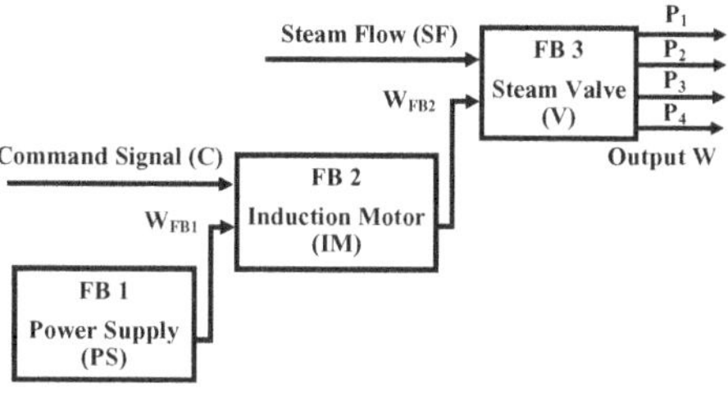

Fig. 2. FBD of Steam-Turbine Governor.

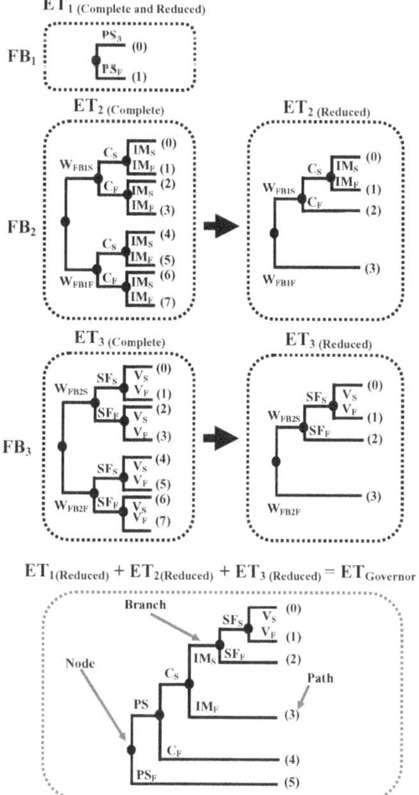

Fig. 3. Steam-Turbine Governor Event Tree (ET) Diagrams.

4. **ET Composition**: Compose all reduced ETs together considering the functional behavior of the steam-turbine governor system to form a complete subsystem level ET model. Here, $ET_{1(Reduced)}$, $ET_{2(Reduced)}$ and $ET_{3(Reduced)}$ are composed to form a subsystem-level $ET_{Governor}$, as shown in Fig. 3, with all possible complete/partial failure and reliability ET consequence paths that can occur.

5. **ET Partitioning**: This step involves extracting the respective paths of the ETs based on the system safety requirements pertaining to the occurrence of certain events, desired by the safety analysts. For instance, if we focus on the Complete Failure (CF) of the IM only, then just the ET Paths 3-5 (Fig. 3) are considered from the $ET_{Governor}$.
6. **FBD based Probabilistic Analysis**: This step evaluates the probabilities of all possible safety classes, ranging from complete failure to partial failure and success, by analyzing the subsystem-level ET paths corresponding to specific events within the system. For example, the probability of CF of the system's component IM, i.e., IM_{CF} event ($ET_{Path3-5}$, Fig. 3) is mathematically expressed as:

$$\begin{aligned} Pr(IM_{CF}) =& Pr(PS_S) \times Pr(C_S) \times Pr(IM_F) + \\ & Pr(PS_S) \times Pr(C_F) + Pr(PS_F) \end{aligned} \tag{1}$$

where $Pr(X_F)$ is the probability of failure for a component X and $Pr(X_S)$ represents the probability of success (correct functioning), i.e., $1 - Pr(X_F)$.

3 FETMA Operation and Structure

Figure 4 illustrates the operational workflow of the FETMA software for the FBD-based modeling and analysis of industrial systems, which consists of 6 main steps as follows: (1) build an FBD for a given system, composed of hierarchical FBs, each representing a subsystem; (2) for each subsystem's FB, identify its components and their operating states, and automatically generate a complete ET capturing all possible subsystem-level outcomes, including complete/partial failure and success paths; (3) refine each generated ET by removing irrelevant branches and nodes to obtain a reduced ET capturing the exact behavior of each subsystem; (4) iteratively combine the reduced ETs associated with all FBs to construct a complete hierarchical ET model of the entire system; (5) Select specific ET paths corresponding to safety classes of interest, guided by system safety requirements; and lastly (6) compute the probabilities associated with all possible safety classes, covering complete/partial failure and success, based on the occurrence of particular events within the system. Algorithm 1 provides a detailed breakdown of FETMA's internal functions that implement these six analysis steps.

The internal structure of FETMA is depicted in Fig. 5, where it consists of 6 core functions dedicated to FBD step-wise analysis and 4 primary functions for ET-based system level analysis. Depending on the required level of detail, users can choose between FBD analysis for subsystem-level insights or ET analysis for broader system-level evaluation. The FETMA software tool is implemented in the Python programming language and is available for download from the project webpage[4].

[4] https://github.com/hvg-concordia/FETMA.

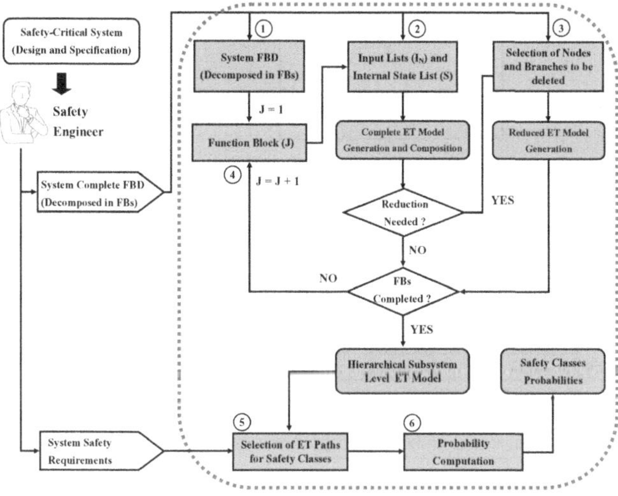

Fig. 4. FETMA Software Operation.

Algorithm 1. FBD Analysis in FETMA

procedure
S1: FBD_modeling
  Input: hierarchical system N FBs
    J = 1
    while (J $\leq$ N)
      S2: complete_gen
        Input: FB (J) inputs and internal states
        Output: subsystem (J) $ET_{Complete}$
          $\mathcal{W}_{Complete}$ (J)
      If Reduction of ET model needed?
      then
      S3: reduction_process
        Input: select nodes and branches
        Output: subsystem (J) $ET_{Reduced}$
          $\mathcal{W}_{Reduced}$ (J)
      S4: composition_process
        Input: $\mathcal{W}_{Complete}$ (J) or $\mathcal{W}_{Reduced}$ (J)
        Output: $\mathcal{W}$ (J) $\bigotimes$ $\mathcal{W}$ (J - 1)
    J = J + 1
  Output: subsystem-level ET graph
    subsystem-level outcome space $\mathcal{W}$
S5: partitioning_paths
  Input: system safety requirements
    select ET path(s)
  Output: system accident events ET graphs
S6: probability_eval
  Input: probabilities of all components states
  Output: occurrence probability of an event
end procedure

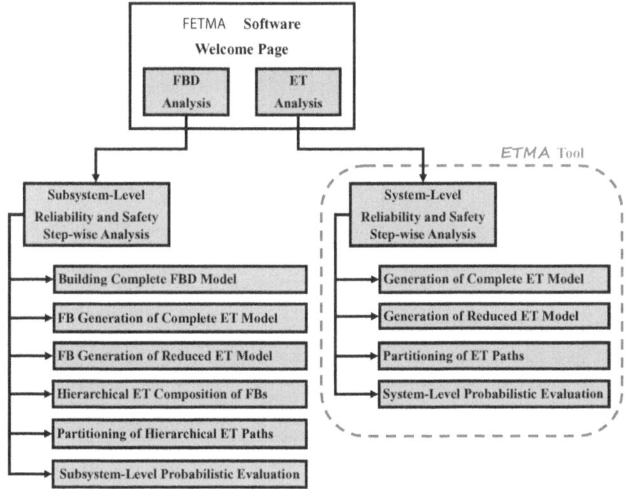

Fig. 5. FETMA Software Internal Structure.

We provide pop-up input windows for all of FBD analysis functions (FBD construction, ET generation, ET reduction, ET composition, ET partitioning, and probabilistic analysis) to enhance users' interaction with FETMA. As noted in Algorithm 1, the ET reduction step is optional and can be bypassed if node or branch deletion is not necessary. To support the generation of hierarchical ET diagrams, the modeling procedures in Algorithm 1 are implemented using the *PyGraphviz* Python package[5], which enables the construction and layout of complex, hierarchical graph structures.

4 Application: Smart Grid Automated Substation

A Smart Grid (SG) is an advanced, interconnected infrastructure designed to deliver electric power efficiently from generation sources to end users [8]. It typically comprises three primary sectors: (i) generation plants, (ii) transmission systems, and (iii) distribution networks [21]. Within this framework, electrical substations play a critical role by transforming voltage levels to facilitate power flow across various stages. In recent years, Smart Automated Substations (SAS) have emerged, incorporating advanced monitoring systems and intelligent control and protection devices to function as integrated, multitasking units [2]. Key substation components, such as Automatic Circuit Reclosers (ACRs), Circuit Breakers (CBs), Disconnecting Switches (DSs), Current Transformers (CTs), and Potential Transformers (PTs), are now equipped with digital transceivers to enable automated control within SAS networks [9].

[5] https://pygraphviz.github.io/.

To ensure reliable and interoperable communication within SAS environments, the IEC 61850 standard [11] is widely adopted, offering enhanced reliability and safety. However, a significant challenge in smart grids with SAS integration lies in safeguarding against potential failures and disturbances. This necessitates comprehensive safety assessments at the subsystem level for all possible accident scenarios. Such analysis is essential for maintaining grid stability and avoiding large-scale blackouts by enabling timely and effective backup responses.

Figure 6 presents the architecture of a real-world smart automated substation, which is organized into three main hierarchical levels, *Process*, *Bay* and *Station*, as follows [7]:

- *Process Level*: It includes Merging Units (MUs) to periodically collect the analog data from sensors and indicators of switchgear equipment, such as CTs, PTs and CBs, through copper wiring. Then, the MUs transit all equipment data to the upper process bus through a digital network.

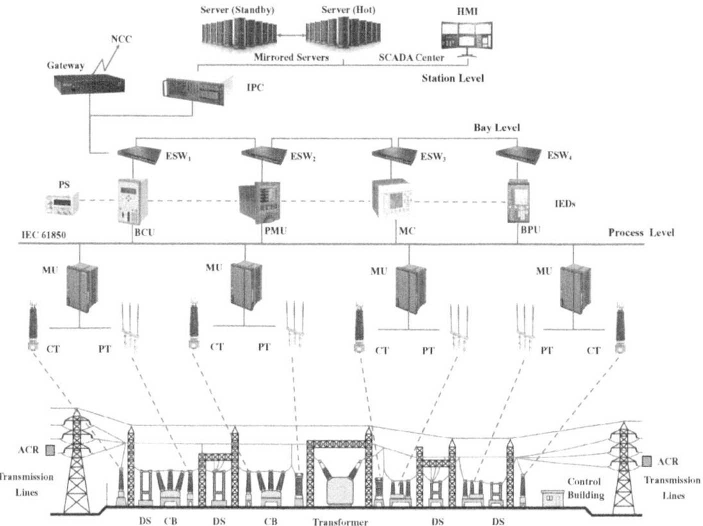

Fig. 6. Automated Substation of a Smart Grid System.

- *Bay Level*: It consists of Intelligent Electronic Devices (IEDs), such as Bay Control Units (BCUs), Bay Protection Units (BPUs), Phasor Measurement Units (PMUs), and Measuring Centers (MCs), which are energized by a DC Power Supply (PS). These IEDs are responsible for gathering all real-time data in each bay and send them to the higher level via communication Ethernet (EI) devices, such as Ethernet Switches (ESWs). There exist five different topologies for IEDs connection configuration, such as simple cascading, redundant cascading, ring, star and hybrid. In this study, we use the simple cascading type for connecting IEDs.

- *Station Level*: It integrates the Supervisory Control and Data Acquisition (SCADA) center to perform remote monitoring and controlling of the SAS system. The SCADA system utilizes Industrial Personal Computer (IPC) and Human Machine Interface (HMI) to display the real-time process data. SCADA also restores all collected data from the Bay Level in a main Server (Hot) as well as a backup mirrored Server (Standby) to prevent the cause of permanent data loss of the SAS. Moreover, the SCADA system utilizes a Gateway (GW) to provide a connection to upper-level Network Control Center (NCC) in the SG.

We now use $\mathbb{FETMA}$ to perform the FBD six step-analysis (cf. Sect. 2) of the SAS system (see Fig. 6) and determine all possible complete/partial safety classes at the subsystem level as follows:

Step 1 (FBD Construction): We enter the FBD multiple-level model of the SAS system, as shown in Fig. 7. The system is susceptible to various sudden Initial Events (IEs) [6], including Transient (T), Semi-Permanent (SP), and Permanent (P) failures. These failures often correspond to common transmission line (TL) faults, such as Line-to-Ground (L-G), Line-to-Line (L-L), Three-Phase (L-L-L), and Three-Line-to-Ground (L-L-L-G), all of which must be promptly isolated. Based on the nature of these IEs, the SAS system can exhibit three safety classes [19], as depicted in Fig. 7: (1) *SUCCESS*: all required functions are operational, and fault isolation is successfully completed; (2) *CLASS I (Manageable Failure)*: Some functions are unavailable, but isolation can still be achieved; and lastly (3) *CLASS II (Complete Failure)*: isolation is not possible due to failure of critical functions. Each Functional Block (FB) within the SAS system is modeled using a multi-state framework for safety analysis, as shown in Fig. 8 [3]. We assume each FB has two operational states: correct functioning (X_1) and failure (X_2). For instance, FB_{11} represents an ACR with states: (a) ACR_1: successful reclosure for fault isolation; and (b) ACR_2: failure to open. Through $\mathbb{FETMA}$'s input interface, we define the operational states for all SAS subsystems across the three hierarchical levels, i.e., *Process level* (ACR, CB_1, CB_2, CT_1, PT_1, MU_1, CT_2, PT_2, MU_2, CT_3, PT_3, MU_3, CT_4, PT_4, MU_4), *Bay level* (PS, BCU, ESW_1, PMU, ESW_2, MC, ESW_3, BPU, ESW_4, EI) and *Station level* (IPC, HMI, $\text{Server}_{\text{Hot}}$, $\text{Server}_{\text{Standby}}$, GW, NCC).

Steps 2–4 (Subsystem-Level ET Generation): We now generate a complete ET graph for each subsystem FB of the SAS system of Fig. 7, then utilise the ET reduction feature in $\mathbb{FETMA}$ to generate a reduced ET model. Next, we use the composition feature of $\mathbb{FETMA}$ to generate a hierarchically composed ET model with all actual complete/partial failure and success scenarios at the subsystem-level (88 ET paths from 0 to 87 out of the complete 2^{31} test cases), as shown in Fig. 9. To the best of our knowledge, this ET composition feature is not available in any other ET analysis tool.

Step 5 (Partitioning): The partitioning process of the generated event outcome space $\mathcal{W}_{SAS}$ is essential as substation safety analysts often seek to evaluate the probabilities of specific event occurrences. Therefore, we can obtain different

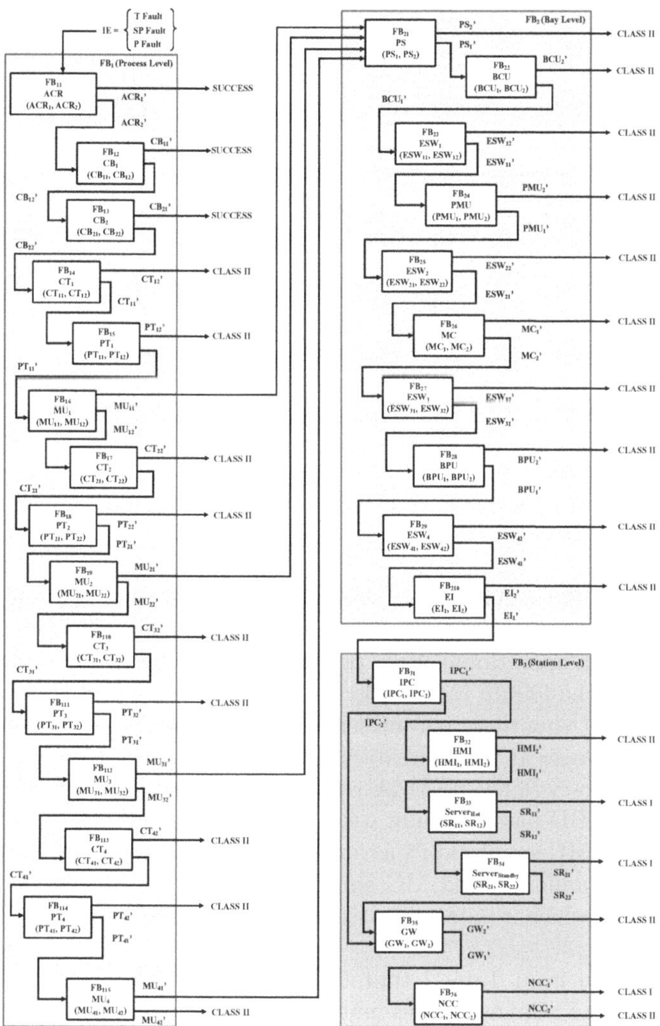

Fig. 7. FBD Multiple-Levels Decomposition of the SAS System.

collections of subsystem-level ET paths, as shown in Fig. 9, by observing the actual behavior of the SAS system as:

- $SAS_{SUCCESS}$ (Complete Success) $= \sum ET_{Paths}(0, 1, 2)$
- SAS_{CLASS_I} (Manageable Failure) $=$
  $\sum ET_{Paths}(3-5, 9, 22-24, 28, 41-43, 47, 60-62, 66)$
- $SAS_{CLASS_{II}}$ (Complete Failure) $= \sum ET_{Paths}(6-8, 10-21,$
  $25-27, 29-40, 44-46, 48-59, 63-65, 67-87)$

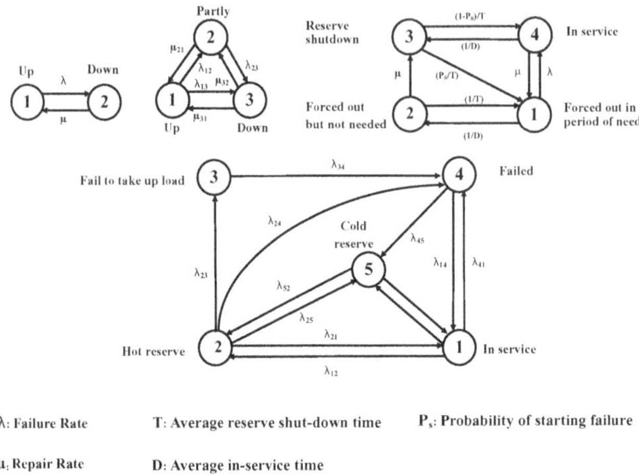

Fig. 8. Multi-State Models for Safety Studies.

Step 6 (Probabilistic Analysis): Assuming that the failure and success events of all SAS subsystem components are continuous exponentially distributed[6] [5] and considering an operational study period of 60 months, i.e., $t = 43,200$ hours, Table 1 presents the failure rates and corresponding state probabilities for each SAS component. Using these parameters, FETMA computes the probabilities of different safety classes at the substation subsystem level, as shown in Table 2. To validate the accuracy of the FETMA results, we perform a comparative analysis against manual FBD-based computation, a commercial software Isograph[7], and MATLAB-based MC simulation[8], as shown in Table 2. Note that the MATLAB software uses a random-based MC simulation algorithm, which examines and predicts the real behavior patterns to estimate the average value of various safety classes.

It can be seen from Table 2 that the results of safety classes for the SAS obtained from the FETMA analysis matches those calculated using the analytical approach and Isograph, while MATLAB provides slightly different results due to its random-based algorithm, which estimates different results at every generation of a random number. Moreover, the CPU time for the SAS FBD analysis in FETMA is much less than MATLAB MC simulations (10x) and Isograph (4x), as shown in Table 2. The experiments were performed on a single-core i5, 2.20 GHz processor, Linux VM with 1 GB of RAM.

During the SAS safety analysis, critical decisions regarding the redundancy of subsystem components must be carefully evaluated, as such enhancements

[6] This distribution is well-known as memoryless and is routinely used in the reliability analysis of real-world substations to determine the probability of failure/success for each SAS component over a time period of interest.

[7] https://www.isograph.com/.

[8] https://www.mathworks.com/products/matlab.html.

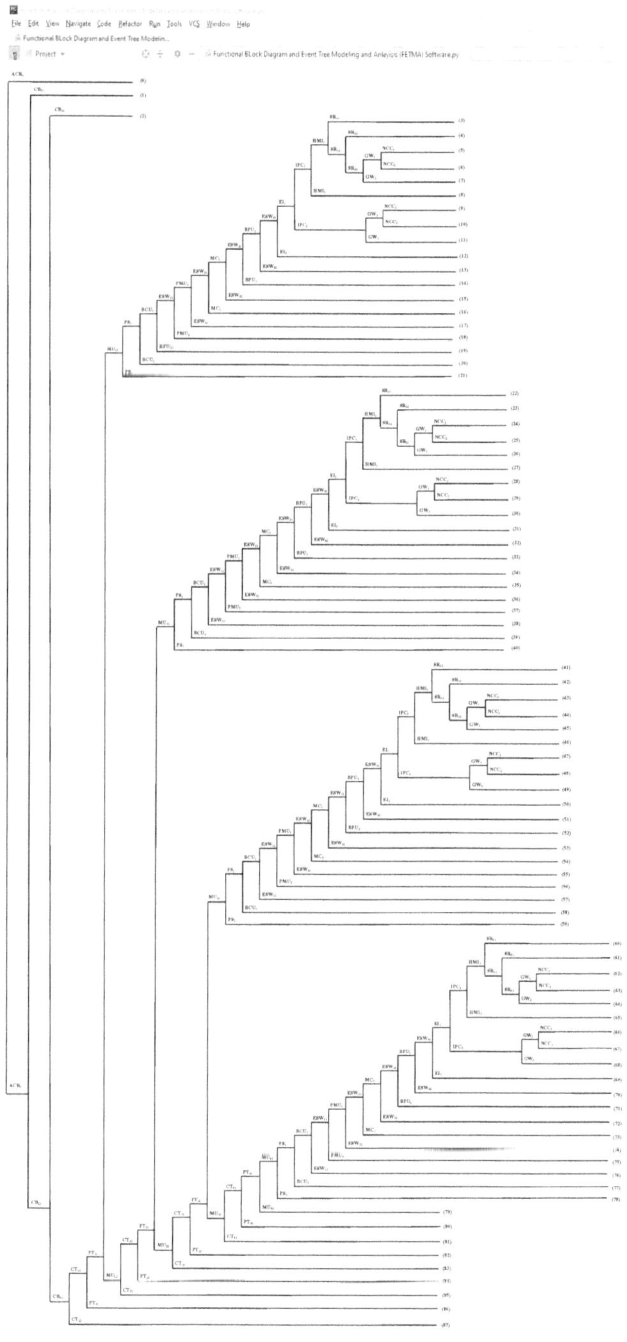

Fig. 9. FETMA: Reduced Subsystem-Level ET Generation of SAS System.

Table 1. SAS Probability of Subsystem Components States

SAS Component (C)	$\lambda(f/yr)$	C_2 After 60 Months	C_1 After 60 Months	SAS Component (C)	$\lambda(f/yr)$	C_2 After 60 Months	C_1 After 60 Months
ACR	0.090	36.24%	63.76%	CB_1	0.085	34.62%	65.38%
CB_2	0.071	29.88%	70.12%	CT_1	0.041	18.54%	81.46%
CT_2	0.057	24.79%	75.21%	CT_3	0.046	20.55%	79.45%
CT_4	0.052	22.89%	77.11%	PT_1	0.045	20.15%	79.85%
PT_2	0.061	26.29%	73.71%	PT_3	0.050	22.12%	77.88%
PT_4	0.063	27.02%	72.98%	MU_1	0.085	34.62%	65.38%
MU_2	0.090	36.23%	63.77%	MU_3	0.075	31.27%	68.73%
MU_4	0.080	32.97%	67.03%	PS	0.029	13.49%	86.51%
BCU	0.050	22.12%	77.88%	PMU	0.040	18.13%	81.87%
MC	0.055	24.04%	75.96%	BPU	0.045	20.15%	79.85%
ESW_1	0.087	35.27%	64.73%	ESW_2	0.094	37.49%	62.51%
ESW_3	0.080	32.97%	67.03%	ESW_4	0.095	37.81%	62.19%
EI	0.083	33.97%	66.03%	IPC	0.069	29.18%	70.82%
HMI	0.100	39.35%	60.65%	$Server_H$	0.020	9.52%	90.48%
$Server_S$	0.032	14.79%	85.21%	GW	0.073	30.58%	69.42%
NCC	0.069	29.18%	70.82%				

Table 2. Comparison for SAS Safety Classes Analysis Results

SAS System Safety Classes	Manual	Isograph	MATLAB	FEMTA
SUCCESS	96.25%	96.251%	94.8743%	96.25117%
$CLASS_I$	1.54%	1.544%	2.3952%	1.54427%
$CLASS_{II}$	2.21%	2.205%	2.7305%	2.20456%
CPU Time	-	23.41 min	52.38 min	5.14 min

significantly impact the total capital cost of the substation. To assess the trade-off between cost and reliability, we conduct a redundancy analysis to examine how adding backup components affects the overall safety of the SAS system. For instance, Fig. 10 illustrates a redundant cascading topology [17] at the bay level, which offers higher reliability compared to a simple cascading configuration, albeit at the expense of increased communication network costs. Additionally, at the process level, we introduce a redundant backup for the critical ACR component to enhance system performance.

Figure 11 presents a comparative histogram of the safety class probabilities before and after redundancy, as computed using the FETMA software. The results reveal a significant reduction in the probability of complete failure ($CLASS_{II}$) from 2.20456% to 0.7592%, a decrease of 1.44536%. Concurrently, the probabilities for SUCCESS and manageable failure ($CLASS_I$) increase from 96.25117% to 97.24692% and from 1.54427% to 1.99388%, respectively. With FETMA, these updated results were obtained within approximately 5 minutes by simply adding the new components and rerunning the analysis. In contrast,

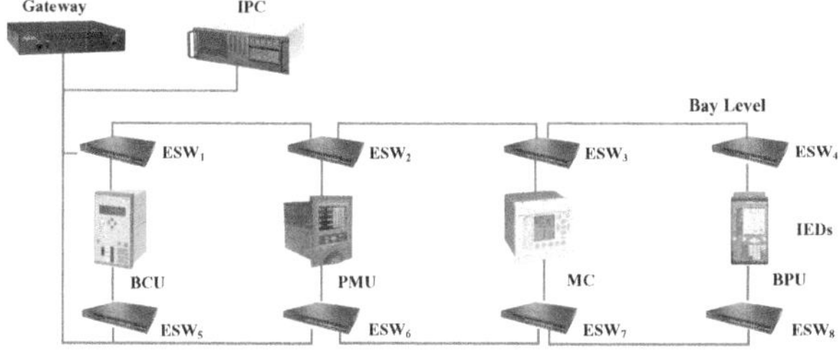

Fig. 10. SAS Redundant Cascading Topology.

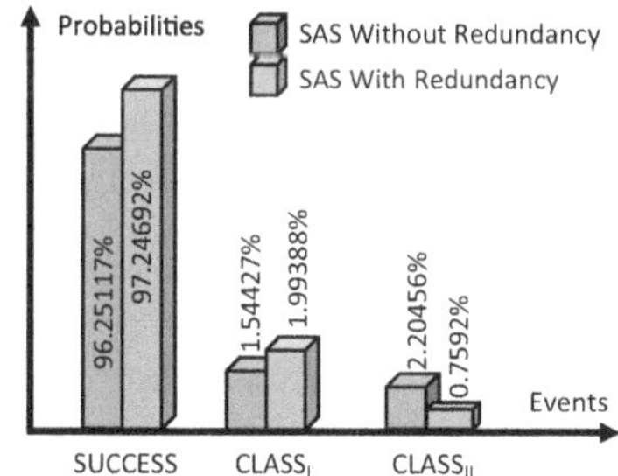

Fig. 11. $\mathbb{FETMA}$: SAS Probabilistic Evaluation.

generating the same results using MATLAB's MC simulation required nearly an additional hour, while manually repeating the FBD-based safety analysis for a system of this complexity was considerably more time-consuming and error-prone. These observations highlight $\mathbb{FETMA}$'s potential to support practicing power and safety engineers in efficiently performing reliability and safety analyses of complex power systems. Its ease of use and ability to deliver accurate results rapidly make it a valuable tool for informed decision-making during the design and assessment phases.

5 Conclusion

In this paper, we introduced $\mathbb{FETMA}$, a novel software tool designed for Functional Block Diagram (FBD) and Event Tree (ET) based safety analysis. Implemented in Python, $\mathbb{FETMA}$ enables the systematic evaluation of the probabilities associated with all possible multi-state safety classes, including complete and partial reliability and failure consequence scenarios. To demonstrate its effectiveness, we applied $\mathbb{FETMA}$ to a real-world industrial application, i.e., a Smart Grid Automated Substation, performing a detailed subsystem-level safety analysis. We validated the accuracy of $\mathbb{FETMA}$ by comparing its results with those obtained through manual analysis, the commercial Isograph tool, and MATLAB-based Monte Carlo simulations, all of which are widely used in ET analysis.

In future, we aim to extend FETMA with cause-consequence analysis capabilities [4], enabling support for Failure Modes and Effects Analysis (FMEA) of complex safety-critical systems.

References

1. Abdelghany, M., Ahmad, W., Tahar, S., Nethula, S.: ($\mathcal{ETMA}$): an efficient tool for event trees modeling and Analysis. In: International Systems Conference, pp. 1–8. IEEE (2020)
2. Aftab, M.A., Hussain, S.S., Ali, I., Ustun, T.S.: IEC 61850 based substation automation system: a survey. Int. J. Electr. Power Energy Syst. **120**, 106008 (2020)
3. Allan, R.N., et al.: Reliability Evaluation of Power Systems. Springer Science & Business Media, Cham (2013)
4. Andrews, J., Ridley, L.: Reliability of sequential systems using the cause-consequence diagram method. J. Process Mech. Eng. **215**(3), 207–220 (2001)
5. Čepin, M.: Assessment of Power System Reliability: Methods and Applications. Springer Science & Business Media, Cham (2011)
6. Chattopadhyay, A., Ukil, A., Jap, D., Bhasin, S.: Toward threat of implementation attacks on substation security: case study on fault detection and isolation. IEEE Trans. Industr. Inf. **14**(6), 2442–2451 (2017)
7. Hajian-Hoseinabadi, H., Golshan, M.E.H.: Availability, reliability, and component importance evaluation of various repairable substation automation systems. IEEE Trans. Power Delivery **27**(3), 1358–1367 (2012)
8. Keyhani, A.: Smart power grids. In: Smart Power Grids, pp. 1–25. Springer (2011)
9. König, J., Nordström, L.: Reliability analysis of substation automation system functions. In: Annual Reliability and Maintainability Symposium, pp. 1–6. IEEE (2012)
10. Li, W., et al.: Reliability Assessment of Electric Power Systems using Monte Carlo Methods. Springer Science & Business Media, Cham (2013)
11. Mackiewicz, R.E.: Overview of IEC 61850 and benefits. In: Power Engineering Society General Meeting, pp. 1–8. IEEE (2006)
12. Palin, R., Ward, D., Habli, I., Rivett, R.: ISO 26262 safety cases: compliance and assurance (2011)
13. Papakonstantinou, N., Sierla, S., O'Halloran, B., Tumer, I.Y.: A simulation based approach to automate event tree generation for early complex system designs. In: International Design Engineering Technical Conferences, vol. 55867, pp. 1–10. American Society of Mechanical Engineers (2013)
14. Papazoglou, I.A.: Functional block diagrams and automated construction of event trees. Reliab. Eng. Syst. Saf. **61**(3), 185–214 (1998a)
15. Papazoglou, I.A.: Mathematical Foundations of Event Trees. Reliab. Eng. Syst. Saf. **61**(3), 169–183 (1998b)
16. Ramanathan, R.: The IEC 61131–3 programming languages features for industrial control systems. In: World Automation Congress, pp. 598–603. IEEE (2014)
17. Salehi, F., Brahman, A., Keypour, R., Lee, W.J.: Reliability assessment of automated substation and functional integration. In: Industry Applications Society Annual Meeting, pp. 1–7. IEEE (2016)
18. Van Rossum, G., Drake, F.L.: Python language reference manual (2003)
19. Wang, F., Tuinema, B.W., Gibescu, M., van der Meijden, M.A.: Reliability evaluation of substations subject to protection system failures. In: Grenoble Conference, pp. 1–6. IEEE (2013)

20. Wei, L., Ya-nan, Y., Wei-dong, D., Bo, Z.: Study on financial risk assessment of substation project based on monte Carlo simulation. In: Communication Software and Networks, pp. 62–65. IEEE (2011)
21. Xu, S., Qian, Y., Hu, R.Q.: On reliability of smart grid neighborhood area networks. IEEE Access **3**, 2352–2365 (2015)

Rail Requirements Tracking and Architectural Verification

Aroua Ben Daya[1](✉), Rim Saddem-Yagoubi[2], and Mohamed Taha Bennani[1]

[1] University of Tunis El Manar, Tunis, Tunisia
aroua.bendaya@etudiant-fst.utm.tn, taha.bennani@fst.utm.tn
[2] Aix Marseille Univ, CNRS, LIS, Marseille, France
rim.saddem@lis-lab.fr

Abstract. The railway signaling system is responsible for managing traffic and ensuring a safe distance between trains in all circumstances. Faced with growing demand for rail transport, renowned for its low carbon footprint, the traditional signaling system, based on the fixed block concept, is reaching its capacity limits. Future signaling systems, based on the moving block concept, aim to reduce the spacing between succeeding trains, thus optimizing the use of existing infrastructure. However, the full requirements for these systems are still under development and require further refinement before they can be considered as a viable and, above all, safe solution for European railways. In this context, European projects X2Rail-1 (2019), X2Rail-3 (2020) and X2Rail-5 (2022) provide detailed descriptions of the functional and safety requirements of these systems in structured natural language. This article presents a method for analyzing these requirements. The study relies on rule-based tools and custom scripts to extract, track, and visualize the evolution of these requirements. The identified requirement changes guided the update of the system's functional architecture to align with the most recent specifications.

Keywords: Requirement engineering · ERTMS/ETCS · Evolution tracking

1 Introduction

System requirements are the cornerstone of critical system engineering, but their formulation in natural language (NL) remains a persistent challenge. Despite its readability and expressiveness, NL is inherently ambiguous and prone to underspecification, leading to interpretation errors, implementation inconsistencies, and costly validation loops in later development stages [9]. These issues are particularly important in safety-sensitive areas, where misunderstandings can lead to widespread failures.

To mitigate these risks, the adoption of Structured Natural Language (SNL) has gained traction. SNL combines the flexibility of NL with structured templates known as boilerplates, which are predefined syntactic patterns like "$< actor >$

B. Ben Hedia et al. (Eds.): VECoS 2025, LNCS 16263, pp. 190–204, 2026.
https://doi.org/10.1007/978-3-032-20440-0_13

shall < *action* > **when** < *condition* >", and strict grammatical constraints that ensure consistency and reduce ambiguity [9]. This structured form facilitates mapping requirement statements to domain-specific ontologies, allowing semantic analyses such as completeness checking, conflict detection, and redundancy elimination. Such semiformal specifications can serve as an intermediate step toward formalization and verification using model checking, simulation, or proof-based techniques [2].

The need for such formalization is even more pronounced in the railway signaling domain. The European Train Control System (ETCS), part of the ERTMS standard, was developed to replace the diverse national Control-Command and Signaling systems with a unified, interoperable European standard [6]. Among its application levels, ETCS Level 3 applies the concept of Moving Block (MB)—already deployed in metro systems—to mainline railways, shifting from traditional fixed-block signaling to a dynamic, train-centered separation principle.

This principle allows trains to operate closer together by continuously updating separation distances based on real-time train location and integrity information. Unlike Levels 1 and 2, which still rely on trackside train detection equipment, Level 3 eliminates much of this infrastructure equipment, enabling higher line capacity, reduced maintenance costs, and improved responsiveness to operational conditions. However, these benefits come with increased system complexity and stringent safety requirements. To ensure reliable operation, onboard and trackside components must interoperate according to precisely defined requirements that evolve across specification versions. These requirements must be formally specified, traced, and validated using model-based verification techniques [12].

To support this evolution, the Shift2Rail initiative has issued successive versions of system requirement specifications through the X2Rail projects (X2R1 in 2019, X2R3 in 2020, and X2R5 in 2022). These documents, though structured, evolve over time, adding, modifying, or removing requirements, which introduces additional challenges for requirement traceability and architectural consistency across versions.

This paper addresses these challenges by proposing an end-to-end approach to requirement engineering in the context of ETCS Level 3 systems. Our contributions are threefold:

1. **Automatic requirement extraction:** We develop a rule-based method to extract functional and safety requirements from structured PDF specifications using syntactic and lexical patterns tailored to the X2Rail format.
2. **Evolution tracking and visualization:** We propose a traceability framework that identifies new, modified, unchanged, or deleted requirements across specification versions, and we introduce an interactive mindmap to visualize the evolution of the requirement space.
3. **Architecture redesign guided by evolved requirements:** We analyze the architectural implications of requirement changes and update the ETCS Level 3 functional architecture accordingly, focusing on communication links between onboard and trackside components.

The remainder of the paper is organized as follows. Section 2 surveys related work on structured requirement extraction, version-aware traceability, and architecture evolution. Section 3 introduces the ETCS Level 3 context, the structure of X2Rail specifications, and the baseline architecture. Section 4 describes our methodology for automated requirement extraction and evolution tracking. Section 6 presents our proposed architectural redesign based on the updated requirements. Finally, Sect. 7 concludes and outlines directions for future work.

2 Related Work

This section reviews previous work in three areas relevant to our study: extracting requirements expressed in Structured Natural Language (SNL), tracking their evolution across specification versions, and updating system architecture based on evolving requirements.

2.1 Requirement Extraction from Structured Natural Language

Extracting requirements from semi-structured documents remains a central challenge in Requirements Engineering, particularly when specifications are encoded in Structured Natural Language (SNL). Several approaches have emerged, varying in complexity and automation level.

Rule-Based Extraction. Rule-based techniques are still widely used to extract requirements from SNL documents. These approaches define syntactic patterns (e.g., modal verbs such as *shall*, *must*, *will*) and lexical patterns (domain-specific terms like *position report*, *integrity*, *RBC*) to detect and isolate requirement clauses [7]. Regular expressions and template matching are typical implementation techniques. This approach aligns well with the structure of the X2Rail specifications (ID, Traceability, Description), making it suitable for our context.

Template-Based and Document-Aware Parsing. Requirements fields in specifications with consistent formatting often follow a known schema. Template-based methods exploit this structure to identify requirement blocks using section headers or formatting cues [10]. These methods are particularly effective when specifications conform to a defined standard, as is the case with X2Rail documents.

Hybrid Rule-Based + NLP Systems. To improve the expressiveness of rule-based approaches, recent work incorporates shallow natural language processing techniques, including tokenization, lemmatization, and part-of-speech tagging [7]. These preprocessing steps help to generalize the syntactic variations and enhance the matching of requirement patterns. Despite the growing interest in machine learning, rule-based methods augmented with linguistic features remain predominant for requirement extraction in structured technical documents due to their transparency and reliability. However, their industrial adoption in safety-critical domains such as ETCS is still limited by strict certification and explainability requirements [13].

2.2 Tracking Requirement Evolution Across Specification Versions

In evolving specifications, tracking the lifecycle of requirements is critical. The main goals are to detect additions, deletions, modifications, and changes in traceability between versions. We identify three approaches: traceability and delta analysis, semantic matching and NLP, and graph visualization.

Traceability and Delta-Based Analysis. Version differencing techniques compare requirements across versions using ID-based alignment and content similarity measures. When IDs are preserved, changes in description or traceability fields are analyzed to classify requirements as *New*, *Modified*, *Unchanged*, or *Deleted* [4]. Our approach builds on this foundation by combining identification and description matching with evolution status annotation and visual mapping.

Semantic Matching and NLP. To align reworded requirements across versions, recent approaches use trained language models such as BERT to compute semantic similarity. These models convert requirements into vector spaces that capture meaning beyond surface-level wording, allowing the detection of semantically equivalent but syntactically different statements [1]. Although promising, these techniques remain largely experimental in safety-critical domains due to explainability and certification constraints.

Graph-Based Visualization. Graph-based visualizations of requirement evolution (e.g., dynamic graphs and temporal networks) provide intuitive insights into change propagation across versions. Our D3-based interactive visualization integrates this idea to enhance human-in-the-loop traceability analysis [8].

2.3 Architecture Updates Driven by Requirement Evolution

The final challenge is to align the system architecture with evolving requirements. Several strategies support this alignment. In this section, we introduce the impact analysis and traceability models, and the synchronization of models.

Impact Analysis and Traceability Models. Requirement changes are propagated to the architecture elements using traceability-driven impact analysis. Rule-based, semantics-aware approaches can identify candidate components or interfaces likely affected by requirement updates [5].

Model Synchronization. Model-driven engineering tools such as Papyrus and ReqCycle enable synchronization between requirement models and architecture (e.g., SysML, UML), supporting semi-automated propagation of requirement changes into system design artifacts [11].

3 Preliminaries

This section introduces the technical background necessary for understanding our methodology. First, we describe the structure of the X2Rail specification documents and the organization of requirements expressed in Structured Natural Language (SNL). Then, we present the baseline functional architecture from X2Rail-3, which serves as the reference model for our architectural analysis.

3.1 Structure of the X2Rail Specifications

The X2Rail deliverables (D5.1 X2R1, D4.2 X2R3, D4.1 X2R5) define hundreds of structured requirements written in *Structured Natural Language* (SNL) and organized by functional topics. Each topic (e.g., *Train Location*) may contain multiple requirements (as formalized by Eq. (1) that describe expected system behaviors under nominal or degraded conditions. This organization can be abstractly formalized as:

$$\langle\texttt{Topic}\rangle\langle\texttt{Requirement}\rangle^{+} \tag{1}$$

Each requirement follows a regular template, which we abstract as:

$$\begin{aligned} &\langle\texttt{Requirement ID}\rangle[\langle\texttt{Mandatory/Optional}\rangle]\ [\langle\texttt{Traceability}\rangle] \\ &\qquad\langle\texttt{Description}\rangle[\langle\texttt{Rationale}\rangle]\ [\langle\texttt{Guidance}\rangle] \end{aligned} \tag{2}$$

where: **Requirement ID** uniquely identifies the requirement; the optional **Mandatory/Optional** label indicates requirement criticality; **Traceability** (present in X2R3/X2R5) links to previous versions; and **Description**, **Rationale**, and **Guidance** provide an explanation of intent and implementation. Figure 1 below illustrates an example requirement following this pattern, extracted from X2R5:

REQ-TrackStatus-1	Mandatory	[X2R3 D4.2: REQ-TrackStatus-1]

The L3 Trackside shall determine the Consolidated Track Status of the entire track within the Area of Control.

Rationale:

It is critical that within a system where the means of locating trains is via Train Position Reports, the Trackside maintains an up to date record of the Track Status within its Area of Control.

Guidance:

An area of track within the Area of Control will be Occupied, Unknown or Clear. The L3 Trackside determines this Consolidated Track Status for the complete Area of Control from all the individual Track Status Areas.

In the absence of any Track Status Area the Track Status of that part of the railway is Clear

Fig. 1. Example requirement structure in X2R5—`REQ-TrackStatus-1`.

Despite this structure, tracking requirement changes across versions remain challenging due to topic reorganization, inconsistent traceability references, and formatting inconsistencies in section titles, which hinder automated parsing.

These structural insights served as a foundation for designing the regular expressions used in our extraction script (discussed later in Sect. 4.1), which target key fields such as the *Requirement ID*, *traceability chain*, and *topic labels*.

3.2 Baseline Functional Architecture (X2Rail-3)

Our architectural analysis is grounded in the functional system view provided in the X2Rail-3 specification. Figure 2 introduces the reference architecture, which includes:

- 13 core functional components (e.g., Train Management, Route Management, Points Management),
- 7 external actors (e.g., Traffic Management System, Train Localization Unit, Driver),
- 59 documented functional interactions, representing control, supervision, or feedback flows.

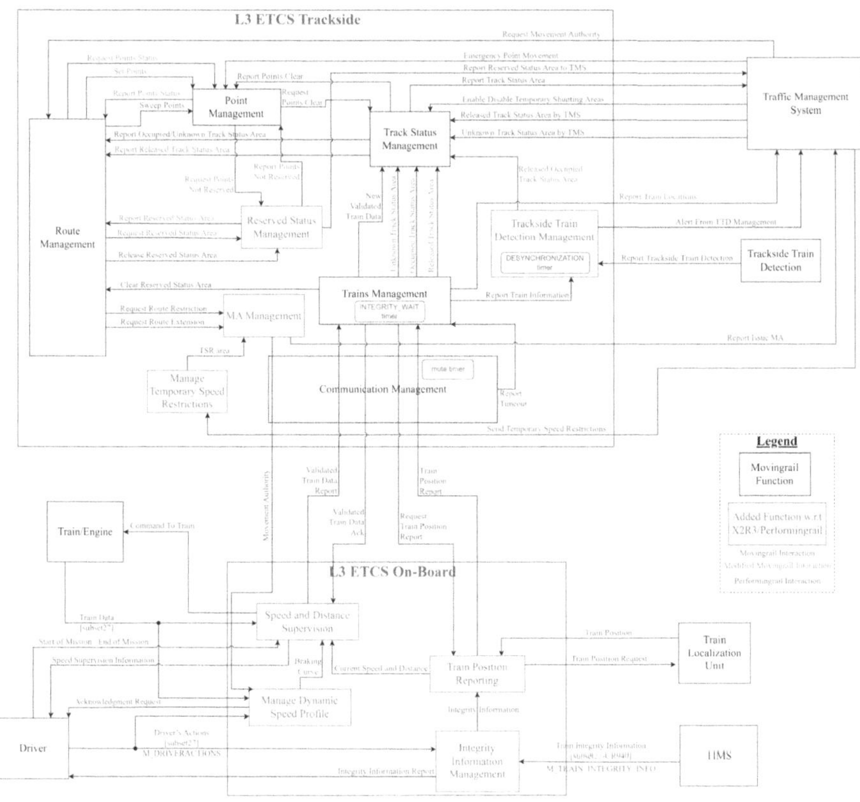

Fig. 2. Baseline ETCS Level 3 architecture (from X2Rail-3).

These interactions define how components exchange information and react to events, forming the baseline against which we assess the impact of requirement evolution in X2Rail-5. While our updates remain consistent with the interaction links defined in X2Rail-3, selected architectural extensions are introduced when explicitly justified by new behavioral requirements in X2Rail-5.

4 Requirement Engineering

To support version-aware analysis of ETCS Level 3 requirements, we adopt a modular process that can be replicated for any new X2Rail deliverable. This process is illustrated in Fig. 3. For each specification version (e.g., X2R1, X2R3, X2R5), requirements are first automatically extracted from semi-structured PDF documents using a dedicated script. These extracted data are then incrementally merged based on traceability and content similarity to build a unified view of requirement evolution across versions.

The resulting merged file encodes all relevant changes—additions, modifications, deletions—alongside metadata such as topic, traceability path, and evolution status. This unified dataset serves as the input for generating an interactive mind map, which visualizes the entire evolution tree of ETCS-L3 requirements.

This procedure is generic and repeatable: each time a new specification is released, it can be processed through the same pipeline, enabling continuous update and visualization of requirement evolution.

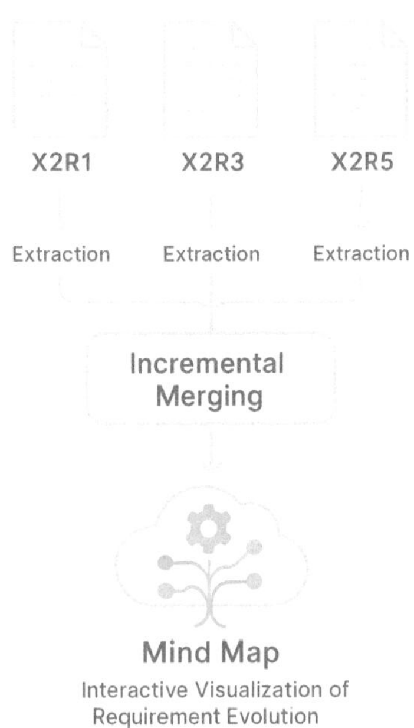

Fig. 3. Version-aware processing pipeline for ETCS Level 3 requirements.

4.1 Pattern-Based Requirement Parsing

To extract structured information from the X2Rail specifications, we rely on regular expressions targeting three main elements: topic headers, requirement identifiers, and traceability references.

Topic Headers. Each functional topic is typically introduced by a section title such as "6.1 - Train Location". We use the following standard pattern 3 to detect such headers:

$$\backslash \mathtt{s} * (\backslash \mathtt{d} + \backslash . \backslash \mathtt{d}+)\backslash \mathtt{s} + ([\mathtt{A} - \mathtt{Za} - \mathtt{z}][\mathtt{A} - \mathtt{Za} - \mathtt{z0} - 9\backslash - /]+) \tag{3}$$

In practice, inconsistent formatting—e.g., missing spaces or compact headings like "6.1TrainLocation"—necessitated a secondary fallback pattern during parsing.

Requirement Identifiers. Each requirement is assigned a unique identifier following the format `REQ-<Keyword>-<Number>` (e.g., `REQ-TrainLoc-5`). These identifiers are extracted using the following regular expression 4:

$$\mathtt{REQ} - [\mathtt{A} - \mathtt{Za} - \mathtt{z0} - 9] + (-\backslash \mathtt{d}+)? \tag{4}$$

Traceability References. Requirements in X2R3 and X2R5 may include backward traceability links to earlier versions, typically enclosed in brackets (e.g., `[X2R3 D4.2: REQ-TrainLoc-2]`). The following expression 5 captures these references:

$$\backslash [(\mathtt{X2R}\backslash \mathtt{d} + \mathtt{D}\backslash \mathtt{d} + \backslash . \backslash \mathtt{d}+ : \mathtt{REQ} - [\mathtt{A} - \mathtt{Za} - \mathtt{z0} - 9-]+)\backslash] \tag{5}$$

Once a requirement identifier is detected, its corresponding description is extracted by reading the subsequent lines until a stopping cue is encountered—typically a keyword such as `Rationale`, `Guidance`. All lines between the identifier and these delimiters are concatenated into a multiline description.

4.2 Mind Map Formalization

To support human-in-the-loop analysis and ensure traceability at scale, the evolution of ETCS Level 3 requirements is visualized through an interactive mind map. This mind map represents the complete lifecycle of each requirement in versions (X2R1, X2R3, X2R5) as an oriented tree structure enriched with semantic annotations.

Node Structure. Each node in the mind map corresponds to a requirement in a specific version. It is labeled using the format: `< Version >:< RequirementID >`

For example, `X2R3:REQ-TrainLoc-7` refers to requirement 7 of the Train Location topic in version X2R3.

Branch Semantics and Traceability. Branches between nodes represent traceability links between versions, showing how a requirement evolves. These branches are constructed by parsing the traceability field during merging. If a requirement in version X2R5 refers to `X2R3:REQ-StartTrain-8`, a direct parent-child link is created between the two. The edge direction always flows from earlier to later versions, forming a forward evolution chain.

Topic and Color Encoding. Topics are encoded using colors. Each unique functional topic (e.g., Train Location, Track Status) is assigned a distinct color. When a requirement changes topic between versions, this is reflected by a change in color between connected nodes. This helps visually detect reclassifications or refactorings of the requirement space.

The following definition 1 formalizes the description of the mind map that expresses the evolution of the requirements.

Definition 1. *Requirement evolution tree (Mind map)*
The mind map is a rooted, oriented, and coloured tree $T =< V, \hat{E}, T, r, c >$. V *is a set of requirements augmented with the root node* r. $\hat{E}$ *is a set of directed edges,* $\hat{E} \subseteq \{(x, y) | (x, y) \in V^2,\ x \neq y, and y \neq r\}$. T *is a set of topics, which corresponds to the different colors. The colouring function* $c : (\hat{E}, V) \rightarrow T$ *is related to four elementary operations: Add, Modify, Unchanged, and Absent.*

Elementary Mind Map Operators. The evolution process is encoded using a set of elementary operators, summarized in Table 1:

Table 1. Elementary operators for mind map requirement evolution

Add ()	**Modify (Topic)**	**Unchanged**	**Absent**
root Add REQ	REQ Topic Change REQ'	REQ No Change REQ	REQ Absent None

The operation *Add* creates a new vertex and connects it to the root of the tree. The colors of the added elements follow the distinctive color associated with the topic. The operation $Modify$ creates a new vertex and connects it to the node representing the previous version of the requirement. A modification can either update the description of a requirement or change its associated topic. In the former case, the color of the edge and the destination node remain consistent with that of the source node. In the latter case, only the destination node adopts the color associated with the new topic, while the connecting edge is drawn in a neutral color, visually decoupled from topic semantics. The *Unchanged* function behaves like the first case of the Modify operation; however, it does not alter the description associated with the destination node. The last function, *Absent*, creates a new vertex and links it to the node corresponding to the removed requirement. The description associated with the newly created node is left empty.

5 Implementation Overview

To support the end-to-end analysis of evolving ETCS Level 3 requirements, we implemented a modular three-step pipeline as depicted in Fig. 4. The complete pipeline—including extraction, evolution tracking, and visualization tools—is available as an open-source repository [3].

To enable automated processing of the X2Rail specifications (STEP 1 - Extraction), we developed a custom Python script, `AutoReqExtract.py`[1], which extracts all functional and safety requirements from a PDF file into a unified, structured Excel format. The script uses pattern-based parsing to detect the fields specified in Sect. 4.1. This extraction process is applied independently to each specification version (D5.1 X2R1, D4.2 X2R3, D4.1 X2R5), serving as the foundation for subsequent comparison and evolution tracking.

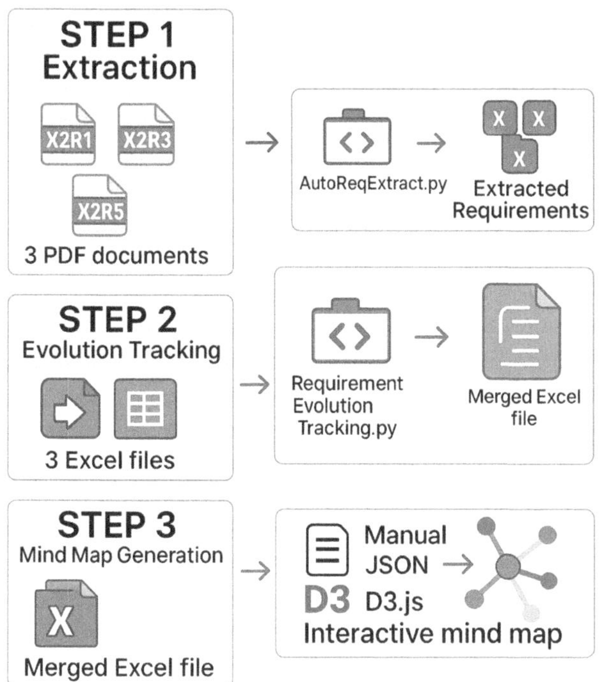

Fig. 4. End-to-end implementation pipeline.

After extracting the requirements from each version, we apply a dedicated Python script, `RequirementEvolutionTracking.py`, to identify changes and

[1] https://github.com/Aroua-Ben-Daya/ETCS-Requirement-Evolution.

classify them across versions (STEP 2 - Evolution Tracking). This script compares the three extracted Excel files from X2R1, X2R3, and X2R5, and produces a consolidated evolution table where each requirement is annotated with an evolution status, which can be one of the following: **New**, **Unchanged**, **Modified**, **Absent**. This process consists of three steps:

1. **Traceability mapping:** The traceability field is parsed to identify base requirements from previous versions (e.g., `X2R3 D4.2: REQ-TrainLoc-2`).
2. **Content and topic comparison:** If a base requirement is found, its topic and description are compared to the current one. Any difference results in a *Modified* label, with the nature of the change recorded.
3. **Status assignment:** Based on the presence or absence of references, and the comparison outcome, an evolution status is assigned.

To avoid conflicting classifications, requirements initially marked as `New` are reclassified if they are reused in a later version. Conversely, requirements not reused in any future version are labeled `Absent`. The final output is a traceable Excel table depicted in Fig. 5, which serves as input to generate the mind map visualization. Each row corresponds to a requirement instance across versions. The first column indicates the specification version (e.g., X2R1, X2R3, X2R5). The second and third columns list the requirement identifier in the current version and its corresponding base identifier, if any. The fourth column encodes the evolution status New, Modified, Unchanged, or Absent. Finally, the last two columns detail the full traceability path and specify whether changes occurred in the topic or description.

Version	Current Requirement ID	Base Requirement ID	Status	Traceability Path	Topic or description change
X2R3	REQ-TrainLoc-3	REQ-TrainLoc-2	Modified	X2R1:REQ-TrainLoc-2 → X2R3:REQ-TrainLoc-3	4 escription changed
X2R5	REQ-EoAExclusionArea-2	REQ-EoAExclusionArea-1	Modified	X2R1:REQ-EoAExclusionArea-1 → X2R3:REQ-EoAExclusionArea-1 → X2R5:REQ-EoAExclusionArea-2	4 escription changed
X2R5	REQ-EoAExclusionArea-3	REQ-EoAExclusionArea-1	Modified	X2R1:REQ-EoAExclusionArea-1 → X2R3:REQ-EoAExclusionArea-1 → X2R5:REQ-EoAExclusionArea-3	4 escription changed
X2R3	REQ-LevelTrans-2	REQ-StartTrain-2	Modified	X2R1:REQ-StartTrain-2 → X2R3:REQ-LevelTrans-2	Topic changed, Description changed
X2R3	REQ-Rev-1	REQ-Rev-1	✓ Unchanged	X2R1: REQ-Rev-1 → X2R3: REQ-Rev-1	
X2R1	REQ-EoM-2		×, bsent	X2R1:REQ-EoM-2	
X2R1	REQ-EoM-3		×, bsent	X2R1:REQ-EoM-3	
X2R1	REQ-EoM-4		×, bsent	X2R1:REQ-EoM-4	
X2R5	REQ-LevelTrans-2		New	X2R5:REQ-LevelTrans-2	
X2R5	REQ-PTS-5		New	X2R5:REQ-PTS-5	

Fig. 5. Example of evolution tracking with status labels.

To complement tabular tracking and support human-in-the-loop analysis, we developed an interactive visualization using the D3.js library (within the third step - Mind Map Generation).

The tree is generated from JSON file representing the merged evolution of requirements. Each node contains an `id` (version and requirement ID), a `topic`, a `status` (e.g., Modified), and a list of `children` pointing to traceability-linked successors.

Figure 6 presents a snapshot of the resulting visualization. It illustrates how requirements are semantically grouped, linked across versions, and annotated for traceability analysis.

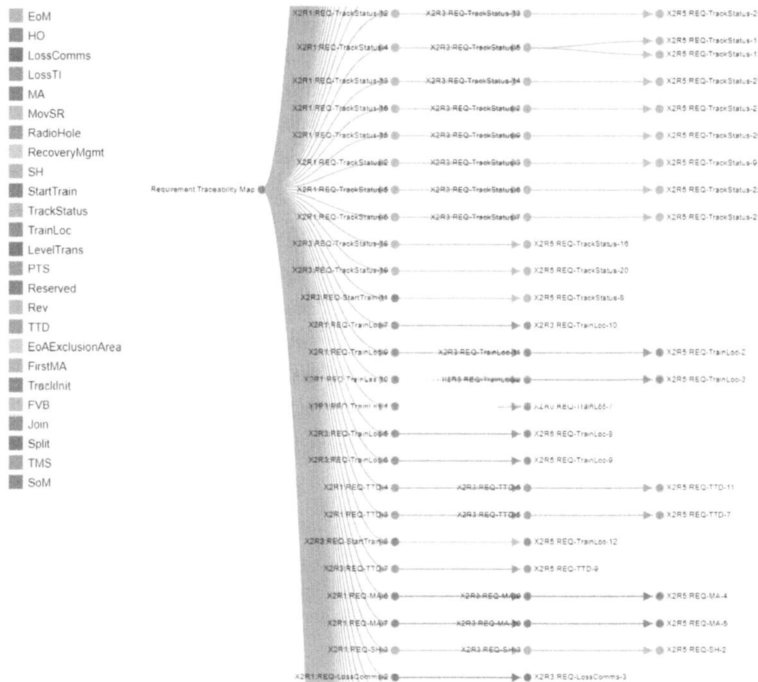

Fig. 6. Interactive mindmap of requirement evolution across versions.

6 Architecture Redesign Based on Requirement Evolution

Building upon the baseline functional architecture described in Sect. 3, we conducted a requirement-driven refinement based exclusively on the 33 new functional requirements introduced in X2Rail-5. Modified, unchanged, and absent requirements were excluded from the scope of this analysis to maintain a focused and realistic workload.

6.1 Methodology

Each newly introduced requirement was analyzed through the following process:

- **Functional interpretation:** Reading and understanding the operational context described in the requirement.
- **Component mapping:** Identifying the functional components involved in the described behavior.
- **Architectural comparison:** Verifying whether the described interaction exists in the X2Rail-3 architecture.
- **Action classification:** Assigning one of the following architectural actions: **Add**, **Modify**, **No Change**. It is important not to confuse architectural actions with Elementary Mind Map Operators.

For component mapping, we consider all functional components defined in X2Rail-3 architecture described in Fig. 2 (Sect. 3.2). A requirement is categorized as **Add** when it introduces a new communication link that does not exist in the current architecture. When the logic or endpoints of an existing link must be updated to accommodate the requirement, the action is classified as **Modify**. Finally, if the described behavior is already fully supported by the X2Rail-3 architecture, no update is necessary and the action is marked as **No Change**. This analysis is performed manually.

The resulting architectural impacts have been compiled in an annotated analysis table, enabling traceable and consistent documentation of the identified changes. Out of the 33 requirements analyzed, Table 2 presents three representative examples that illustrate how new requirements from X2Rail-5 were mapped to architectural actions. These were deliberately selected to reflect the three possible architectural outcomes: *Add*, *Modify*, and *No Change*. The first column indicates the requirement ID from X2Rail-5. The second column provides the requirement description. The third column identifies the impacted functions in the form (source, destination). The fourth column describes the corresponding architectural action, and the fifth column specifies the name of the flow between the impacted functions.

Table 2. Excerpt from the architectural impact analysis of new X2Rail-5 requirements

Req ID	Description	Impacted Functions	Action	Flow(s)
Train Loc-4	When receiving a Start of Mission Train Position Report from a train where the reported position is unambiguous to the L3 Trackside, the L3 Trackside shall create a new Train Location for that train from the Max Safe Front End to the Min Safe Front End derived from the Train Position Report.	(Train Position Reporting, Train Management)	Add	SoM-TPR
TTD-10	For a system using TTD, when detecting an unexpected TTD occupancy adjacent to an existing Unknown Track Status Area which has a Recorded Train Length greater than zero, the L3 Trackside shall extend the Unknown Track Status Area up to the next boundary of this TTD section.	(TTD Management, Track Status Management)	Modify	ReleasedOccupied UnknownTrack Status Area
Track Status-7	When the L3 Trackside has updated the Train Location for a train, then the Track Status Area associated with this train shall be updated accordingly.	(Train Position Reporting, Train Management); (Train Management, Track Status Management)	No Change	–

6.2 Interpretation of Selected Examples

The three requirements in Table 2 were chosen to reflect the full range of architectural outcomes observed during the analysis:

REQ-TrainLoc-4 (Add). Introduces a new communication flow between *Train Position Reporting* and *Train Management*. This flow captures how the system reacts to a Start of Mission report with an unambiguous position, triggering the creation of a new Train Location. It formalizes an entry point into the system, previously absent from the X2Rail-3 architecture.

REQ-TTD-10 (Modify). Updates the behavior of an existing link between *TTD Management* and *Track Status Management*. The flow, already present in X2Rail-3, is extended in X2Rail-5 to handle unexpected occupancy in Unknown Track Status Areas. This refinement reflects how existing interactions are adapted to evolving operational needs.

REQ-TrackStatus-7 (No Change). Describes a behavior already handled by the current architecture. The requirement is fully covered by existing flows between *Train Position Reporting*, *Train Management*, and *Track Status Management*, requiring no architectural change. This confirms the relevance and completeness of previously defined interactions.

7 Conclusion and Future Work

This paper presents a structured approach for tracking the evolution of ETCS Level 3 requirements across successive versions of the X2Rail specifications. We introduced rule-based scripts to automatically extract functional and safety requirements from semi-structured PDFs, developed a version-aware comparison method to detect and classify requirement changes, and proposed architectural refinements grounded in traceability analysis. The approach ensures that proposed updates remain consistent with the reference architecture and traceable to evolving specifications.

Short-Term Perspectives. As a natural extension of this work, we plan to extend the architecture redesign process to incorporate requirements marked as *Modified* and *Absent*.

Mid-Term Objectives. This work serves as a stepping stone toward the author's upcoming doctoral research, which will explore formal modeling and verification of evolving requirements in railway systems. A central objective is to assess how incremental requirement updates can be systematically propagated to formal models while preserving correctness and safety guarantees.

Disclosure of Interests. The authors have no competing interests to declare that are relevant to the content of this article.

References

1. Ajagbe, M., Zhao, L.: Retraining a bert model for transfer learning in requirements engineering: a preliminary study. In: Proceedings of the RE Next! Track at the 30th IEEE International Requirements Engineering Conference (2022). https://doi.org/10.1109/RE54965.2022.00046, https://www.researchgate.net/publication/365112611
2. Baier, C., Katoen, J.P.: Principles of Model Checking. MIT Press, Cambridge (2008)
3. Daya, A.B.: Etcs-requirement-evolution: Scripts for extraction, tracking, and visualization (2025). https://github.com/Aroua-Ben-Daya/ETCS-Requirement-Evolution. Accessed June 2025
4. De Lucia, A., Fasano, F., Oliveto, R.: Traceability management for impact analysis. In: FoSM. IEEE (2008)
5. Göknil, A., Kurtev, I., Berg, K.V.d.: A rule-based change impact analysis approach in software architecture for requirements changes (2016). arXiv preprint; uses formal semantics & traceability to detect impacted architecture
6. Hoang, T.S., Butler, M., Reichl, K.: The hybrid ERTMS/ETCS level 3 case study. In: Butler, M., Raschke, A., Hoang, T.S., Reichl, K. (eds.) ABZ 2018. LNCS, vol. 10817, pp. 251–261. Springer, Cham (2018). https://doi.org/10.1007/978-3-319-91271-4_17
7. Luttmer, J., Prihodko, V., Ehring, D., Nagarajah, A.: Requirements extraction from engineering standards systematic evaluation of extraction techniques. In: Procedia CIRP, vol. 119, pp. 794–799. Elsevier (2023). https://doi.org/10.1016/j.procir.2023.03.125
8. Madaki, A.A., Wan Zainon, W.M.N.: A visual framework for software requirements traceability. Bull. Electr. Eng. Inform. **11**(1), 426–434 (2022). https://doi.org/10.11591/eei.v11i1.3269, https://beei.org/index.php/EEI/article/view/3269
9. Mokos, K., Katsaros, P.: A survey on the formalisation of system requirements and their validation. Array **7**, 100030 (2020). https://doi.org/10.1016/j.array.2020.100030
10. Rauf, R., Antkiewicz, M., Czarnecki, K.: Logical structure extraction from software requirements documents. In: Proceedings of the 29th IEEE/ACM International Conference on Automated Software Engineering (ASE), pp. 405–416. ACM (2014). https://doi.org/10.1145/2642937.2642973, https://www.researchgate.net/publication/266682045_Logical_Structure_Extraction_from_Software_Requirements_Documents
11. Marrone, S., et al.: PERFORMINGRAIL D2.2 - Moving Block Specification Development. Technical report (2022). https://www.performingrail.com/
12. Saddem-Yagoubi, R., Beugin, J., Ghazel, M.: A methodology framework for modelling a rail moving block system. In: Transport Research Arena (TRA) Conference (2023)
13. Tambon, F., et al.: How to certify machine learning based safety-critical systems? a systematic literature review. arXiv preprint arXiv:2107.12045 (2021). https://arxiv.org/abs/2107.12045

Author Index

B. Ben Hedia et al. (Eds.): VECoS 2025, LNCS 16263, p. 205, 2026.
https://doi.org/10.1007/978-3-032-20440-0

The manufacturer's authorised representative in the EU is Springer Nature Customer Service Centre GmbH, Europaplatz 3, 69115 Heidelberg, Germany. If you have any concerns regarding our products, please contact ProductSafety@springernature.com

Printed and bound by CPI Group (UK) Ltd, Croydon, CR0 4YY
07/07/2026
02160917-0002